The Alternative Tradition

Religion and Society 18

MOUTON PUBLISHERS · THE HAGUE · PARIS · NEW YORK

The Alternative Tradition

Religion and the Rejection of Religion in the Ancient World

JAMES THROWER
University of Aberdeen

MOUTON PUBLISHERS · THE HAGUE · PARIS · NEW YORK

ISBN: 90-279-7997-9

Printed in Great Britain.

For Judith

Οἱ μὲν ἰππήων στρότον, οἱ δὲ πέσδων,
οἱ δὲ νάων φαῖσ' ἐπὶ γᾶν μέλαιναν
ἔμμεναι κάλλιστον, ἔγω δὲ κῆν' ὄτ–
τω τις ἔραται·

Sappho of Ephesus
fl. 600 BC

Preface

The belief is still widely held that the rejection of a religious understanding of the world, and of life, is something of a modern phenomenon, or at least, if not strictly modern, that it is something which begins no earlier than the period of the European eighteenth century *Aufklärung*.

A corollary of this belief is the further belief that such rejection of religion as can be found in human cultures is found only in European culture, and in other cultures only in so far as they have come under the influence of that culture.

The principal aim of this work is to show, by an appeal to such historical evidence as has come down to us, the groundlessness of both of these commonly held assumptions. The rejection of religion – and by 'rejection of religion' I mean, overall, just that, and not merely the rejection of some particular, localised, contingent form of religion – is, in fact, almost as old as human thought itself and just as widespread.

I begin my study of the rejection of religion, therefore, in ancient India, with those doubts concerning ancient Indian religion – and often, by implication, of all forms of religion – which we find in the literature of the late Vedic period (ca. 1000 BC) and in some of the *Upaniṣads*, and which gave rise to the first fully articulated naturalistic outlook on life in recorded history – the system known to later Indian thought as Lokāyāta, the philosophy of the people. From Lokāyāta – or Cārvāka, as some would call it – I pass to consider the naturalism inherent in the earliest forms of the Sāṃkhya and Vaiśeṣika philosophies, and to the non-supernaturalistic strains discernible in the earliest forms of Buddhism and Jainism.

Next, I consider Chinese culture – never a very religious one – but one where Confucian humanism continued to do battle with religion, both indigenous and imported, for well over two thousand years, and which threw up a number of thinkers whose thought was avowedly naturalistic.

From China I turn my attention to Western Classical Antiquity, and more particularly to ancient Greece, where a similar disatisfaction with traditional religion to that discernible in ancient India gave rise, not only to that metaphysical theology which was to prove so influential in articulating early Christian religion, but to a philosophical outlook on life which was the very antithesis of this, and which has haunted the Western world from that time to the present day – the philosophy of Epicurus. I also look at the naturalistic strains in the philosophy of Aristotle and at the irreligious implications of the thought of the Sceptics and of some of the other thinkers of the late Hellenistic and Roman worlds.

Finally, I look at ancient Israel and the ancient Near East. Here overt naturalism and irreligion are rare, though not entirely unknown, but it is here that many today would see the true beginnings of those secularising forces which, over the past half-millennium, have all but dispossessed religion of the dominant influence it once had within Western culture.

We in the Western Hemisphere live in a post-religious age, and are, in fact, the first persons in the history of our race to do so. But the spirit which animates our concerns is not new, for it is one, as I hope to show, that can be found from the time of man's earliest recorded speculations; at times overt, even stridently overt, at times subtle and barely self-conscious, at times cowed and well-nigh indiscernible; but always it has been there, in all cultures and at all times – for it is one polarity of the questing human spirit. The purpose of this study is to listen to those voices from the past which foreshadow the concerns of the present, and to trace the earliest and often multiform beginnings of what, in the light of the underlying unity of spirit that I discern, and which I have termed 'naturalism', I would call 'the alternative tradition' – in contradistinction to the overwhelmingly predominate religious tradition.

Religion itself is a notoriously difficult phenomenon to define, and I have no intention of trying to do so. Rather, in an introductory chapter, I have sought to characterise what I take to be the essential features of the traditional religious understanding of reality – archaic, primitive and contemporary – and to which I counterpose the understanding I have termed naturalistic. The growth of this juxtaposition is long and complex and is, perhaps, not even today complete or even clearly and precisely definable. I have had no hesitation, therefore, in this work, in glancing at criticisms of religion which are not, in the strict meaning of the term, naturalistic, but which have, I hold, contributed to the general climate of opinion which has allowed naturalism, in all spheres, to grow and develop.

Naturalism is equally difficult to define. Certainly I would want to distinguish naturalism, as I understand it, from vulgar materialism and most certainly from mechanico-materialism – though at times, as we shall see, it has been identified, especially in its earliest stages, with these. Just as religion has become more refined and sophisticated as it has developed within the historical process, so too has naturalism. In fact much of the ongoing development of religion has been in response to the critique which naturalism has brought against it. Rarely, however, has the reverse been the case. Naturalism has developed almost entirely by its own momentum, conditioned only by an increasing awareness of the actualities of the external world; for naturalism holds the meaning of the world to lie – in all spheres – within itself. It makes no reference to those 'powers' which religious men see lying beyong space and time and which they hold to be operative in history determining the destiny of men. The whole meaning of man's life is, for naturalism, to be found, if at all, within this world. Herein lies the crux of the ongoing argument between a religious and a non-religious response to the world. One of the aims of this work is to show just how early in human culture this argument begins.

A work such as this, which covers almost all of the major cultural traditions of mankind is, of course, heavily dependent on the first hand labours of others in the primary source materials of the cultures concerned – a debt which I seek to acknowledge in the notes and bibliography appended to this volume. An inability to work with all the primary source materials of world cultures has not, however, prevented scholars in the discipline of the history of religions from giving to the general reader introductory volumes of considerable interest, and of varying merit, to that vast field.

It is in the spirit of this enterprise from within the discipline of the history of religions that this all too brief attempt at a survey of the beginnings of 'the alternative tradition' is offered to the same general reader. It is, so far as I am aware, the first such attempt made to survey this field, and if it does no more than stimulate others to offer a fuller and better treatment of this important area of man's self-understanding then it will have fulfilled its purpose. It is, after all, the tradition itself that is important, for it is our own – some would say, fatal – inheritance.

Acknowledgements

First and foremost I would like to express my gratitude to those who have commented on the manuscript of this book either whole or in part: to Mr. James Forsyth of the University of Aberdeen who read through the whole of the final draft and who made innumerable suggestions for the improvement of the style and who saved me from some of the worst excesses of my highly idiosyncratic misuse of the English language; to Mr. Christopher Macy of the British Rationalist Press Association who first suggested that I write this book and whose comments on an earlier version drove me to write what I hope he will agree is at least an improvement on that earlier attempt; to Dr. Jacques Waardenburg of the University of Utrecht, one of the editors of the series in which it appears; to Mrs. Karin Kvideland of the University of Bergen; to Professor Zigmunt Poniatowski of the Polish Academy of Sciences and to the scholars of the Museum (and Library) of the History of Religion and Atheism in Leningrad – all of whom made constructive suggestions with regard to particular sections of this work. I would also like to thank my own students at the University of Aberdeen, as well as those students of the University of Helsinki who in 1974 heard sections of this book delivered to them as lectures. From both groups of students I have learnt much. To these and others, who in various ways have helped me – my thanks. Such shortcomings as remain are, of course, solely my responsibility.

Dr. Joselyn Murray helped me with the bibliography and with the index, as indeed did my eldest daughter Pene, and I would also like to put on record the help given to me, in ways known only to ourselves, during the then final stages of the production of this book by Bill and Iris Scott and by one of my final year students, Bob Middleton.

I would also like to record my gratitude to the University of Aberdeen University Studies Committee and to the Carnegie Trust for the Universities of Scotland for generous financial assistance towards the publication of this book. In the harsh economic climate in which scholarly publishing finds itself in the commercial world of today, publication without such assistance would have been virtually impossible.

Finally I would like to thank my wife for providing an environment conducive to both work and relaxation during the writing of this book; to her it, with all its faults, this book, as is its author, is dedicated.

JAMES THROWER

Contents

1

Introduction

1.1 RELIGION AND MYTH

My theme is the beginnings of the growth of a consistently held naturalistic view of the world, but before turning to these beginnings in ancient India, China, Greece, Rome and the ancient Near East, I have thought it advisable to look at the outlook on the world which naturalism seeks to supplant and which I call 'mythological' or 'mythico-religious'. I do not, however, intend these terms to be construed in the popular sense of 'fictitious', for the question of the validity of the mythico-religious response to the world is one that I wish to leave open. I intend, therefore, to use the terms 'mythological' and 'mythico-religious' in the sense in which they are now widely used by ethnologists, social anthropologists and historians of religion – a sense which I hope to make clear in the chapter which follows.

It is in this, as yet to be defined, sense of 'mythological' that the term can be said to express what is most characteristic of the religious approach to the world. As one of the foremost scholars working in the field of the phenomenology of religion today has written:

> Common as it may be to define religion by reference to belief in God, gods, etc. (a procedure which runs up against troubles in any case in regard to, for example, Therevada Buddhism), there may be merit in looking at the focus or foci of religious activity through the medium of the mythic, that is, in a context where such entities are acting, not just so to say quietly existing. (Ninian Smart 1973: 79)

The influential German theologian Rudolf Bultmann has likewise identified the religious approach to the world – at least within traditional Christianity – with mythology, and he too concentrates on the notion of divine activity, of the interplay of natural and supernatural forces, as being the distinctive feature of the mythico-religious approach to reality.[1] He writes:

> The whole conception of the world presupposed in the preaching of Jesus as in the New Testament generally is mythological; i.e. ... the conception of the intervention of supernatural powers in the course of events; the conception of miracles, especially the conception of the intervention of supernatural powers in the inner life of the soul.... This conception of the world we call mythological because it is different from the conception of the world which has been formed and developed by science since its first inception in ancient Greece and which has been accepted by all modern men. In this modern conception of the world the cause-and-effect nexus is fundamental. Although modern physical theories take account of chance in the chain of cause and effect in subatomic phenomena, our daily living, purposes and actions are not affected. In any case, modern science does not believe that the course of nature can be interrupted, or, so to speak, perforated, by supernatural powers. The same is true of the study of modern history.... Modern men take it for granted that the course of nature and history, like their own inner life and their practical life, is nowhere interrupted by the intervention of supernatural powers. (Bultmann 1960: 15-16)

In this, of course, 'modern men' differ, not only from ancient and from 'primitive', but also from modern *religious* men.[2] As, however, my approach in this work is historical, it is to the world of ancient man that I wish first to turn, leaving the relevance of ancient man's response to reality to later and more sophisticated religious responses to emerge as the story which I have to tell progresses.

1.2 MYTH AND REALITY: THE PRIMAL VISION

For modern man to attempt to enter the mythological world of ancient man might seem at first sight a well-nigh impossible task – so great is the distance in time which separates our world from that of the myth makers and so greatly has our whole conception of reality changed since their time. And so it might be, were it not for the fact that, within the last half century, intensive work by a number of gifted social anthropologists, studying at first hand societies where myth is still — or was until quite recently — a living force, has to a great extent succeeded in articulating for us the *Weltanschauung* of peoples for whom myth is a natural mode of expression, and so aided our understanding of the mythological response to the world.[3]

If it be felt that some justification is needed for utilising the study of contemporary 'primitive' societies to illuminate past periods of history, I would instance the light which present day studies of witchcraft in 'primitive' societies has shed on witchcraft beliefs in Western Europe in the sixteenth and seventeenth centuries.[4] I would also remind the reader of Sir James Frazer's well-known words in his book, *The Gorgon's Head*:

> Now when we examine side by side the religions of different races and ages, we find that, while they differ from each other in many particulars, the resemblances between them are numerous and fundamental, and they mutually illustrate and explain each other, the distinctly stated faith and circumstantial ritual of one race clearing up ambiguities in the faith and practice of other races.... (Frazer 1927: 281-282)

Words which I still believe to be apposite today.

From the work of contemporary social anthropologists, together with the explorations of ancient cultures by such historians of culture and religion as Henri Frankfort (1949) and Mircea Eliade (1960; 1964), a number of tentative conclusions regarding 'primitive' man's relationship to the world can be drawn.

Perhaps the greatest single difference between modern Western man's relationship to the world and that of 'primitive' man — ancient and contemporary — lies in the fact that for modern man the phenomenal world is experienced as impersonal — as an 'It' set over against him — whereas for the 'primitive' the world is, at times, experienced as personal, as a 'Thou' confronting him as a living presence,[5] to the extent that natural phenomena are often conceived by him in terms of human experiences and human experiences conceived in terms of cosmic and supernatural events. This way of conceiving of the relationship between man and the world goes, as Frankfort notes (1949: 12-13), far beyond the 'animistic' theory of religion, so popular in the nineteenth century and not unknown in the writings of scholars today. Nothing could, in fact, be further from the way in which 'primitive' man responds to the world than this theory, which sees 'primitive' man as asking and answering, in his own charming, if immature, way questions similar to those which now preoccupy ourselves. Whatever mythology may be, it is certainly not proto-philosophy or proto-science. Living mythology, as we shall see, betrays an entirely different apprehension of reality from that which now characterises the predominant Western approach to the world.[6]

It would, therefore, be a mistake to see 'primitive' man – ancient or modern – as arguing by analogy from the human world in order to explain natural phenomena for, as Frankfort again notes:

> Primitive man simply does not know an inanimate world and for this reason he does not 'personify' phenomena. (1949:14)

At certain times the 'natural' world which confronts him is one which is alive as he is alive and he has, therefore, only one mode of discourse – the personal.

Another way of bringing out the difference between the 'primitive', mythico-religious response to reality and our own, would be to say that whereas, for us, reality is something to be investigated and explained – according to the most general and impersonal principles that we can find – for 'primitive' man reality is something which reveals itself to him. Reality is apprehended as people are apprehended – as will, as presence, and as something unique. 'Primitive' man's relationship to reality is, therefore, a dynamic and a reciprocal one. Frankfort sums this up as follows; he writes:

> The world appears to primitive man neither inanimate nor empty but redundant with life; and life has individuality, in man and beast and plant, and in every phenomenon which confronts man – the thunderclap, the sudden shadow, the eerie and unknown clearing in the wood, the stone which suddenly hurts him when he stumbles on a hunting trip. Any phenomenon may at any time face him not as an 'It' but as 'Thou'. In this confrontation, 'Thou' reveals its individuality, its qualities, its will. 'Thou' is not contemplated with intellectual detachment; it is experienced as life confronting life, involving every faculty of man in reciprocal relation-

> ship. Thoughts, no less than acts and feelings, are subordinated to this experience. (1949:14)

The difference between seeing the natural world as impersonal, and seeing it as personal, brings into sharp focus the way in which the mythico-religious response differs from the contemporary scientific approach to reality, for an object, unlike a person, can always be related to other objects and appear as part of a group or series. Just so is science able to see objects and events as expressions of universal laws which make their behaviour to a large extent predictable. As W. K. C. Guthrie has written:

> Philosophy began when the conviction began to take shape in men's minds that the apparent chaos of events must conceal underlying order, and that this order is the product of impersonal forces. (1962: 26)

The development of the 'new philosophy' of nature in sixteenth and seventeenth century Europe was to undermine the current Christian mythico-religious understanding of the world on just such an account.

But to return to archaic, 'primitive' mythology and to its connection with speculative thought. It is likely, as Frankfort says, that ancient man recognised certain intellectual problems connected with the why, wherefore and whither of his life, but it is important to see that he asks and answers these problems in his own distinctive way. As Frankfort himself puts it:

> In primitive society thought does not operate autonomously. The whole man confronts a living 'Thou' in nature; and the whole man – emotional and imaginative as well as intellectual – gives expression to that experience. All experience of 'Thou' is highly individual; and early man does, in fact, view happenings as individual events. An account of such events and also their explanation can be conceived only as action, and necessarily takes the form of a story. In other words, the ancients told myths instead of presenting an analysis or conclusions. (1949: 14-15)

In telling myths ancient man was not, therefore, simply seeking for an intelligible and detached explanation of phenomena, but recounting events in which he was involved to the extent of his very existence – events which he experienced as the result of the interplay of personal forces. This is most evident in those myths which relate to the origin of the world, of man, and of disease and death. As Frankfort writes:

> The imagery of myth is therefore by no means allegory. It is nothing less than a carefully chosen cloak for abstract thought. The imagery is inseparable from the thought. It represents the form in which the experience has become conscious. (1949: 15)

Malinowski makes a similar point with regard to myth among the Trobriand islanders of his day. He writes:

> Studied alive myth ... is not symbolic, but a direct expression of its subject matter; it is not an explanation in satisfaction of a scientific interest, but a narrative resurrection of a primeval reality, told, in satisfaction of deep religious wants, moral cravings, social submissions, assertions, even practical requirements. Myth fulfils in primitive culture an indispensable function: it expresses, enhances, and codifies beliefs, it safeguards and enforces morality; it vouches for the efficiency of ritual and contains practical rules for the guidance of man... it is not an intellectual explanation nor an artistic imagery, but a pragmatic charter of primitive faith and moral wisdom.... These stories ... are to the natives a statement of a primeval, greater, and more relevant reality, by which the present life, fates and activities of mankind are determined, the knowledge of which supplies man with the motive for ritual and moral actions, as well as with indications as to how to perform them. (1954: 101-108)

More recent investigations have borne him out (cf. Beattie 1964: ch. 12 and 13).

Similarly, the historian of religions E. O. James, after reviewing some of the theories currently put forward as interpretations of myth, and which would see myth as, for example, proto-philosophy, proto-science, poetry, legend, and saga, comments:

> Myth cannot be identified with any of these theories for myth is not the product of imagination in the sense of speculative thought or philosophising about the origins of phenomena in the form of an aetiological tale invented to explain objects and events that arouse attention. It is not idealised history or allegorised philosophy, ethics or theology; still less is it an idle story told for intellectual

> amusement ... or a day dream to be interpreted by the symbols of psycho-analytic exegesis.

He goes on:

> All these may retain elements of myth, but the myth itself is distinct from the fantasy, poetry, philosophy and psychology with which it has become associated in its ramifications, developments and degenerations and their interpretations.

He insists myth is essentially none of these things, but that

> however naive and fantastic some of these stories, beliefs and practices (of the 'primitive') may appear today, to the modern mind, they are in fact perfectly rational, intelligible and logical once their premises and presuppositions are granted.

He claims:

> It is not lack of logic, that characterises their outlook but a particular attitude to the relationship between sacred and profane, the natural and the supernatural, mind and matter, cause and effect. (James 1958: 279-281)

This, I take it, is the point, as Evans Pritchard had insisted against Lévi-Bruhl, in his now well-known Cairo papers published in 1934, that it was the point (cf. 1965: ch. 4). It is not that 'primitives' are somehow deficient in rationality, but quite simply that the premises upon which they base their whole response to the world are different from the premises upon which the majority of us base our understanding of the world today. The illiciting of these premises is the task of the present chapter.

I should like, however, before going further, to guard against a common misunderstanding of myth and of the mythico-religious understanding of the world. I am not in the least suggesting that 'primitive' man's entire outlook on the world is characterised by the premises that make up the distinctiveness of the mythico-religious response to the extent that he is totally incapable of adopting a non-mythological attitude to his environment, for such would be patently untrue. In fact, as Malinowski noted, 'every primitive community is in possession of a considerable store of knowledge, based upon experience and fashioned by reason' – a fact substantiated by his own first hand researches. Writing of the Trobriand Islanders of Melanesia, he pays tribute to their quite highly developed agricultural knowledge and he notes that here they were guided 'by a clear knowledge of weather, seasons, plants and pests, soil and tubers, and by a conviction that this knowledge is true and reliable and that it can be counted upon and must be scrupulously obeyed'. But, as he added, 'mixed up with all their activities is magic, a series of rites performed every year over the gardens in rigorous sequence and order'. Further, although magico-religious rituals[7] are regarded as absolutely indispensible, and although no one can tell exactly what would happen without them since, Malinowski wrily adds, no garden has ever been made without them, 'despites thirty years of missionary activity', to suggest to the Trobriander that gardens should be made entirely by magic would evoke a smile on the face of the Trobriander at one's simplicity, for 'he knows as well as you do', writes Malinowski, 'that there are natural causes and conditions, and by his observations he knows also that he is able to control these natural forces by mental and physical effort' (1954: 26-28) – together, however, with magico-religious rituals. To the Trobriand Islander *both* are necessary.

Frankfort notes a similar admixture of natural and supernatural causation – as they now appear to us to be – in ancient Babylonian and Egyptian cultures. He writes:

> When the Egyptians claim that Osiris, and the Babylonians that Oannes, gave them the elements of their culture, they include among these elements the crafts and agriculture as well as ritual usages. These two groups of activities possessed the same degree of reality. It would be meaningless to ask a Babylonian whether the success of the harvest depended on the skill of the farmers or on the correct performance of the New Year's Festival. Both were essential to success. (1949: 22)

I would like to point out here that the same can be said of religious men within our own society – a society where, even today, prayers for the sick and for fruitful harvests go hand in hand, in the minds of many, with the practice of the most advanced medical and agricultural knowledge known to man. This is surely the enduring and essential stuff of the magico-religious approach to the world.

Taking cognisance then of the admixture, in ancient, 'primitive' and contemporary religious approaches to the world, of what we would now term 'natural' and 'supernatural' forces, it is essential that we see the magico-religious response to the world in its proper context, for it would appear to arise at that point where man comes up against the ultimate questions with regard to his existence – for the 'primitive', perhaps, somewhat sooner than for contemporary man. Here, at the limit, is where ancient, 'primitive' and some modern religious men see the world as grounded in and admixed with personal supernatural forces – a vision which they express mythologically.

To complete our phenomenological analysis of myth a number of further points need to be stressed.

1.3 MYTH AND RITUAL

The first is that ancient society not only recounted its myths but did so within the framework of a dramatic re-enactment of them.[8] To understand this it will be necessary to look a little more closely at the character of myth.

Myths, by and large, relate to origins. They narrate a sacred history and tell of events that took place in 'primordial time' – the fabled time of the beginnings. They tell how, through the deeds of supernatural beings, a reality came into existence, whether this be the whole of reality (the Cosmos) or only a fragment of reality (an island, a species, an activity, an institution, death etc.). As Mircea Eliade says:

> Myth then, is always an account of a 'creation'; it relates how something was produced, began to *be*. Myth tells only of that which *really* happened, which manifested itself completely. The actors in myths are Supernatural Beings. They are known primarily by what they did in the transcendent times of the 'beginnings'. Hence myths disclose their creative activity and reveal the sacrednes [or simply the 'supernaturalness'] of their works. In short, myths describe the various and sometimes dramatic breakthroughs of the sacred [or the 'supernatural'] into this World. It is this sudden breakthrough of the sacred that really *establishes* the World and makes it what it is today. (1964: 6)

If to this we now add that for ancient man (as for modern 'primitives') events in time are not, as they are for us, irreversible, but that what happened *ab origine* can be repeated – nay, must be repeated if the 'strength' of the cosmos is to be upheld – in sacred rites, then we are in a position to understand why ancient man not only recited his myths as an explanation of the existence of the Cosmos and of his own mode of being in it, but periodically re-enacted them, for in re-enacting them he was able to repeat what the gods, heroes and ancestors did *ab origine*, and so strengthen and preserve the Cosmos and everything in it.

Two examples will suffice to make this clear – the first drawn from a contemporary primitive society, the second from an ancient society.

Australian Aborigine myths consist for the most part of the recital of the perigrinations of mythical ancestors of totemic animals. They tell how in the *alcheringa* [Dream Time] i.e. mythical time, these supernatural beings made their appearance on earth and set out on long journeys, stopping now and then to change the landscape or to produce certain animals and plants, before finally vanishing underground. Knowledge of these myths is essential for the on-going life of the Aborigines, and they are taught to the male youth during the rituals which mark their passage into adulthood. Periodically, rituals take place in which not only are these myths recited but in which male Aborigines act the part of the supernatural beings concerned (whether animal or superhuman) and imitate their action (Strenlow, quoted in Lévi-Bruhl 1935: 123). This, it is believed, brings about the multiplication of such-and-such an animal or plant.

At a rather more sophisticated level we may instance the Babylonian New Year Festival – known in Akkadian as *Akitu*. During this festival, which was one of ritual renewal of nature and society and celebrated the primordial conflict between the Cosmos and the Chaos out of which it had emerged, the great Myth of Creation – known from its opening words, 'When on high', as *Enuma Elish* – was liturgically recited on the fourth of the eleven days of celebration. The myth envisages the primordial situation as one of watery chaos:

When on high the heaven had not been named,
Firm ground below had not been called by name,
There was nought but primordial Apsu, their begetter,
And mother Tiamat, who bore them all,
There waters commingling in a single body;
No reed hut had been matted, no marsh land had appeared,
When no gods whatever had been brought into being,
uncalled by name, their destinies undetermined,
Then it was the gods were formed within them.
(Table I, lines 1-9. Translation of the myth by E. A. Speiser, in Pritchard 1955: 60f.)[9]

The gods having being born, strife breaks out among them and a god called Ea (or Enki) kills his father Apsu with the result that Ti'amat prepares to kill all the gods. They are saved, however, by Ea's son Marduk, who himself kills Ti'amat and makes the world from her body. John Gray summarises the story as follows:

> The inert forces of Apsu and Tiamat and the primordial gods resent the purposeful activity of the younger effective gods of the Mesopotamian pantheon. Anu, the sky-god and the divine king paramount, Enki also called Ea and Nudimmud, the god of controlled waters and others. Apprehending repression by the primordial powers, Ea, who is also the god of wisdom, cunning and spells as well as of water, overcomes Apsu by his art and imposes his control over him.... Then Marduk is born to Ea.... The resentment of the forces of primordial Chaos mounts, and their menace under the championship of Tiamat is great enough to dismay Anu and his celestial court.... The second part of the myth describes how Marduk is singled out as the champion of the divine court, undertakes the commission and is invested with the kingship to sustain the royal authority of Anu and the heavenly court against the menace of primeval Chaos.... The allies of Tiamat are slain or captured and imprisoned and the Tablets of Destiny are... fixed by Marduk to his own breast, so that control of the world should be under the proper authority of the heavenly court. (1969: 29-31)

As a first token of his efficient power to uphold Order against the menace of Chaos, Marduk proceeds to complete creation. The myth recounts this as follows:

> The Lord trod on the legs of Tiamat,
> With his unsparing mace he crushed her skull.
> When the arteries of her blood he had severed.
> [...]
> He split her like a shell-fish into two parts;
> Half of her he set up and ceiled it as sky,
> Pulled down the bar and posted guards.
> He bade them to allow not her waters to escape.
> He squared Apsu's quarters the abode of Nudimmud,
> As the Lord measured the dimensions of Apsu.
> The Great Abode, its likeness, he fixed as Esharra,
> The Great Abode, Esharra, which he made as the firmanent.
> Anu, Enlil, and Ea he made occupy their places.
> [...]
> He constructed stations for the great gods,
> Fixing their astral likeness as constellations,
> He determined the year by designating the zones.
> [...]
> The moon he caused to shine, the night [to him] entrusting.
> (Table IV, lines 129-131, 137-146; Table V, lines 1-3 and 12. Translation by E. A. Speiser, in Pritchard 1955: 67-68)

Lastly the creation of man out of the blood of the slain god Kingu is described.

As well as the ritual recitation of the Creation Myth there was also, as part of the festival, both the re-enactment of the ritual combat in which Marduk triumphed over his enemies and a re-enactment of the sacred marriage between the god and the fertility-goddess to ensure the fertility of the land for the coming year. Finally, there was the 'fixing of the destinies' in nature and society for the coming year.

This, in bald outline, is the myth and ritual of the *Akitu* festival, the purpose of which was to re-establish the world and the nation and to ensure fertility, during the coming year.

We thus see that 'primitive' man – both archaic and contemporary – believes that by knowing the myth he knows the origin of things and so can control and manipulate them. It is only in this sense that myth can at all be regarded as proto-science.

1.4 MYTH, REALITY AND SCIENCE

We turn now to the way in which the mythico-religious understanding of the world regards the subject-object distinction – so fundamental to the scientific understanding of the world – appearance and reality, symbol and what is symbolised, time, space and causality.

On the distinction between subject and object modern science has based a critical and analytical procedure by means of which it progressively reduces individual phenomena to typical events subject to general laws, thus creating a wide gulf between our immediate perception of phenomena and the conceptual apparatus by means of which we make them intelligible. The mythico-religious world view knows no such distinction and makes no distinction, therefore, between subjective knowledge – how the world appears to me – and objective knowledge – how the world is in reality. Both coalesce.

Meaningless too to the mythico-religious understanding is our distinction between appearance and reality, for whatever is capable of affecting a man – whether it be dream, vision, evil influences, the will of the dead, the will of the gods or god – has the same substantial reality as have our more ordinary and intra-personal perceptions. Symbols are regarded in the same way. A name, a part of a person, or a figurine can all stand for and be regarded as essentially identical with the thing which, for us, they symbolise. Here once more we see in the 'primitive' response to the world a coalescence of what we would distinguish. A similar coalescence can be seen in the belief that rituals enacted on earth effect what happens in the supernatural sphere – which brings us to the ancient and 'primitive' notion of causality.

'Primitive' man recognises, of course, the relationship of cause and effect, but, his relationship to nature being as we have described it, he does not see cause and effect functioning in an impersonal, systematic manner. On the contrary, for him, confronted as he believes himself to be by wills in nature like unto his own, he frequently looks, not for the 'how?', but for 'who?'. If the rains do not come we, with our increasing meteorological knowledge and technical skills ask 'why?' and look for 'how' we might alter the situation. For ancient and 'primitive' man the rain has *refused* to come – perhaps the rain-god is angry – and he must, therefore, be placated and persuaded by sacrifice to fulfil the will of man.

For ancient, 'primitive', and, we might add, for many religious men within our own society, general explanatory laws fail to do justice to the felt individual character of certain events. A tree falls on a man when he is out hunting and he is killed, sickness strikes, a road accident occurs, or whatever, and he knows and his friends know that falling trees can kill, that sickness is due to, perhaps, contaminated water, that cars can go out of control and injure people – and why and how – but this fails to do justice to some people's sense of meaning and purpose and so they go on to ask, 'But why to me or this person at this particular time?' or 'Who has done this?'. In the mythico-religious understanding – whether ancient or modern – there is little conception of chance or coincidence.[10]

Similarly, in cases where a naturalistic approach would see no more than association, the mythico-religious response finds a causal connection. 'Every resemblance, every contact in space and time, establishes a connection between two objects or events which makes it possible to see in the one the cause of changes observed in the other,' writes Frankfort (1949: 27). The 'primitive' mind sees an initial situation and an end situation and rarely, if ever, inquires into the process by which the one might be said to emerge from the other. There is little conception of change in 'primitive' societies beyond a vague notion of transformation or metamorphosis. This is yet one more feature of the mythico-religious approach which has survived into the present – so characteristic is it of the religious understanding of the world – and we would do well to note it. We can discern it today, for instance, in talk about 'grace', 'providence', 'miracle' and the like. Rarely, if ever, do theologians who use such language tell us anything about such activities on the part of the Divine beyond the bare assertion that such divine intervention has occurred or is occurring.

Space too, in the mythico-religious world outlook, is conceived existentially – that is, as not dissociated from subjective experience of it – as is time also. Both can be either sacred or profane, and both can be regarded as beneficial or hostile to man – and intentionally so. Man has, however, in his sacred specialists, the means at his disposal to determine, to some extent, the influence that these might have upon him.

This then is the mythico-religious universe of ancient, contemporary 'primitive', and of many modern religious men. It is not totally alien to any of us, however, for much of our 'thought' in certain spheres – in art and in poetry, for instance, – moves along not dissimilar lines. Indeed, we have all, if the Swiss psychologist Jean Piaget is right, passed through such a stage of development in childhood (Piaget 1929).[11] The mythico-religious response to the world and that of the child bear remarkably close similarities, for as Piaget has shown, until about the age of eleven a child's conception of matter, space, time and causality differs fundamentally from those of normal adults. Basing his conclusions on wide ranging, yet quite simple experiments, Piaget concluded that the young child is incapable of distinguishing clearly between his own person and the outside world – that, in effect, he cannot differentiate clearly between psychical and physical phenomena. Children's thoughts, feelings and desires get mixed up with what the adult comes to regard as reality external to himself. Psychological processes are objectified and objects endowed with subjective attributes. Dreams, for example, appear to come from outside, words are inextricably linked with the objects to which they refer, and speaking is often felt to be a way of acting on things. Conversely, the physical world is not sharply divided off from the personal as material and impersonal, but regarded as if it possessed or mediated life, consciousness and will.

Piaget's own view on the origin of such ways of responding to the world focusses attention on the diffuse nature of the cognitive relationship between the child and his environment and he sees a regression to childhood responses – as, of course, had Freud – in those situations in adult life where the boundary between a person and his environment temporarily loses its sharpness – situations such as those involving intense anxiety or the exclusive obsession with a particular desire. It was thus, perhaps, a correct diagnosis on the part of Immanuel Kant when, towards the close of the eighteenth century – a century which saw great advances in the naturalistic understanding of the world in all spheres – he described this century as the one in which man had 'come of age' (1838-1842, IV: 174).

Before passing to describe the beginnings of this process of 'coming of age' in the cultural traditions of mankind, there are two features of the mythico-religious outlook as a whole that we must notice. The first provides a link between this outlook and the emerging naturalistic outlook; the second describes a very important function of the mythico-religious understanding of reality, which perhaps helps us to understand some of the reasons for its persistance and for the, sometimes virulent, opposition that the alternative outlook of naturalism has aroused.

The link between the mythico-religious understanding of the world and that of naturalism rests on a fundamental characteristic of the cognitive process – the innate tendency of man to organise his environment into coherent patterns, to find meaning in the most diverse phenomena and so to find both intellectual and emotional satisfaction. Phenomena which cannot be so organised are felt to be threatening or disturbing.[12] This is particularly so in 'primitive' societies, whether ancient or contemporary. In such societies elaborate edifices are constructed on the basis of resemblances and analogies which, to the naturalistic mind, no longer form part of the structure of its formal reasoning. A good example of this tendency is the resemblance which older societies have felt between the macrocosm and the microcosm – a view which dominated the ancient world and which persisted in Western Europe until the 'scientific revolution' of the seventeenth century. This view did not just involve the idea of a general connection between celestial and human affairs, but led to a detailed and fantastically elaborate working out of the details of this relationship. It was only with the advent of the 'scientific revolution' in the Western world, with its accompanying widening of the gulf between the person and the external world, that such a harmonious and emotionally satisfying mode of thinking disappeared. I would venture to suggest that it is because the naturalistic approach, whilst not entirely lacking the emotional satisfaction afforded by the older mythico-religious outlook, appeals only to a minority within our society, that many today feel a nostalgia for a paradise which they know has, in fact, gone for ever. Max Weber's description of the onward progress of naturalism as one of 'disenchantment' aptly describes such feelings.[13]

The touchstone for naturalism, however, is not simply internal harmony among ideas, nor whether man feels 'at home in the world' – to use a phrase of Martin Buber – but a demonstrable relationship between ideas and reality. Both mythology and naturalism, as is now generally recognised, seek order, structure, pattern; but the question is, of course, what order, structure, pattern? The mythico-religious understanding will seek to establish order – that is, correlations between events – at almost any cost; the naturalistic, scientific understanding will seek for order only upon the satisfaction of certain rigorous criteria, and, in the absence of evidence, will quite often simply suspend judgement. Therein lies one of the major differences between these two approaches to understanding the world.

One further dimension of the mythico-religious view of the world remains to be considered – and in some ways it is the most important of all – and that is the tendency inherent in this way of understanding the world to see the socio-political structure of society as 'given'; that is, a tendency to bestow ultimate, and therefore definitive, ontological status on existing social and moral structures by locating them within a sacred and cosmic frame of reference.[14]

The ancient way of doing this was to see the order of the microcosm reflecting that of the macrocosm, or to hold that the social and moral order reflected the will of the gods or god. Criticism of the socio-political structure, or of the accepted moral code, was thus seen as blasphemy, and criticism of the mythico-religious response to the world was, therefore, seen as something subversive. As one of the protagonists in Cicero's dialogue *De Natura Deorum* says:

> When piety goes, religion and sanctity go with it. And when these are gone, there is anarchy and chaos in our way of life. I do no know whether, if our reverence for the gods were lost, we should not also see the end of good faith, of human brotherhood and even of justice itself, which is the keystone of all virtues. (*De Natura Deorum*, I, 3; translation by McGregor 1972: 70)

Shakespeare expressed similar sentiments some fifteen hunderd years later when he wrote in *Troilus and Cressida*:

> The heavens themselves, the planets and this centre,
> Observe degree, priority and place...
> O, when degree is shak'd
> Which is the ladder to all high designs,
> The enterprise is sick! How could communities,
> Degrees in schools, and brotherhoods in cities,
> Peaceful commerce from dividable shores,
> The primogenity and due of birth,
> Prerogative of age, crowns, sceptres, laurels,
> But by degree, stand in authentic place.
> (Act 1, Scene 3, v. 85-108)

Although, as we shall see, there are intimations of the breakdown of this view of society in the writings of the Sophists in ancient Greece, it persisted, certainly within Western culture, so long as a religious understanding of the world remained the dominant cultural force.[15] It was only with the advent of Marxism in the nineteenth century that the possibility of a revolutionary, humanistic transformation of society, in accordance with a naturalistic understanding of man and of society, became a serious possibility. Prior to the nineteenth century revolutionary thinking about the transformation of society was invariably millenarian, in that what was sought was divine intervention to implement that new social order in which men might find their true fulfilment.

Whilst a consideration of the naturalistic critique of society belongs outwith the scope of this volume, such a critique has more often than not been preceded by a naturalistic critique of the mythico-religious understanding of man and of nature, and to the beginnings of this – in ancient societies – we now turn.

2

India

2.1 INTRODUCTION

Within the four-millenia-old cultural tradition of the Indian subcontinent religious unbelief has had rather different connotations from those which it has had in the West; for whereas the great divide between a religious and a non-religious interpretation of life over much of Western culture has been between those who saw the world as created and directed by a transcendent God and those who did not or who were agnostic on the issue, the dividing line in Indian culture has been drawn in terms of the acceptance or rejection of the authority of the *Vedas* or sacred scriptures – of what in Sanskrit, the sacred language of Hinduism, is called *śruti*[1] – and, as the subsequent development of post-Vedic thought shows, the *Vedas* have been susceptible to both theistic and non-theistic interpretation. Atheism in Indian thought need not necessarily, therefore, be irreligious. It is quite possible to be an atheist and an orthodox Hindu. The great monistic tradition of the *advaita* (or non-dualistic) Vedānta, which was articulated as a systematic philosophy of life by the medieval Hindu thinker Śankara in the early years of the ninth century of the Christian Era but which traces its origins at least as far back as the age of the *Upaniṣads* (i.e. to the period 800-400 BC), denies the existence of a transcendent creator-God but is none the less religious for that. Similarly, the heterodox systems of Jainism and Buddhism, which broke away from Hinduism in the sixth century BC – religions by almost any definitions of that term – also denied the existence of a transcendent God, although later non-Theravāda Buddhism has, at times, developed in a theistic direction.

But whilst, on the whole, Indian philosophising, whether theistic or atheistic, has undergirded a religious outlook on life, sceptical, agnostic and naturalistic strains are not unknown and, in fact, one great naturalistic school – that of the Cārvākas, known also as Lokāyāta – flourished for well over a thousand years before virtually disappearing about the seventh century AD under the rising tide of religious Idealism. It was, however, still thought worthy of mention as late as the fourteenth century, when Mādhavācārya wrote his *Sarva-darśana-śaṅgraha*, one of our major sources for knowledge of the Cārvāka system.

It is, of course, a truism that much agnosticism and unbelief can be understood only against the background of the religious belief that it was concerned to question or deny, and this is certainly so in India during the early period of philosophical speculation. It will, therefore, be necessary to look briefly, before outlining such scepticism, agnosticism and naturalism as can be found in India, at the religion of the earliest period of the Aryan settlement of that subcontinent.

2.2 THE RELIGION OF THE VEDIC PERIOD

The earliest civilized inhabitants of India, whose remains at Harrapa and Mohenjo – Daro in the Indus Valley have only recently been uncovered, worshipped a Mother Goddess and a Horned God. They had sacred trees and animals, and ritual ablutions would appear to have played an important part in their religious life. Beyond this, despite a vast amount of speculative, and for the most part imaginative, reconstruction of their religion, and in the absence of any intelligible texts – their script has not yet been deciphered – it is not safe to go.[2]

Of the religion of the Aryans, however, we know a good deal, for in the hymns which form the earliest strata of the *Vedas*, and in the *Ṛg Veda Samhitā* in particular, composed somewhere between 1500-900 BC, they have left us a fairly extensive account of their outlook on the world.

Their religion as we would expect – they being of Indo-European origin – is not dissimilar to that which we find in ancient Iran, Greece, Rome and Northern Europe. It also betrays some resemblance to the myth and ritual pattern of the ancient Near East.

Four features need to be noticed. At one level the religion of the

Aryans can be regarded, as indeed it was by early Western commentators on the religion such as Max Müller, as a form of nature polytheism – the gods representing the mysterious forces of nature upon which the life of man is dependent; fire (*Agni*), thunder and rain (*Indra*), air (*Vayu*) and sun (*Surya*). Here the gods are every whit as anthropomorphically conceived as are the gods of Homer in ancient Greece and are just as capricious!

Secondly, the invading Aryans were a warrior people and many of their gods were also war-gods (Indra in particular); so much so that many of the (later) myths which tell of their doings may well reflect the actual historical circumstances of the conquering of the land.[3]

Thirdly, the invaders possessed an elaborate sacrificial ritual and this too is represented in many of the hymns of the early *Vedas*, which were used liturgically in the rites performed by the priestly class, the Brahmins; rites designed to uphold the stability and fertility of the Cosmos, which the phenomenology of religion shows to be a well-nigh universal feature of the mythico-religious response to reality (cf. Eliade 1964: chap. 1). As a leading scholar of this period has said:

> The Ṛg Veda poets were deeply affected by the apparently mysterious working of the awe-inspiring forces of nature. Their hymns reflect in places that primitive attitude of mind which looks upon all nature as a living presence, or as an aggregate of animated entities. The luminaries who follow a fixed course across the sky are the *devas* [*lit.*: the shining ones] or gods.... The attempt of the human mind, more poetic than scientific, to account for the various forces and phenomena of nature with which man is confronted, leads to the rise of myths. When the imagination interprets a natural event as the action of a personified being resembling a human agent, a myth is born. The creative fancy of the Rigvedic poets goes on adding new touches to the picture, so that a natural phenomenon ultimately appears as a drama of human passions and not as an unintelligible and chaotic happening. (Majumbar 1951: 360-361)

There are, however, in the *Ṛg Veda*, traces of a more anthropomorphic conception in which sacrifices to the gods are regarded as little more than bribes.

Lastly, underlying the polytheism of the Vedic hymns, there is the notion of *Ṛta*, or cosmic order, to which even the gods are subject; a notion not unlike that of *Moira* among the ancient Greeks and of *Tao* among the Chinese.

From the *Ṛg Veda* it is also possible to reconstruct something of the development of Aryan religion. We read, for instance, of a high-god, Dyaus, cognate with the Greek Zeus and the Roman Jupiter, but he is a distant shadowy figure whose place in the Ṛg Vedic pantheon is often usurped by other lesser gods. We can also discern tendencies in some of the later hymns, first towards a rationalisation of the function of the gods and secondly, towards monotheism and monism. For example:

> I ask, unknowing, those who know, the sages,
> as one all ignorant for the sake of knowledge;
> What was the one who in the unborn's image hath
> stablished and fixed firm these worlds' six regions.
>
> They call him Indra, Mitra, Varuna,
> Agni, and he is heavenly noble –
> winged Garutman (The sun),
> To what is one, sages give many a title.
> (*Ṛg Veda* 1. 164. v. 4 [Griffith])[4]

2.3 THE BEGINNINGS OF SPECULATION: SCEPTICISM AND AGNOSTICISM

It is in passages such as the above that we can discern the earliest recorded speculation of ancient man, and it is highly likely that such speculation was connected with the growing practice of asceticism – as practised by the Munis or silent ones, of whom we read in a late hymn of the *Ṛg Veda* that they 'wear the wind as a girdle, and who, drunk with their own silence, rise on the wind and fly in the paths of the demi-gods and birds' (*Ṛg Veda* X. 136 [Basham]). It is from such circles that the newer strains, which we find coming to the fore in Indian culture from about 800 BC, and which have been preserved for us in the *Āraṇyakas* and the *Upaniṣads*,[5] came.

Asceticism was more than an escape from an unhappy and unsatisfying world, for it had a positive aspect in that it was, in part, inspired by a desire for knowledge – for a wisdom which the early *Vedas* could not give. All through the first millenium BC intelligent minds were striving for convincing explanations of the cosmic mystery, and it is as early as the later hymns of the *Ṛg Veda* that we witness the beginnings of that break with mythico-religious explanations and the search for other and more satisfying solutions which was to become a feature not only of Indian culture, but of Chinese and Greek as well.

The first stage of this breakdown, and the first glimmers of philosophical speculation, can be seen in the way in which in many of the later hymns of the *Ṛg Veda* the gods became identified with each other, or became evoked in pairs, or in groups of three or more. Occasionally one god is evoked as supreme and the attributes of other gods are transferred to him. We see this happening in the case of Varuna and also of Indra. We also have references to 'the One', or simply to 'He' or 'It' – a tendency which passes easily, as it did in ancient Greece, into either monotheism or pantheistic monism, especially when it is combined both with a resurgence of interest in *Ṛta*, the principle of cosmic order to which both gods and men are subject, and with speculation regarding the primary substance or 'stuff' out of which the multiplicity of the world as we observe it came.

Whilst, initially, doubts regarding the existence of one or other of the gods tend to centre on Indra as, for instance, at that point in the *Ṛg Veda* where reference is made to those who say:

> Indra is not, who ever saw him
> Who is he that we should praise him?
> (*Ṛg Veda* XI. 12. v. 5 [Macdonnell 1922])

and which may simply reflect the interests of a rival cult, we also come across passages, such as the following, which is a hymn to an unknown God and where there would seem to be a half-sceptical questioning which (if any) god is real. The refrain to each verse 'Who is the God to whom we shall offer sacrifice?' is significant, although later commentators, puzzling at a time when the orthodoxy of the *Vedas* was established as to how to interpret this passage, were led to hypostatise the 'Who?', which in Sanskrit is *Ka*, as the name of a God!

> He who gives breath, he who gives strength,
> whose command all the bright gods revere,
> whose shadow is immortality, whose shadow is death:
> Who is the God to whom we shall offer sacrifice?
>
> He through his might became the sole King
> of the breathing and twinkling world,
> who governs all this, man and beast:
> Who is the God to whom we shall offer sacrifice?
>
> He who through whose might these snowy mountains are,
> and the sea, they say, with the distant river,
> he of whom these regions are indeed the two arms:
> Who is the God to whom we shall offer sacrifice?
>
> He through whom the awful heaven and the earth were made fast
> he through whom the ether was established, and the firmament;
> he who measured the air in the sky:
> Who is the God to whom we shall offer sacrifice?
> (*Ṛg Veda* X. 121. v. 2-5 [Müller])

Similar questioning can also be found in the following passage:

> That which is earlier than this earth and heaven,
> before the Asuras and the gods had being,
> What was the germ primeval which the waters received
> where all the gods were seen together?
>
> The Waters, they received that germ primeval
> wherein the gods were gathered all together.

It rested upon the unborn's navel, that One
wherein abide all things existing.

Ye will not find him who produced these creatures:
another thing has risen up among you.
Enrapt in misty cloud, with lips that stammer,
hymn – chanters wander and are disconcerted!
(*Ṛg Veda* X. 82. v. 5-7 [Griffith])

More pronounced is the agnosticism regarding both the existence of the Primal Being (from which in the earlier myths the world is thought to have originated) and of the soul which we find in verses such as the following:

Who has ever seen the Primeval (Being) at the time of his being born:
What is that endowed with substance which the insubstantial sustains:
From earth are the breath and blood, but where is the soul;
Who may repair to the sage to ask this?
Immature [in understanding], undiscerning in mind,
I enquire of those things which are hidden [even] from the gods.
(*Ṛg Veda* 1. 164 [Dutt])

There is also evidence of a growing moral criticism of the gods and again the target is Indra, a drunken, brawling, arrogant warrior-god if ever there was one! The song which he sings, half-intoxicated on the sacred *soma* drink, itself worshipped as a god in other parts of the *Ṛg Veda*, is typical and worth quoting, if only because it is probably the oldest recorded drinking song in the world!

Thus indeed, thus is my mind: kine and horses I will win,
Have I not drunk of the Soma?
Like the roaring winds the draughts of Soma have roused me up.
Have I not drunk of the Soma?

The draughts have roused me up, as swift horses a chariot.
  Have I not drunk of the Soma?
The hymn has drawn nigh to me, as a lowing cow to her dear calf.
  Have I not drunk of the Soma?
As a carpenter making a seat for the chariot, round my heart I bend the hymn.
  Have I not drunk of the Soma?
In no wise are the five peoples aught to me
  Have I not drunk of the Soma?
Not the half part of me are both worlds [heaven and earth]
  Have I not drunk of the Soma?
The Heaven have I overpassed in greatness and this great earth.
  Have I not drunk of the Soma?
Lo, I will put down this earth here or yonder.
  Have I not drunk of the Soma?
Swiftly will I smite the earth here or yonder.
  Have I not drunk of the Soma?
In Heaven is one half of me. Down below I have drawn the other.
  Have I not drunk of the Soma?
I am most mighty. Nigh to the clouds I have risen.
  Have I not drunk of the Soma?
I go to the house of him who is ready. To the gods goes the oblation bearer.
  Have I not drunk of the soma?
(*Ṛg Veda* X. 119 [Thomas])

Other stories tell us of Indra's assuming the guise of the husband of a girl whom he desires in order to seduce her! It is not, therefore, surprising that in the *Ṛg Veda* we find those who mock and criticise him, as well as those who feel the need to apologize for him (cf. *Ṛg Veda* II. 12. v. 5).

The difficulties of speculation, particularly upon such topics as the origin of the world, is also recognized in the *Ṛg Veda*, and nowhere better than in superb *Hymn of Creation*, known as the *Nāsadīya*, which one noted scholar has called 'one of the oldest surviving records of philosophical doubt in the history of the world' (Basham 1954: 247):

> Non-being then existed not, nor being:
> There was no air, nor heaven which is beyond it.
> What motion was there? Where? By whom directed?
> Was water there? and fathomless abysses?
>
> Death then existed not, nor life immortal:
> Of neither night nor day was any semblance.
> The One breather calm and windless by self-impulse:
> There was not any other thing beyond it.
>
> Darkness at first was covered up by darkness;
> The universe was indistinct and fluid.
> The empty space that by the void was hidden,
> That one was by the force of heat engendered.
>
> Desire then at first arose within it,
> Desire, which was the earliest seed of spirit.
> The bond of being in non-being sages,
> Discovered searching in their hearts with wisdom.
>
> Who knows it truly? Who can here declare it?
> Whence was it born? When issued this creation?
> And did the Gods appear with its production?
> But then who knows from whence it has arisen?
>
> This world-creation, whence it has arisen,
> Or whether it has been produced or not,
> He who surveys it in the highest heaven,
> He only knows or ev'n he does not know it.
> (*Ṛg Veda* X. 129 [Macdonnell 1922])

Similar questioning can also be found at other points in the *Ṛg Veda*; for instance:

> Which of these two (heaven or earth), is prior,
> which posterior: how were they engendered;
> (declare) sages, who knows this?
> (*Ṛg Veda* I. 185. v. 1 [Dutt])

and,

> Who knows what is the truth or who may here declare it?
> What is the proper path that leads to the gods?
> Their inferior abiding places are beheld, as were
> Those which are situated in superior mysterious rites.
> (*Ṛg Veda* III. 54. v. 5-6 [Dutt])

While such verses are, of course, capable of being developed, as indeed they were, in the direction of a revised and more sophisticated theism, they are also evidence of a questioning, sceptical and speculative spirit; a spirit which, as we shall see, was capable of developing in an altogether different direction.

For such questioning Max Müller coined the term 'adevism'—the doubting of the 'devas', as the gods of the Ṛg Vedic pantheon were called, and, as he pointed out, such doubting and questioning is a vital principle in all living religion. His fine words are worth quoting:

> Their atheism [he is referring to the breakdown of belief in the older 'nature gods', as he designates them] such as it was, would more correctly be called Adevism, or a denial of the old Devas. Such a denial, however, of what was once believed, so far from being the destruction, is in reality, the vital principle of all religion. The ancient Aryans felt from the beginning, aye, it may be more in the beginning than afterwards, the presence of a Beyond, of an Infinite, of a Divine, or whatever else we may call it now; and they tried to grasp and comprehend it, as we all do, by giving it name after name. They thought they had found it in the mountains and the rivers, in the dawn, in the sun, in the sky, in the heaven, and the Heaven-

Father. But after every name, there came the No.! What they looked for was like the mountains, like the rivers, like the dawn, like the sky, like the father, but it was not the mountains, not the rivers, not the dawn, not the sky, it was not the father. It was something of all that, but it was also more, it was beyond all that. Even such general names as Asura, or Deva could no longer satisfy them. There may be Devas and Asuras they said; but we want more, we want a higher word, a purer thought. They foresook the bright Devas, not because they believed or desired less, but because they believed and desired more than the bright Devas.

There was a new conception working in their mind; and the cries of despair were but the harbingers of a new birth. (Müller 1878: 303-304)

We can also discern in the *Ṛg Veda* the beginnings of philosophical enquiry into the origin and nature of the 'world-stuff' and we have here, some centuries before its appearance in ancient Greece, those first steps which were to take the human race along the path to that consistent naturalism with which we to-day are so familiar.

What was the primal matter [*adhisthana*]? What the beginning?
How and what manner of thing was that from which
The Maker of All, see-er of all, brought forth
The Earth, and by his might the heavens unfolded?

What was the wood? What was the tree
From which heaven and earth were fashioned forth?
Ask, ask, ye wise in heart, on what did he rely
That he should (thus) support (these worlds)?
(*Ṛg Veda* X. 81. v. 2-4 [Zaehner])

Further, *Ṛg Veda* X. 190 tells us that from heat were produced *Ṛta* (the cosmic order) and *Sarya* (beings); then, the night, the ocean, and the year were produced in succession. *Ṛg Veda* X. 72. 2. says that *sat* (being) was produced from *asat* (non-being). *Ṛg Veda* X. 121, some centuries before Thales, postulates water as the primal substance. As these references show, we are now some way from the mythological accounts, such as we find in the *Puruṣa – Sukta* (*Ṛg Veda* X. v. 90), where the original material of the universe is the body of *Puruṣa*, the primal man, and the agents of creation are the gods, who sacrifice him to make the world (a sacrifice which was re-enacted in the Vedic ritual to sustain and uphold the Cosmos).

Such theorising is not, of course, systematic, but it is a beginning, and it contains the germs of the more overtly naturalistic views which we find referred to in the *Upaniṣads* to which we now turn.

2.4 THE UPANIṢADIC PERIOD

The reflective tendencies found in some of the later hymns of the *Ṛg Veda* are even more pronounced in the *Upaniṣads* – those forest treatises, composed from about the eighth to the fourth centuries BC, which were later included in the canon of sacred scripture. Here hymns to the gods disappear and are replaced by the search for the underlying reality behind or within the plurality of the phenomenal world. It is during this period that those doctrines were developed which were to become normative for orthodox Hinduism, doctrines such as *saṁsāra*, the round of birth and rebirth according to the law of *karma*, and the identification of the *Brahman*, which pervades the universe, with the *ātman* or self in man; knowledge of which leads to *mokṣa* or release from *saṁsāra*.

This of course is still religion, but it would seem that during this great creative period in Indian culture there were also those whose speculation ran in a rather different direction and who denied these doctrines and avowedly asserted what can only be described as a naturalistic view of man and the world; so much we can deduce from the polemical references to such people which we find in the *Upaniṣads* themselves, although, as we shall see, there is further evidence, outwith the *Upaniṣads*, to support this.

As good an example as any of these tendencies is the discourse, recorded in the *Chāndogya Upaniṣad*, between Śvetakatu Aruneya and his father Uddālaka. The father answers his son's question regarding the primordial reality as follows:

> In the beginning this world was just Being (*sat*),
> one only without a second.
> To be sure, some people say,
> 'In the beginning this world was just Non-Being (*a-sat*),
> one only without a second;
> from that Non-Being Being was produced.'
> But verily, whence could this be?...
> How could Being from Non-Being be produced?
> On the contrary, in the beginning this world was just Being,
> one only without a second.
> (*Chāndogya Upaniṣad* [Hume 1921: 241])

The *Upaniṣad* next passes to relate how, out of Being, by a process of emanation, the plurality of the world as we know it was produced.

> It (Being) bethought itself: 'Would that I were many!
> Let me procreate myself!' It emitted heat.
> The heat bethought itself: 'Would that I were many!
> Let me procreate myself!' It emitted water.
> (*Chāndogya Upaniṣad* [Hume 1921: 241])

And so on until we come to the emanation of man, the main constituents of whom are taken to be food and water.

> Food when eaten, becomes divided into three parts.
> That which is its coarsest constituent, becomes faeces;
> that which is medium, the flesh;
> that which is finest, the mind.
>
> Water, when drunk, becomes divided into three parts.
> That which is its coarsest constituent becomes urine;
> that which is medium, the blood;
> that which is finest, the breath.
>
> Meat, when eaten, becomes divided into three parts.
> That which is its coarsest constituent, becomes bone;

that which is medium, the marrow;
that which is finest, the voice.

For the mind consists of food;
the breath consists of water;
the voice consists of heat.
(*Chāndogya Upaniṣad* [Hume 1921: 243])

The analogy which Uddālaka evokes to substantiate this claim is interesting:

Of coagulated milk when churned,
that which is the finest essence moves upward;
it becomes butter.

Even so food, when eaten,
that which is the finest essence all moves upward;
it becomes the mind.

Of water, when drunk,
that which is the finest essence all moves upward;
it becomes the voice.

For the mind consists of food;
the breath consists of water,
the voice consists of heat.
(*Chāndogya Upaniṣad* [Hume 1921: 243])

The proof which he adduces in support of this view is also worth noticing. Uddālaka asks his son to recite the *Vedas*, and the story continues:

The son said: 'Verily they do not come to me Sir.'
The father explained. 'Just as a single coal ...
may be left over from a great kindled fire,
but with it the fire would not thereafter burn much –

so of your sixteen parts, of a single sixteenth,
part may be left over, but with it
you not now apprehend the Vedas.
Eat then you will understand from me.
(*Chāndogya Upaniṣad* [Hume 1921: 244])

The son does so, and again approaches his father, but this time he is able to answer all that he is asked. Uddālaka explains this as follows:

Just as one may, by covering it with straw,
make a single coal ...
blaze up and with it
the fire would thereafter burn much –
so of your sixteen parts
a single sixteenth part has been left over.
After having been covered with food it has blazed up.
With it you now apprehend the Vedas;
for the mind consists of food,
the breath consists of water,
the voice consists of heat.
(*Chāndogya Upaniṣad* [Hume 1921: 245])

The real purpose of the discourse, however, is to get behind the principles of heat, water, and food to the fundamental reality behind everything that is – which is again identified with Being:

'All creatures have Being as their root,
have Being as their home,
have Being as their support ...'
[says Uddālaka]
'That which is the finest essence –
this whole world has that as its soul.
That is reality (*satya*). That is *ātman* (soul).
That art you, Swetakatu.
(*Chāndogya Upaniṣad* [Hume 1921: 245-246])

The East German Indiologist, Walter Ruben, argues that the views expressed by Uddālaka are similar to those of the 'Breath-Wind' magicians, as he calls them, who held that 'breath' was the most important constituent of the universe, and he gives a list of eighteen such thinkers mentioned by name in the older *Upaniṣads.*[6] Whilst accepting the existence of (rather earthy) gods, these thinkers sought to explain phenomena in terms of the fluctuations of breath and air, instead of by the creative activity of the gods; although some certainly did take 'air' for a deity.

Dale Riepe goes further and states that Uddālaka broke with the cosmological and theogonic tradition and held as an alternative a hylozoistic and perhaps even materialistic view of reality (1961: 27-32). Against his Idealistic opponent Jajnavalkya, who held that the great Spirit of the universe was like a musical instrument and the 'world-stuff' like a tone struck off it, Uddālaka, according to Riepe, stated that Being was like a tone only in the sense that a tone must arise from material 'stuff'. He further held, says Riepe, that nothing can come out of nothing – not even by divine power – and thus whatever is thought must be dependent on Being, which for him meant physical matter. Riepe thus holds that Uddālaka is important for the subsequent development of naturalism on four counts: (1) his hints at a monistic natural universe, (2) his suggestion that natural elements are made up of physical being, (3) his proto-atomistic theory, and (4) his analysis of meaning in terms of the physically observable (1961: 31).

This is surely going too far. Tempting as it is to see fully materialistic theories in the views put forward by Uddālaka in the early part of the dialogue given above, Uddālaka himself was certainly no materialist, as the concluding section of the discourse shows. There, as elsewhere in the *Chāndogya Upaniṣad*, the Soul of the Universe, Being itself, is identified by Uddālaka with the *ātman* or soul in man, ultimately a spiritual and not a material principle. Whether or not the views expressed in the early part of the dialogue are the relics of an older materialism, as some have maintained (e.g. Chattopadhyaya 1959: 434), or the prototype of views which later, in the Sāṃkhya philosophy, for instance, developed in a fully materialistic direction is a debatable point (e.g. Jacobi 1884-85; cf. Belvakar and Ranade 1926: 415f.). What is certain is that Uddālaka himself is no fully-fledged materialist, although there certainly are elements in his thinking which would suggest a physical basis for that which many people would call spiritual.

Better evidence of near-naturalistic speculation can, however, be found in other *Upanisads*. The *Śvetāśvatara Upaniṣad*, for instance, speaks of those deluded sages who take 'time' or 'nature' to be the cause of everything:

> Some wise men, deluded, speak of Nature,
> and others of Time (as the cause of everything):
> but it is the greatness of God
> by which this Brahma-wheel is made to turn.
> (*Śvetāśvatara Upaniṣad* IV. VI [Müller])

While earlier, after raising such questions as:

> ... Is Brahman the cause? Whence are we born?
> Whereby do we live, and whither do we go?
> O ye who know Brahman, [tell us] at whose command we abide,
> whether in pain or in pleasure?

the same *Upaniṣad* goes on:

> Should time, or nature, or necessity, or chance,
> or the elements be considered as the cause,
> or he who is called the person (*Paruṣa*)?
> (*Śvetāśvatara Upaniṣad* I. VI. 2 [Müller])

The denial of *saṁsāra*, and, therefore, of the need for *mokṣa* or release from it, is also referred to in the *Upaniṣads*. The *Kaṭha Upaniṣad*, for instance, says that there are grave doubts among certain people (*nāstikas*) whether one does or does not exist after death.

> Naciketus said: 'There is that doubt,

when a man is dead, –
some saying he is; others, he is not.
This I should like to know, taught by thee....'

To which Death, who is being addressed, replies,

'... On this point even the gods have doubted formerly,
it is not easy to understand.
Choose another boon, O Naciketas,
do not press me, and let me off that boon.'
(*Kaṭha Upaniṣad* I. v. 20 [Müller])

Naciketas, however, refuses to be put off and eventually is given the answer which became orthodox Indian teaching about the nature of the self, and its destiny.

Again, in the *Bṛhad-āraṇyaka Upaniṣad*, we come across references to those who maintain that consciousness arises from a combination of the primary elements of matter and vanishes when this combination disintegrates at death.

As a lump of salt, when thrown into water
becomes dissolved into water,
and could not be taken out again,
but wherever we taste [the water] it is salt, –
verily, O Maitreyi, does this great Being [the self]
endless, unlimited, consisting of nothing
but knowledge; and having risen from out of these elements,
and vanishes again in them.
When he has departed there is no more knowledge....
(*Bṛhad-āraṇyaka Upaniṣad* II, v. 12 [Müller])

and again,

As a mass of salt has neither inside nor outside,
but is altogether a mass of taste,
thus indeed has that Self neither inside nor outside,

but is altogether a mass of knowledge;
and having risen from out of these elements,
vanishes again in them.
When he has departed there is no more knowledge.
(*Bṛhad-āraṇyaka Upaniṣad* IV, 5. v. 13 [Müller])

Whilst most references to naturalistic views in the *Upanisads* are polemical, there is one *Upaniṣad*, the *Swasanved*, which is avowedly naturalistic (*Swasanved Upaniṣad*, Sutra 11). Its thesis has been summarised as follows:

> There is no incarnation, no God, no heaven, no hell; all traditional religion is the work of conceited fools; nature, the originator, and time the destroyer, are the rulers of things and take no account of virtue and vice in awarding happiness or misery to men; people deluded by flowery speeches cling to God's temples and priests, when in reality, there is no difference between Visnu and a god. (Roy 1952: 561)

2.5 THE BEGINNINGS OF LOKĀYĀTA

It is out of tendencies such as those which we have considered, and which belong to the earliest period of Indian speculation, that there emerged, sometime before the sixth century BC, the materialistic and hedonistic outlook known as Lokāyāta. The origins of this school are obscure and with the exception of one late treatise – the *Tattvopaplavasiṇha*, or *The Lion that Devours all (religious) Categories*, of Jayāraśi Bhaṭṭa – from the seventh century AD, what we know of this school must be reconstructed almost entirely from polemical references in the writings of its opponents. There would appear to have once existed a major work of this school known as the *Bṛhaspati Sūtra*,[8] but this is now lost, although reference to it, and perhaps even brief quotations from it, can be found in later writers. The teachings of the school were certainly known to the early Buddhists and it is from their writings, together with references in the *Visnu Purana*, the *Mahābhārata*, the *Rāmāyana*, the *Sarva-siddhānta-saṁgraha*,[9] and the *Sarva-darśana-*

saṁgrha of Mādhavācārya, that what is known is for the most part derived. The *Laws of Manu* mention 'nihilists, heretics and revilers of the Vedas' (Bühler 1886: 11, ii), but whether this is a reference to the Lokāyātikas is not certain.

Various theories have been put forward to account for the origins of Lokāyāta.[10]

Radhakrishnan, for instance, argued that Lokāyāta was the product of the unsettled conditions existing in India during the period 600 BC to 200 AD – a period when the faith of previous centuries was crumbling and the hold of authority over the people was being shattered (1948, I: 271-276). He wrote:

> In such an atmosphere ever so many metaphysical fancies and futile speculations were put forward.... We have the materialists with their insistence on the world of sense, the Buddhists with their valuable psychological teachings and high ethics. (1948, I: 272)

Despite his obvious distaste for the Lokāyāta – he writes, of course, as an orthodox Vedāntin – Radhakrishnan saw Lokāyāta as a progressive force, in that it repudiated the old religion of custom and magic, declared the spiritual independence of the individual, rejected the principle of authority, and so helped to pave the way for the Vedānta. He wrote:

> The Carvaka philosophy is a fanatical effort made to rid the age of the past that was oppressing it. The removal of dogmatism which it helped to effect was necessary to make room for the great constructive efforts of speculation. (1948, I: 283)

For Dasgupta, the origins of Lokāyāta were to be found in ancient Sumer, although on being imported into India the beliefs underwent, so he held, considerable modification (1940, III: 528f). An important piece of evidence regarding Lokāyāta, to which Dasgupta sought to give due weight, is a passage in the *Chāndogya Upaniṣad* where the body and the mind are said, by people identified as Asuras, to be identical (1940, III: 529) – a view which, as we shall see, was indeed held by the Lokāyātikas. Dasgupta identified these Asuras with the ancient Sumerians who buried their dead with clothing and other possessions, in the belief that they would be required when the dead were resurrected. He wrote:

> Probably the Lokāyāta doctrines had their beginnings in the preceeding Sumerian civilization in the then prevailing customs of adorning the dead and the doctrine of bodily survival after death. This later on became so far changed that it was argued that since the self and the body were identical and since the body was burned after death, there could not be any survival after death and hence there could not be another world after death.... We thus know that Lokāyāta views are very old ... being current among the Sumerian people of pre-Aryan times. (1940, III: 529, 531)

The link which Dasgupta saw between the Asuras and the Lokāyāta is, as we shall see shortly, an important one. The rest of his theory is not one, however, that need be taken too seriously.

The Italian Indiologist Professor Tucci saw Lokāyāta as originally a part of Indian priest-craft. He, like Rhys Davids, was aware of the fact that in the writings of early Buddhism *Lokāyāta* was spoken of as a branch of Brahmanical learning. Unlike Rhys Davids, however, who took Lokāyāta to refer to Nature-Law (Davids 1889: 171), Tucci understood it as referring to state-craft or political science (Tucci 1925: 40). In the *Artha-Sāstra* of Kutilya Lokāyāta is also designated as a science – along with Sāṃkhya and Yoga – to be studied by all accomplished persons, which would seem to suggest that it was once perfectly acceptable to orthodoxy. If this is so, then it would appear that from the point of view of orthodoxy it later degenerated. This is certainly the view taken of it by Buddhist writers. Buddhaghoso calls it a *vitaṇḍā-vāda-satthaṃ* (cf. Davids 1889: 167). *Vitaṇḍā* means that tricky logical discussion designed rather to criticise an opponent's thesis without upholding a counter-thesis of one's own. *Vāda*, on the other hand, means just the reverse – and refers to logical discussion undertaken to uphold a particular thesis. There would thus appear something odd in calling Lokāyāta both *vitaṇḍā* and *vāda*. Dasgupta, however, suggests that early Buddhism, which had little sympathy with philosophical speculation, did not distinguish between the two, but used *vāda* to denote both forms of argument (1940: 512-513).

Certainly it would appear that logic, as so often in its relationship with religious belief, proved more the enemy than the friend, capable of being wielded with destructive and annihilating force. 'Follow not the Lokāyāta that works not for the progress in merit' says Vidhura the Pundit (cf. Davids 1889: 168) – a sentiment which was echoed in 12th century Europe by Bernard of Clairvaux in his dispute with Abelard (cf. Thrower 1973: 58-68).

There is further evidence that the debate between faith and reason occurred early in India. The art of disputation was certainly very old, for we read in the *Yayur-veda* and in the *Nyaya-sūtras* that the orthodox took the trouble to learn the art of logic, if only to defend themselves against attack (Dasgupta 1940: 516-517). Reference can also be found to this in the *Mahābhārata* epic (*Mahābhārata* III, 13034; V, 1983; XIII, 789). Dasgupta even suggests that the orthodox Hindu doctrine that ultimate truth can only be ascertained by appeal to the sacred scriptures, since no finality can be reached by rational argument (the arguments of one logician contravening the arguments of another) can be traced back to the negative influence of these early dialecticians, who sought to refute by argument the Vedic doctrine of birth and rebirth, with its presupposition of an immortal soul, and who also attacked the efficacy of the sacrificial ritual (Dasgupta 1940: 517). Further the *Laws of Manu* demand that those Brahmins who through confidence in reason ignore the authority of *śruti* and *smṛti*, and who are, therefore, no better than the *nāstikas*, should be driven out by all good men. But this is to look too far ahead. Our concern at the moment is with the origins of Lokāyāta rather than with its later development.

A further interesting suggestion regarding Lokāyāta was that put forward by H.P. Shastri (1925: 4f.), who saw Lokāyāta not simply as belonging to some ancient period of Indian history, but as surviving into the India of today among certain obscure and neglected sects. Arguing on the basis of evidence from the *Bṛihaspati Sūtra* (recovered by Thomas) and the writings of the Jain commentator Gunaratna, he saw a close connection between Lokāyāta and an ancient sect called the *Kapalīkas*. Whilst the *Bṛihaspati Sūtra* sees them as distinct sects, Gunaratna identifies the two. On the basis of this identification Shastri wrote:

... the influence of the Lokāyātikās and the *Kapalīkas* is still strong

> in India. There is a sect, and a numerous one too, the followers of which believe that *deha*, or the material human body, is all that should be cared for, and their religious practices are concerned with the union of men and women.... These call themselves *Vaiṣṇavas*, but they do not believe in *Viṣṇu* or *Kṛiṣṇa* or his incarnations. They believe in *deha*. They have another name, *Sahajia*, which is the name of a sect of Buddhists which arose from *Mahāyāna* in the last four centuries of its existence in India. (1925: 6)

His son, D.R. Shastri, took this suggestion a stage further. Degenerates, he believed, attract each other and he saw an amalgam taking place between degenerate Lokāyāta and degenerate Buddhism. He wrote:

> Some of the sects of degenerated Buddhists, in which laxity in sexual morals was one of the features, became gradually affiliated to the Lokāyāta school. One of these sects was the Kapalīka sect. The Kapalīkas are a very ancient sect. They drink wine, offer human sacrifices and enjoy women. They strive to attain their religious goal with the help of human corpses, wine and women.... As *kama*, or the enjoyment of sensual pleasure was the goal of this sect, it came gradually to be affiliated to the *Nāstika* form of the Lokāyāta school, according to which the summum bonum of the human life is ... the enjoyment of gross sensual pleasure. (1930: 35-36)

And a little later:

> After the great Brahmanic renaissance the *Lokāyāta* sect took shelter under different forms in different parts of India. In Bengal, an old sect of the Buddhist Mahāyāna school chiefly concerned with sexual romance gave up its independent existence and like the Svabhavavadins and the Kapalīkas became at one with the *Nāstika* Lokāyātikas and the Lokāyātikas on their part incorporated themselves with that community. The old element of sensualism of the festival of Madanotsava of the Nāstikas, sanction for the gratification of grosser pleasures, is still found to linger in this sect. The name of this sect is the Sahajin sect. (1930: 37)

The problem with regard to the origin of Lokāyāta is that of reconciling in a single theory the various pieces of evidence noticed by those whose theories we have outlined above. Basically these are: (1) that in its earliest period Lokāyāta would appear to have been a respectable branch of Brahmanical learning, (2) that it would appear to have some connection both with views called Asura and with the rites and outlook of a number of other obscure sects – some of which survive to the present day, and (3) that it would also appear to have some connection with early non-Vedic speculation.

Evidence to the effect that early Lokāyāta was not just a speculative philosophy but that, whilst opposed to Vedic ritualism, it had ritual practices of its own, has been put forward recently by the Bengali Marxist historian Deprisad Chattopadhyaya in a stimulating study of the origins of Lokāyāta (1959: 37ff.). He notes that in the Buddhist text *Saddharma Pundarika* (cf. Müller, ed. 1879-1910, *S.B.E.*, XXI: 263) we come across a passage in which the words *lokāyāta-mantra-dharka* and *lokāyātika* are mentioned together. Kern translates the passage as follows:

> ... when he does not serve, not court, not wait upon adepts of wordly spells (*lokāyāta-mantra-dharka*) and votaries of a world-philosophy (*lokāyātika*).... (*Ibid.*, *S.B.E.*, XXI: 263)

From this passage it is clear that the Lokāyātikas were thought of as practising some kind of spell (*mantra*).

Similarly in another Buddhist text, the *Divyavandana* (*Ibid.*, *S.B.E.*, XXI: 619), we come across the phrase lokāyāta-yajna-mantresunisnstah which may mean either expert in *lokāyāta-yajna* [ritual] and spell [*mantra*] or expert in the *yajna* and *mantra* of Lokāyāta or expert in the *mantras* of the *lokāyāta-yajna*. However understood, the text sees a connection between Lokāyāta and ritual and spell.

Another Buddhist text, the *Vinaya Pitaka*, makes it overwhelmingly clear that early Buddhism understood Lokāyāta as being largely a matter of magic spells.

> Now at that time the Chabbaggiya Bhikkhus learnt the Lokāyāta system.

People murmured, etc. saying. 'Like those who still enjoy the
   pleasures of the world!'
The Bhikkhus heard of the people thus murmuring; and those
   Bhikkhus told the matter to the Blessed One.
'Now can a man who holds the Lokāyāta as valuable reach up,
O Bhikkhus, to the full advantage of it, or attain to full growth
   in,
to full breath in this doctrine and discipline?'
'This cannot be Lord!'
'Or can a man who holds this doctrine and discipline to be
   valuable learn the Lokāyāta system?'
'This cannot be Lord!'
'You are not, O Bhikkhus, to learn the Lokāyāta system ...
to teach the Lokāyāta system ... to learn or teach the low arts
(of divination, spells, omens, astrology,
sacrifices to gods, witchcraft and quakery).'
(*Ibid., S.B.E.,* XX: 151-152)

Rhys Davids too has noted that the seven 'low arts' are mentioned in
association with Lokāyāta in the *Maha Sila.* The connection between
Lokāyāta and religio-magical practices would therefore appear to be
clearly established.

If this is so, then the clash between Brahmanical orthodoxy and
Lokāyāta is not simply a clash between those who asserted and those
who denied certain religious beliefs but a clash between two cultures
— the latter, as the name suggests, being deep-rooted in the lives of
the ordinary people (Chattopadyaya 1959: 40).

This suggestion is reinforced if we now take cognisance of the fact,
noted by Dasgupta, but before him as early as 1862 by Muir (Dasgupta
1940: 531; Muir 1862: 302), that a number of ancient sources — the
Chāndogya Upaniṣad, the *Viṣṇu Purāṇa* and the *Mahābhārata* epic in
particular — attribute views very like those attributed by later sources
to the Lokāyātikas to people called Asuras.[11]

The *Viṣṇu Purāṇa* describes these Asura views as follows:

   The great Deceiver, practising illusion, next beguiled other Daityas [i.e. heretical Indians] by means of many other forms of heresy. In a very short time these Asuras, deluded by the deceiver, abandoned the entire system founded on the ordinances of the triple Veda.

Some reviled the Vedas, others the gods, others the ceremonial of sacrifice, and others the Brahmans. This, they declared is a doctrine which will not bear discussion; the slaughter [of animals in sacrifice] is not conducive to religious merit.

[To say that] oblations of butter consumed in the fire produce any future reward, is the assertion of a child.

If Indra, having attained to godhead by numerous sacrifices, feeds upon sami, and other woods, then an animal which eats leaves is superior to him. If it be a fact that a beast slain in sacrifice is exalted to heaven, why does not the worshipper slaughter his own father?

If a man is really satiated by food which another person eats, then sraddhas should be offered to people who are travelling abroad, and they, trusting to this, should have no need to carry any food along with them.

After it has been settled that this doctrine is entitled to credence, let the opinions which I express be pondered and received as conducive to happiness.

Infallible utterances, great Asuras, do not fall from the skies; it is only assertions founded on reasoning that are accepted by me, and by other intelligent persons like yourselves. (*Viṣṇu Purāṇa* III. 18. 14-20 [Muir])

Similarly in that portion of the *Mahābhārata* epic known as the *Bhagavad-Gītā* Kṛṣna speaks as follows:

Two orders of contingent beings in this world there are:
The godly and the devilish [*asuras*].
Of the godly I have discoursed enough,
Now listen to my words about the devilish.

Of creative action and its cessation

The devilish folk know nothing;
In them thou'lt find no purity nor yet
Seeming behaviour or truthfulness.

'The world's devoid of truth' they say,
'It has no ground, no ruling Lord,
It has not come to be by mutual causal law;
Desire alone has caused it, nothing else.'
[*or variant reading*, 'random and without any cause']

Fast holding to these views,
Lost souls with feeble minds,
They embark on cruel and violent deeds, – malignant
[In their lust] for the destruction of the world.

Insatiate desire's their starting-point –
Possessed of hypocrisy, pride and frenzy,
Clutching at false conceptions, deluded as they are,
Plying their several trades; impure are their resolves.

Unmeasured care is theirs
Right up to the time of their death,
[For] they aim at nothing but to satisfy their lusts,
Convinced that this is all.
(*Bhagavad Gītā* XVI. 7-18 [Zaehner])

Earlier sources, such as the *Maitrayani Upaniṣad*, also mention the myth recounted in the *Viṣṇu Purāṇa* concerning the origin of the devilish and un-Vedic views of the Lokāyātikas (*Maitrayani Upaniṣad* VII. 9). The important question is therefore: who were the Asuras? In the myths of the *Upaniṣads* they are, of course, regarded as 'devils', but as Chattopadhyaya has argued, it is highly likely that they represent a real and despised section of the early populace of India (1959: 42ff.).

He begins answering the question of their identity by looking at the views attributed to them in the *Upaniṣads* (cf. *Maitrayani Upaniṣad*

VII. 10; *Chāndogya Upaniṣad* VIII. 788). For the most part these concern the nature of the self and the origin of the universe. Of their view of the self the *Chāndogya Upaniṣad* speaks as follows:

> Oneself is to be made happy here on earth.
> Onself is to be waited upon.
> He who makes his own self happy here on earth,
> who waits upon himself – he obtains both worlds,
> both this world and the yonder.
> (*Chāndogya Upaniṣad* VIII. 788 [Hume])

The Asuras it would seem identified the self with the body, as did the later Lokāyātikas. This view – known as the *deha-vada* in Buddhist sources – was not, however, by them identified with Lokāyāta. Buddhist sources, as we have seen, identify Lokāyāta with magico-religious practices. Chattopadhyaya thus raises the question, 'Do we come across in the cultural history of ancient India any *deha-vada* which was at the same time characterised by its distinctive spells and rituals?' (1959: 48). His answer is that we do, for in those obscure beliefs and practices which are broadly referred to as Tantrism we find just that combination of *deha-vada* belief and magico-religious practice which, combining the evidence from all the ancient sources, was said to characterise early Lokāyāta. As Chattopadhyaya understands Tantrism it was originally non-Vedic, atheistic and materialistic. The latter description is doubtful, but Chattopadhyaya's identification of original Lokāyāta with Tantrism has much to commend it.[12]

But whatever the origins of Lokāyāta, there is considerable evidence that from about the sixth century BC the Lokāyātikas emerged as a definite school of philosophy associated with the name of Cārvāka.[13]

There is also evidence from Buddhist sources that other heretical thinkers were abroad – which would substantiate Muir and Radhakrishnan's claim that the sixth century was one in which a considerable amount of free-thinking was taking place. These thinkers and their views are interesting in themselves irrespective of their possible influence on Lokāyāta, and we will consider them now before turning to look in detail at the Lokāyāta system. The most important are Purana Kassapa, Ajita Kesakambali and Makkhali Gosala, a contemporary of the Buddha and of Mahavira, who founded the sect of the Ajivikas.

2.6 SOME EARLY FREETHINKERS

Purana Kassapa — a wandering ascetic — attacked the fundamental Hindu doctrine of *karma* and held that there was no such thing as virtue or vice and thus that no action could lead, as the doctrine of karma taught, to any fruit hereafter. In reply to King Ajatasatru, who asked him what visible reward their was in the life of a recluse, he answered:

> To him who acts, O king, or causes another to act,
> to him who mutilates or causes another to mutilate, —
> to him who causes grief or torment, ...
> to him who commits robbery, ... adultery, or who speaks lies,
> to him thus acting there is no guilt....
> Were he to go along the south bank of the Ganges
> giving alms and ordering gifts to be given,
> offering sacrifices or causing them to be offerred,
> there would be no merit thence resulting,
> no increase of merit.
> In generosity, in self-mastery, in control of the senses,
> in speaking truth,
> there is neither merit, nor increase of merit.
> (*Samanna-Phala-Sūtra — The Fruits of the Life of a Recluse*, (52) 17 [Davids 1889: 69-70])

The teaching of Ajita Kesakambali (Ajita of the garment of hair) is very similar; for he is reported as saying that not only is there

> no such thing as alms or sacrifice or offering. There is neither fruit nor result of good and evil deeds. There is no such thing as this world or the next.

Going further he attacks not only Upaniṣadic doctrines but the persons of the Brahmins themselves when he asserts that:

> There are in the world no recluses or Brahmins who have
> reached the highest point who walk perfectly and who,
> having understood and realised, by themselves alone, both
> in this world and the next, make their wisdom known to others.

He also puts forward an anthropology every whit as naturalistic as that which we later find attributed to Cārvāka:

> A human being, [he says] is built up of the four elements;
> when he dies the earth in him returns and relapses to the earth,
> the fluid to the water, the heat to the fire, his wind to the air,
> and his faculties pass into space.
> The four bearers, with the beirs the fifth, take the dead body away;
> till they reach the burial ground men utter eulogies,
> but there his bones are bleached and his offerings end in ashes.
> It is a doctrine of fools this talk of gifts.
> It is an empty lie, mere idle talk,
> when men say there is profit therein.
> Fools and wise alike, on the dissolution of the body,
> are cut off, annihiliated and after death they are not.
> (*Samanna-Phala-Sūtra*, (55) 23 [Davids 1889: 73-74])

Makkhali Gosala, the founder of the Ajīvikas – a sect which survived until at least the thirteenth century AD (cf. Basham 1951) – also denied the doctrine of *karma* and would appear to have held something approaching a naturalistic conception of man:

> All animals, all creatures (with one, two or more senses),
> all beings (produced from eggs or in a womb),
> all souls are without force and power and energy of their own.
> They are bent this way and that by their fate,

> by the necessary condition of the class to which they belong, by their individual nature....
> (Davids 1889: 71)

On the other hand Gosala believed not only in the doctrine of *saṁsāra*, but also introduced a doctrine of re-animation. However, there are other heretics referred to in early Buddhist writings whose anthropology is certainly wholly naturalistic.[14] They are reported as holding that,

> Upwards from the soul of the feet up to the bottom of the tips of hair and in all transverse directions the soul is up to the skin; so long as there is the body there is the soul and there is no soul apart from this body; when the body is dead there is no soul.
>
> When the body is burnt no soul is seen and all that is seen is but the white bones. When one draws a sword from a scabbard, one can say that the former lies within the latter, but one cannot say similarly of the soul that it exists in the body; there is in reality no way of distinguishing the soul from the body such that one may say that the former exists in the latter. (*Sutra-Kṛtanga-Sutra* 11.1.9-10 [Gupta])

This certainly sounds like the view attributed to Cārvāka/Lokāyāta by other (non-Buddhist) sources, as we shall see shortly.

One other source shows acquaintance with similar views. The *Ramayana* epic puts into the mouth of the Brahman Jabali views which are intended to shake the faith of Rama in the arrangements made for him by his late father, whereby he lived the life of a forest recluse, so that he might return from the forest and take possession of the throne now offered to him by his dutiful younger brother. The conflict is in a way perhaps to be read as symbolical of the conflict of earthly over against spiritual and other-worldly satisfactions. Jabali, who is described as a logician (*naiyāyika*), addresses Rama as follows:

> You, descendent of Raghu, ought not, like an ordinary person,

to entertain such unprofitable notions, the contemptible ideas of an ascetic....
How can any person be of kin to any other? What has anyone to do with any other? Seeing that every creature is born alone and dies alone.
Hence a mother and a father resemble a lodging; the man who feels any attachment to them is to be regarded as insane....
Permit yourself to be enthroned in opulent Ayodha; that city eagerly expects you....
Enjoying, Prince, the exquisite gratifications of royalty, disport yourself there as Indra does in paradise.
Dasaratha [Your Father] is now nothing to you, nor you to him; that kin [was] one person, and you [are] another; do therefore what I advise.
A father is nothing more than the seed of a creature; his seminal principle, with blood and air, combined with the seminal substance of the mother – such is a man's generation of a son.
That monarch has gone to the place where he had to go; such is the course of human beings; but you are being needlessly injured.
Wherefore I inquire of such as adhere to justice, and of no others; for the just suffer affliction here, and when they die they incur annihilation.
Oblations are offered to projenitors and to the gods; men are intent upon the ceremony, but see what a destruction of food! What is left for the dead?
If an oblation eaten here by one [really] passes into the body of another, then let a sraddha be offered to a man who is travelling abroad, and let him carry no provisions for his journey.
These books composed by wise men [containing such precepts as] worship, bestow, offer sacrifice, practise austerities, abandon [the world] are merely meant to multiply gifts.
Understand, intelligent [prince], that no one exists hereafter; regard not that which is beyond the reach of our senses, but only that which is an object of perception.
Acting upon this principle, which should be the guide of all man-

kind, allow yourself to be persuaded by Bharata [his younger brother], and accept your kingdom.
(*Ramayana* Sect. III [Muir])

These sentiments are exactly those which are attributed to Cārvāka by other writers. But before turning to Cārvāka, one other figure should certainly be noted — Sangaya, of the Belattha clan, whose reply to certain questions asked of him illustrate the supreme prevarication of the agnostic. He says:

> If you ask me whether there is another world — well, if I thought there were, I would say so. But I don't say so. And I don't think it thus or thus. And I don't think it otherwise. And I don't deny it. And I don't say there neither is, nor is not, another world. And if you ask me about the beings produced by chance; or whether there is any fruit, any result, of good or bad actions; or whether a man who has won the truth continues, or not, after death — to each or any of their questions do I give the same reply. (*Samann-Phala-Sūtra* (59) 31 [Davids 1889: 75])

2.7 PHILOSOPHICAL LOKĀYĀTA OR CĀRVĀKA

Whether the name of Cārvāka, which in the later tradition becomes an alternative designation of the more ancient Lokāyāta, refers to an historical personage is a matter for dispute. As already mentioned, some later writers name the founder of this school as Bṛhaspati — although this may simply reflect the legend, to which we have referred, to the effect that Bṛhaspati in order to deceive those enemies of the gods, the Asuras, propounded a materialistic philosophy. Cārvāka, which could mean 'sweet-tongued', may, of course, not be a proper name at all but simply a pejorative designation of a philosophy which later Idealistic philosophers despised. A Cārvāka is mentioned, however, in the *Mahābhārata Epic*, where he plays the part of the moral accuser of Yudhisthira, whom he accuses, at the moment of his triumph, of killing kith and kin; for which outrage he, Cārvāka, is burnt by the Brahmins. Thus the designation 'Cārvāka' may derive from this legend, for Cārvāka is there mentioned as an Asura, whose views, as we have seen, were close to Lokāyāta.

But whatever the historicity of Cārvāka, and whatever the early origins of Lokāyāta, what is certain is that from about the sixth century BC there arose in India the philosophical articulation of views which we would now call naturalistic and which later tradition designated as Lokāyāta or Cārvāka; views which challenged and continued to challenge the dominant religious interpretation of life for something like a thousand years.

Professor Tucci (1926) after an extensive examination of all surviving references to this school, reconstructs its tenets as follows:

1. Sacred literature should be disregarded as false.
2. There is no deity or supernatural.
3. There is no immortal soul and nothing exists after the death of the body.
4. Karma is inoperative and an illusion.
5. All (that is) is derived from material elements.
6. Material elements have an immanent force.
7. Intelligence is derived from these elements.
8. Only direct perception gives true knowledge.
9. Religious injunctions and the sacerdotal class are useless.
10. The aim of life is to get the maximum amount of pleasure.

This philosophy, as can be seen from the above summary of its main tenets, is naturalistic (and therefore atheistic in the Western sense of the term) in epistemology, metaphysics and ethics.

The foundations of Cārvāka lie in its realist epistemology which asserts that all knowledge is derived from the five senses. According to the *Sarva-siddhānta-saṅgraha* Cārvāka held that,

> Only the perceived exists; the unperceivable does not exist, by reason of its never having been perceived. (Radhakrishnan and Moore 1973: 234)

Perception can be of two kinds, as we learn from the *Sarva-darśana-saṅgraha* of Mādhavācārya. It can be neither external, in so far as it is produced by the five senses, or internal, in so far as it is produced by the inner sense or mind. (*Ibid.*: 229)

On the basis of this epistemology the Cārvāka drew a number of conclusions, among them that reality consists only of four elements – earth, air, fire and water. Ether, which was generally accepted as a fifth element, they denied, as it was not perceivable. The validity of inference from particular to universal propositions was also denied. Their ontology was thus an unqualified materialism. The world, including man, they held, is made up of the four elements and is neither created nor directed by any supernatural agency and this is the only world that there is. There is no heaven and no hell, and no rebirth; in fact no life at all hereafter. Consciousness arises out of the combination of the elements in the body and disintegrates upon the death of the body.

> In this school, [Mādhavācārya tells us] the four elements are the original principles; from these alone, when transformed into the body, intelligence is produced, just as the inebriating power is developed from the mixing of certain ingredients; and when these are destroyed, intelligence at once perishes also. They quote the Sruti for this (Brhadaranyaka Upaniṣad 11. iv. 12) 'Springing forth from these elements, itself solid knowledge, it is destroyed – after death no intelligence remains.' Therefore the soul is only the body distinguished by the attribute of intelligence, since there is no evidence for any self distinct from the body, as such cannot be proved, since this school holds that perception is the only source of knowledge and does not allow inference. (*Ibid.*: 234-235)

This is confirmed by the *Sarva-siddhānta-saṅgraha*, which states:

> According to the Lokayata doctrine the four elements alone are the ultimate principles – earth, water, fire and air, there is none other.
>
> Only the perceived exists; the unperceivable does not exist, by reason of its never having been perceived; even the believers in the invisible say that the invisible has been perceived.
>
> If the rarely perceived be taken for the unperceived, how can they call it the unperceived?
>
> How can the ever-unperceived, like things such as the horns of a hare, be an existent?

> Others should not here postulate [the existence] of merit and demerit from happiness and misery.
> A person is happy or miserable through [the laws] of nature; there is no other cause.
> Who paints the peacocks, or who makes the cuckoos sing?
> There exists here no cause excepting nature.
> The soul is but the body characterised by the attributes signified in the expressions, 'I am stout', 'I am youthful', 'I am grown up', 'I am old' etc. It is not something other than the body.
> The consciousness that is found in the modifications of non-intelligent elements [i.e. in organisms formed out of matter] is produced in the manner of the red colour out of the combination of betel, areca-nut and lime.
> There is no world other than this, there is no heaven and no hell; the realm of Siva and like regions are invented by stupid impostors of other schools of thought. (*Ibid.*)

and again, from the *Sarva-darśana-saṅgraha*, where the author quotes from what is evidently a Cārvāka/Lokāyāta text, which he attributes to Bṛhaspati,

> The fire is hot, the water cold, refreshing cool the breeze of the morn;
> By whom came this variety? from their own nature was it born.
> There is no heaven, no final liberation, nor any soul in another world,
> Nor do the actions of the four castes, orders, etc. produce any real effect.
> The Agnihotra, the three Vedas, the ascetics three staves, and smearing oneself with ashes,
> Were made by nature as the livelihood of those destitute of knowledge and manliness. (*Ibid.*: 233)

Here a new note is struck. The priests with their sacrificial ritual are not just mistaken – they are frauds. Bṛhaspati goes on:

> If a beast slain in the Jytishoma rite will itself go to heaven, why then does not the sacrifice forthwith offer his own father?
> If the Sraddha produces gratification to beings who are dead,
> Then here, too, in the case of travellers when they start, it is needless to give provisions for the journey.
> If beings in heaven are gratified by our offering the Sraddha here,
> Then why not give food down below to those who are standing on the housetop?
> While life remains let a man live happily, let him feed on ghee even though he runs into debt;
> When once the body has become ashes, how can it ever return again?
> If he who departs from the body goes to another world,
> How is it that he come not back again, restless for love of his kindred?
> Hence it is only as a means of livelihood that Brahmans have established here.
> All ceremonies for the dead – there is no other fruit anywhere.
> The three authors of the Vedas were buffoons, knaves and demons.
> All the well-known formulae of the pundits, jarphari, turphari, etc.,
> And all the obscene rites for the queen commanded in the Aswamedha.
> These were invented by buffoons, and so all the various kinds of presents to the priests. (*Ibid.*: 234)

From the writings of the early Buddhists – who had certain things in common with the Cārvākas, such as the rejection of the sacrificial system and of caste, but who disagreed on others, such as the Cārvāka denial of transmigration – it is possible to reconstruct the actual arguments which the Cārvākas brought against the notion of a substantial soul and its transmigration (cf. Dasgupta 1940: 540f.). Why, the Cārvākas argued, if the soul has existed before now, does it not remember its previous existences? Why does it not return, if it survives death, in such a way as to be observed? Believers themselves show their belief in rebirth to be absurd by their actions, for they do not behave as though they believed, since, for instance, they fear death. They further argued against the Buddhist view that the series of conscious states in any life (the early Buddhists, of course, denied a substantial self) are due to the last conscious state before death in a previous life, and that the state of consciousness in any life can be the cause of a series of conscious states in another future life. The Cārvākas asserted, against the Buddhists, that no consciousness that belongs to a different body and a different series can be regarded as the cause of a different series of conscious states belonging to a different body; in short, that consciousness appertaining to one body cannot be said to be the cause of consciousness in another body. Again they argued that no consciousness is carried over into foetal life. A child must learn what it knows from outwith itself. And lastly, and this is in accord with their realistic epistemology, no one, they argued, has ever observed the transference of consciousness from one body to another.

Such then is the Cārvāka metaphysic. The ethical consequences which they drew from this outlook on the world were, as one might expect, thoroughly hedonistic – something which ran counter to the whole tenor of the ascetic approach to life of higher Hinduism and for which they were violently attacked. As the *Sarva-darśana-saṅgraha* says, in their ethic,

> The only end of men is enjoyment produced by sensual pleasures.

If it be replied to this that such cannot be the true end of man, for all pleasure is mixed with some kind of pain, the Cārvāka had a ready reply:

> It is our wisdom to enjoy pure pleasure as far as we can, and to avoid the pain which inevitably accompanies it; just as the man who desires fish takes the fish with their scales and bones, and having taken as many as he wants, desists; or just as the man who desires rice, takes the rice, straw and all, and having taken as much as he wants, desists. It is not therefore for us, through

> fear of pain, to reject the pleasure which our nature instinctively recognises as congenial. Men do not refrain from sowing rice, because forsooth there are wild animals to devour it, nor do they refuse to set the cooking-pots on the fire, because forsooth there are beggars to pester us for a share of the contents. If one were so timid as to forsake a visible pleasure, he would indeed be foolish like a beast. (Radhakrishnan and Moore 1973: 229)

And they quoted the words of a popular poet:

> The pleasure which arises to men from contact with sensible objects,
> Is it to be relinquished as accompanied by pain?—such is the reasoning of fools;
> The berries of paddy, rich with the finest white grains,
> What man, seeking his true interest, would fling away because covered with husk and dust?
> (*Ibid.*: 229)

The *Sarva-siddhānta-saṅgraha* expands on this. According to the Lokāyata doctrine, it says:

> The enjoyment of heaven lies in eating delicious food, keeping the company of young women, using fine clothes, perfumes, garlands, sandal paste, etc.
> The pain of hell lies in the troubles that arise from enemies, weapons, diseases; while liberation [mokṣa] is death which is the cessation of life-breath.
> The wise therefore ought not to take pains on account of that [i.e. liberation]; it is only the fool who wears himself out by penances, fasts etc.
> Chastity and other such ordinances are laid down by clever weaklings....
> The wise should enjoy the pleasures of this world through the proper visible means of agriculture, keeping cattle, trade, political administration, etc. (*Ibid.*: 235)

No wonder then, that as the author of the *Sarva-darśana-saṅgraha* rather despairingly remarks at the outset of his account of the Cārvāka system:

> The efforts of Cārvāka are indeed hard to be eradicated, for the majority of living beings hold by the current refrain:
> While life is yours, live joyously;
> None can escape Death's searching eye:
> When once this frame of ours they burn,
> How shall it e'er return?
> (*Ibid.*: 228)

As one student of them has remarked, 'Probably no other school in the history of philosophy endorsed the seeking of pleasure and enjoyment so unqualifiedly as did the Cārvāka (Riepe 1961: 73). And so far as we can tell, they did not make any qualitative distinction between pleasures, although, as the lines quoted above show, the Cārvākas were extremely practical in their approach to the production of pleasure; agriculture, political organisation, trade etc. were to be the means for ensuring the good life for men.[15]

Many other later writers testify to Cārvāka doctrines and influence and seek to refute them. Buddhists, Jains and the philosophical school of the Naiyayikas all argued against them. Śaṇkara sought to refute their denial of a substantial soul in his commentary on the *Brahma-Sūtra*, and Sriharsa in his *Naisadha-scarita* gives us yet another account of their doctrines which tallies with what we have already learnt.

Something of the popular influence of the Lokāyāta materialism can be got from the ancient drama *Prabodha-candrodaya* (The Rise of the Moon Intellect) of Kṛṣṇa Miśra, which has a Materialist as one of its major characters, along with Passion as another. Both Passion and Materialist put forward views similar to those which we have found attributed to Cārvāka and the Lokāyāta. For example:

> *Passion*: Uncivilised ignorant fools, who imagine that spirit is something different from the body and reaps the reward of its

actions in a future state; we might as well expect to find excellent fruit drop from trees growing in air. But assuming the existence of what is the mere creature of their own imagination they deceive the people. They falsely affirm the existence of what does not exist.... Who has seen the soul existing in a state separate from the body? Does not life result from the ultimate configuration of matter?

and similarly:

Materialist: [speaking to one of his pupils] My son, you know that Legislation [the law of punishment by fear of which alone men are influenced in their conduct] is the only Science.... The three Vedas are a cheat. Behold if Heaven be obtained through the officiating priest, sacrificial rites, and the destruction of the substances employed, why is not abundance of excellent fruit obtained from the ashes of a tree which has been burnt up by the fire of the forest...?
Pupil: Venerable tutor, if to gratify the appetites be the principle end of life, why do these men renounce sensual pleasures and submit to pain arising from the severest mortifications?

To which the Materialist replies:

These fools are deceived by the lying Sastras, and are fed with the allurements of hope. But can begging, fasting, penance, exposure to the burning heat of the sun, which emaciate the body, be compared with the ravishing embraces of women with large eyes, whose prominent breasts are compressed with ones arms?[16] (Radhakrishnan and Moore 1973: 247-249 [Taylor])

The pupil is convinced!

Why the Cārvākas disappeared we do not know. Their rejection of the autority of the *Vedas* and their denunciation of the Brahmans may have helped, especially as orthodoxy crystallised and became established, but this would not seem a wholly satisfactory explanation since both Jains and Buddhists followed them in this. Their rejection of theism is also something which they shared not only with Buddhists and Jains but with the orthodox schools of the Sāṃkhyas and the Mīmāmsākas. All we can say is that they were either forcibly suppressed – which seems unlikely, and for which there is no evidence – or, as is more likely, they simply ceased to appeal as Indian thinking moved more and more towards monistic Idealism and theism. Something of their teaching survived in the well-known *Kāma-sūtra* of Vatsyayāna, but Vatsyayāna, whilst recommending the desirability of pleasure, including sensual pleasure, kept within the bounds of orthodoxy by regarding *dharma*, the following of the moral law, as the supreme end of life and by saying that the acquisition of pleasure should be in conformity with *dharma*. The ideal man of the *Kāma-sūtra* cultivates all three values of life – *dharma*, *artha* and *kama*. In this he is not unlike the ideal man that Aristotle holds up for our emulation in his *Nichomachean Ethics*.

But although the Cārvāka's pass out of Indian culture towards the beginning of the Indian middle-ages (i.e., from about 800 AD), naturalistic tendencies can be found surviving not only in Jainism and Hināyāna Buddhism, but in the philosophical schools of both the Sāṃkhya, and the Vaiśeṣika as well.

2.8 EARLY SĀṂKHYA AND VAIŚEṢIKA NATURALISM

Sāṃkhya is one of the six orthodox schools of Hindu philosophy. It is also the oldest, originating during that creative period of Indian culture which saw not only the rise to pre-eminence of Upaniṣadic Idealism, but the rise of the heterodox systems of Cārvāka, Jainism and Buddhism as well.[17] The name Sāṃkhya means 'enumeration' and the philosophy would appear to be so-called on account of its enumerating categories of thought – these originally being twenty-four or twenty-five in number, but later being expanded to twenty-six. Of the legendary founder of the school, Kapila, little is known and none of his works survive; the earliest extant text that has come down from this school being the *Sāṃkhya-karīka* of Iśvara Kṛṣṇa, which was probably composed in the third century AD. From the earliest times Sāṃkhya has been closely associated with another of the six orthodox systems, Yoga (cf. *Śvetāśvatara Upaniṣad* b. 13, and *Bhagavad-Gītā* 2. 39ff.) – the composite system being a practical way to liberation worked out against the background of a cosmology and metaphysics supplied by the earlier philosophy. Sāṃkhya would appear to have been originally atheistic – if not naturalistic[18] – although later, when it became officially associated with Yoga, the category of *Iśvara* [Personal Lord] was added to it to make the twenty-sixth category; and it may be that the atheism which we find in Jainism and early Buddhism derives from this source.[19] Ninian Smart summarises the Sāṃkhya system as follows:

> Sāṃkhya depicts the universe as made up of innumerable souls [*puruṣas*] on the one hand, and nature [*prakṛti*] on the other. Typically souls are embedded in nature and pursue the round of rebirth until such a time as they attain liberation. The psychophysical organism, including the intellect [*buddhi*] is regarded as part of physical nature, and the conscious functioning of the individual occurs through the association of a soul with a psychophysical organism.... In the state of liberation, which accrues upon the existential realisation of the fundamental distinction [*viveka*] between itself and nature, the soul is no longer capable of suffering, which characterises all material existence.... The emergence of the cosmos out of chaos at the beginning of each cycle [of the universe] is explained through an evolutionary theory. Nature is composed of three strands or qualities [*gunas*] in tension.... These are *sattva* [essence], *rajas* [energy] and *tamas* [mass].... The whole process is explained without reference to a personal Creator. (in Brandon 1970: 553-554)

But although Sāṃkhya is atheistic it is not a thorough-going naturalistic system, for it postulates, rather in the manner of Aristotle, a transcendent first-cause – *Paruṣa* – as the initiator of movement or change in the universe. Although this was the position of the Sāṃkhya system as expounded in the *Sāṃkhya-Karīka* of Īśvara Kṛṣṇa there is considerable evidence that the Sāṃkhya philosophy was originally not only atheistic but thoroughly naturalistic as well (Chattopadhyaya 1959: 383ff. Cf. also Roy 1951: 556f.). By the ancients it was referred to as the doctrine of the *pradhāna* — matter in its pre-evolved state, primordial matter; and this, as we shall see, is the way in which Śaṇkara and Rāmānuja, in their commentaries on the *Vedānta-Sūtras* (cf. Müller, ed. 1879-1910, *S.B.E.*, XXIV and XXXVIII), certainly understood it. The other term for *pradhāna* is *prakṛti* [nature] or, more correctly, *rula-prakṛti* or root-*prakṛti*. Apart from this, as we have seen, the Sāṃkhya system also recognised the primary element of *paruṣa*, (or rather as we shall see a multiplicity of them), by which was meant the principle of consciousness or the Self, although originally, in Vedic mythology, the word had meant simply 'male' — the original 'Person' out of the sacrifice of whose body the world was made. A question therefore arises — if original Sāṃkhya is taken as being consistently naturalistic — as to the significance of the inclusion of *paruṣa* in the Sāṃkhya system.

As contrasted with *prakṛti*, *paruṣa* is secondary in the Sāṃkhya system. The commonest designation for it is *udasina* or the indifferent.[20] *Paruṣa* is indifferent to the actual world-process and has no part to play in the actual evolution of the phenomenal world from the primary 'world-stuff'. That it was later included would seem to be the result of the influence of the Vedanta.

The incongruity of including *paruṣa* in the Sāṃkhya system was noted by Śaṇkara in his commentary on the *Vedānta-Sūtras*. He writes:

> Beyond the *pradhāna* there exists [according to the *Sāṃkhya*] no external principle which could either impel the *pradhāna* to activity or restrain it from activity. The soul (*paruṣa*) as we know, is indifferent [*udasina*] — neither moves to, nor restrains from action. As, therefore, the *pradhāna* stands in no relation, it is impossible to see why it should sometimes modify itself into the great principle [*mahat*] and sometimes not. (*S.B.E.*, XXXIV: 370)

And later, commenting on the assertion by Īśvara Kṛṣṇa (in his *Sāṃkhya Karīka*) that *paruṣa* acts on *prakṛti* as a loadstone acts on iron, that is passively, he says that such a defence would amount to a surrender of the fundamental principles of Sāṃkhya:

> ... according to which the *pradhāna* is moving of itself, and the [indifferent and inactive] soul possesses no moving power. And

how should the indifferent soul move the *pradhāna*? [he asks]. A man, although lame, may make a blind man move by means of words and the like; but the soul which is devoid of action and qualities cannot possibly put forth any moving energy. Nor can it be said that it moves the *pradhāna* by its mere proximity, as the magnet moves the iron; for from the permanence of proximity [of the *parusa* and the *pradhāna*] a permanency of motion would follow.

The proximity of the magnet, on the other hand [to the iron], is not permanent, but depends on a certain activity and the adjustment of the magnet do not supply really parallel instances. The *pradhāna* being non-intelligent and the *paruṣa* indifferent, and there being no third principle to connect them, there can be no connection of the two. (*S.B.E.*, XXXIV: 374)

That the original doctrine of Sāṃkhya was simply a doctrine of *pradhāna* and *pariṇāma* [change], that is, an assertion of the reality of the world, as against the Vedantist doctrine of the world as *māyā* or illusion, (known as *vivartavada*) is shown, not only by the fact that the Vedantist notion of the 'Self' as the ultimate principle (in later Sāṃkhya as First Cause) of the world is never fully reconciled in the Sāṃkhya system and remains throughout incongruous, but also by the fact that in original Sāṃkhya *paruṣa* was not thought of at all in this way but simply, as in Jainism, as a multiplicity of selves (*paruṣa bahutvam*), having nothing to do with cause in the world (so in fact Īśvara Kṛṣṇa, *op. cit.*: 8). This Śaṇkara recognised. He wrote:

Kapila, by acknowledging a plurality of selves, does not admit the doctrine of their being one universal Self.

and he quotes the *Mahābhārata* in support of this interpretation of the Sāṃkhya:

In the *Mahābhārata*, also, the question is raised whether there are many persons [souls] or one; thereupon, the opinions of others is mentioned, 'There are many persons [*paruṣas*], O King, according to the Sāṃkya and the Yoga philosophers'. (*S. B. E.*, XXXIV: 295).

That Sāṃkya took a much more naturalistic (and common-sense) view of the soul than did Vedanta is shown by the arguments which this philosophy put forward in support of its view of a plurality of souls. Gaudapada, the eighth century commentator, for example, explaining the argument in his *Commentary On The Kapila Aphorisms* writes:

> Thus, if there was but one soul, then when one was born, all would be born; when one died, all would die; if there was any defect in the vital instruments of one, such as deafness, blindness, dumbness, mutilation, or lameness, then all would be blind, deaf, dumb, maimed and halt: but this is not the case; and therefore, from the several apportionment of death, birth and instruments of life, multiplicity of souls is demonstrated. (*Sāṃkhya-Karīka*, in Colebrooke 1887: 57-58)

Gaudapada offers two further arguments along the same lines. The first is that individuals differ in their activities; the second, that they differ in having differences in the three *gunas*, that is, in the three constituents of matter (*prakṛti*) (*Ibid.*: 58). This anti-metaphysical view of the soul is about as far removed as anything can be from the view of the soul found in the Idealistic Vedanta tradition.

The assumption behind the Sāṃkhya argument is that the phenomenal world, in which persons, exhibiting the differences outlined above are found, is real, and not, as the Vedanta maintained, ultimately unreal. This was the essential difference between the two philosophies, as evidenced in the *Brahma-Sūtra* and the commentaries upon it. That the world was of the nature of an effect and that the effect was contained potentially in the cause, neither philosophy doubted; where they differed was over the nature of the effect and so over the nature of the cause, for Vedanta the effect being unreal (*vivarta vada*), for Sāṃkhya the effect being real (*parinama vada*).

The important question, however, concerned the genuine participation of *paruṣa* in the world-process. As we have stated, the introduction of *paruṣa* as the cause of the world in the *Sāṃkhya-Karīka* of Īśvara Kṛṣṇa leads to a number of incongruities within the Sāṃkhya system. Of this Śaṇkara was aware, for he designated the Sāṃkhya system as follows:

> Just as jars, dishes and other products which possess the common quality of consisting of clay are seen to have for their cause clay in general; so we must suppose that all outward and inward [i.e.

inanimate and animate] effects which are endowed with the characteristics of *sattva*, *rajas* and *tamas* have for their causes *sattva*, *rajas* and *tamas* in general. These, in their generality, constitute the threefold *pradhāna*. This *pradhāna*, which is non-intelligent, evolves itself spontaneously into multiform modifications, in order thus to effect the purposes [i.e. enjoyment, release, and so on] of the intelligent soul. (*On the Brahma Sūtra*, 11.2.1. *S.B.E.*, XXXIV: 364)

What it is important to note in the above quotation is that Śaṇkara takes the Sāṃkhya to be holding that the non-intelligent (i.e. unconscious or material) *pradhāna* evolves itself spontaneously into this phenomenal world, a point which he makes the main target of his criticism. The real issue between himself and Sāṃkhya he regards as one concerning the cause of the world and its claim to ultimate reality. This is why, despite the introduction into Sāṃkhya of the Idealistic conception of the Self and of the teleological view that the process of evolution was meant to serve the purpose of the Self, he still regards the system as being strongly opposed to his own version of Vedanta. He believed this because he takes the Sāṃkhya philosophy to hold that consciousness has no role in the production of the world. As the *Brahma-Sūtra* had said:

> That which is inferred [by the *Sāṃkhya*'s, *viz.* the *pradhāna*] cannot be the cause [of the world], on account of the orderly arrangement [of the world] being impossible [on that hypothesis]. (*Ibid.*: 363)

This hypothesis that non-intelligent (*acetana* – unconscious or material) *pradhāna* and nothing else is the cause of the world, is what Śaṇkara sets himself to refute, and he identifies it as the thesis put forward by Sāṃkhya.

That this was how Śaṇkara understood Sāṃkhya is made even clearer if we consider the further arguments that he brings against this exposition. The Sāṃkya argument for the existence of *pradhāna* was based on its doctrine of causality, to the effect that the nature of the cause of the world is to be inferred from a consideration of its effect, namely the world. The basis of this doctrine was the observation in the world of those facts of nature which were used as analogies (what Śaṇkara called 'parallel instances' – *dristana vala*) –

jars, dishes and other products. Śaṇkara argues as follows:

> If you Sāṃkhyas base your theory on parallel instances merely, we point out that a non-intelligent thing which, without being guided by a non-intelligent being, spontaneously produces effects capable of subserving purposes of some particular person is nowhere observed in the world. We rather observe houses, palaces, couches, pleasure-grounds and the like – things which according to circumstances are conducive to the obtainment of pleasure, or the avoidance of pain – are made by workmen endowed with intelligence. Now look at this entire world.... (*Ibid.*)

and there follows an argument not unlike the one popularly but mistakenly attributed to the eighteenth century English theologian Paley[21] which concludes:

> and then say if a non-intelligent principle like the *pradhāna* is able to fashion it! (*Ibid.*: 364-365)

Our concern is not, however, with Śaṇkara's argument and the consequences – so different from those of Paley – that he drew from it, although it is interesting to come across this argument in eighth century India, but with the fact that the Sāṃkhya which Śaṇkara is seeking to refute was a Sāṃkhya which held (unlike later Sāṃkhya) that the material cause – *pradhāna* – was a sufficient cause of the existence of the phenomenal world as we know it. Śaṇkara continues the same line of argument in his commentary on the next sutra of the *Brahma-Sūtra*, and he again takes the Sāṃkhya system as maintaining that the activity whereby the world is produced – leaving on one side the actual arrangement which we find in it – is again 'non-intelligent *pradhāna* left to itself (*Ibid.*: 367).

It would thus appear that despite the introduction of the Vedantist notion of the Self into the Sāṃkhya system, its philosophers were still thinking of the principle of *prādhana* or primordial matter as a sufficient explanation of both change in the world and of that change within primordial matter that began the evolution of the world. This of itself, of course, is not sufficient to show that original Sāṃkhya did not postulate *paruṣas* as co-eternal elements with *pradhāna* or *prakṛti*, but what it does show is that, according to Śaṇkara, such were not considered to be the cause of the world-process.

However, according to the *Caraka-Saṃhitā* – a work which according to Dasgupta is considerably older than the *Sāṃkhya-Karīka* of Īśvara Kṛṣṇa (1923: 217) – *paruṣa*, which is simply equated with consciousness, is on a par with the five well-known elements and is itself, therefore, a form of material element (*dhatu*). Dasgupta also notes that, from other points of view than that of Īśvara Kṛṣṇa, Sāṃkhya was said to postulate only twenty-four categories; namely, the ten senses (five cognitive and five conative), *manas* [mind], the five objects of the senses and the eight-fold *prakṛti*,[22] (*prakṛti*, *mahat*, *ahamkara*, and the five elements) (*Ibid.*: 213, and 217-218). It is thus possible, indeed highly likely, that in the earliest formulations of Sāṃkhya, *paruṣa* was either simply another (near) material element or omitted altogether.

Accepting as they did – against the Vedanta – the reality of the material universe and of change within it, the question arises as to how the Sāṃkhya philosophers accounted for change without postulating a controlling intelligence. Their answer – which it would take us too far from our purpose to expound in detail – brings us very close towards what in the Western would be called 'laws of nature'. Śaṇkara gives their answer as follows:

> As non-sentient milk flows forth from its own nature [*svabhavenaeva*] merely for the nourishment of the young animal, and as non-sentient water, from its own nature, flows along for the benefit of mankind; so the *pradhāna* also, although non-intelligent, may be supposed to move from its own nature.... (*S.B.E.*, XXXIV: 369)[23]

and again, commenting on the sūtra which reads:

> Nor [can it be said that the *pradhāna* modifies itself spontaneously] like grass, etc. [which turns into milk]; for [milk] does not exist elsewhere [but in the female animal].

Śaṇkara represents the Sāṃkhya philosophers as arguing as follows:

> Just as grass, herbs, water etc., independently of any other instru-

mental cause transform themselves, by their own nature [*shabhavat eva*], into milk; so, we assume, the *pradhāna* also transforms itself... and if you ask how we know that grass transforms itself independently of any instrumental cause; we reply, 'Because no such cause is observed'.... Hence the transformation of grass and the like must be considered to be due to its own nature merely; and we may infer therefrom that the transformation of the *pradhāna* is of the same kind. (*Ibid.*: 371)

This doctrine of *svabhavenaeva*, or natural law, is also (reluctantly) recognised as characteristic of early Sāṃkhya by Gaudapada, who remarks that 'according to the Sāṃkhya philosophers there is a certain kind of cause called *svabhava* (nature) (Colebrooke 1887: *Sāṃkhya-Karīka* 27).

If Sāṃkhya was originally asserting such doctrines as we have outlined above, then, of course, it must have been extremely close to Lokāyāta, which was also described as *Svabhava vada*, and in fact this is just what the Jain commentator Silamka notices (cf. Hastings, ed. 1908-1926, XI: 190). Śaṇkara too points out that the Sāṃkhya philosophers cited the authority of the Lokāyāta in defence of their thesis that activity could appertain to *pradhāna* alone. He wrote:

For this reason, namely, that intelligence is observed only where a body is observed while it is never seen without a body, the Lokāyātikas consider intelligence to be a mere attribute of the body. Hence activity belongs only to what is non-intelligent. (*S. B. E.*, XXXIV: 368)

We thus see that although Idealistic Vedanta eventually came to dominate the Indian philosophical scene, not only in Lokāyāta, but in Sāṃkhya as well, there had once lain the germs of a very different approach to the world, and in Sāṃkhya naturalistic strains were to remain within the mainstream of the Indian philosophical tradition as a constant challenge to other more world-denying outlooks.

But although Sāṃkhya eventually takes into itself – somewhat incongruously as we have argued – the notion of *Paruṣa* as the cause of the world, it never in fact identifies this Cause with God. In fact it explicitly rejects such an identification.

The universe, even later Sāṃkhya maintained, required no other explanation than uncreated and eternal *prakṛti* being acted upon by uncreated and eternal *paruṣa*. The existence of a transcendent Lord or Īśvara was held, not only to be unproven, but to be impossible of proof, and Sāṃkhya put forward counter-arguments to show why such a Creator-God could not exist.

> [And, further,] it is not proved that he [the 'Lord'] exists; because [whoever exists must be either free or bound; and] of free and bound, he can be neither the one nor the other.
> (a) The 'Lord' whom you imagine; tell us, is he free from troubles, etc.? Or is he in bondage through these? Since he is not, cannot be, either the one or the other, it is not proved that there is a 'Lord': Such is the meaning.
> (b) He explains this very point:
> [Because] either way, he would be inefficient.
> (a) Since, if he were free, he would have no desires, etc., which [as compulsory motives] would instigate him to create; and, if he were bound, he would be under delusion; he must be [on either alternative] unequal to the creation, etc., of this world. (Ballantyne 1885: aph. 93 and 94 of Bk. 1)[24]

In his commentary on the *Sāṃkhya-Kārīka* Gaudapada repeats this argument. He says:

> ... How can beings composed of the three Gunas proceed from Isvara (God), who is devoid of Gunas? Or how can they proceed from the soul, equally devoid of qualities? Therefore they must proceed from Prakriti. Thus from white threads white cloth is produced; from black thread, black cloth, and so from Prakriti, composed of the three Gunas, the three worlds composed of the three Gunas are produced. God (Isvara) is free from Gunas. The production of the three worlds composed of the Gunas from him would be an inconsistency. (Gaudapada, *Bhadya* 61., in Īśvara Kṛṣṇa, *Sāṃkhya-Kārīka* [Śāstri 1935])

This, of course, was a problem that worried thinkers within the Greek tradition – particularly in the second and third centuries AD. It had also worried Plato, who had solved it in the *Timaeus* by means of the notion of a demiurge – a view which survived in the systems of Gnosticism and in the Christian heresy of Marcion.

Having rejected belief in a transcendent Creator, Sāṃkhya, as an orthodox system committed to upholding the authority of the *Vedas*, had to account for the references to such a personal Creator found in the sacred Scriptures. This it did by a piece of demythologising as well as by a concession to popular piety. The scriptural texts which make mention of the 'Lord' (Īśvara) are, it says:

> ... either glorifications of the liberated Soul, or homages to the recognised [deities of the Hindu pantheon].
> (a) That is to say: accordingly as the case may be, *some* text [among those in which the word 'Lord' occurs] is intended in the shape of a glorification [of the Soul], as the 'Lord', [as Soul is held to be,] merely in virtue of junction [with Nature], to incite [to still deeper comtemplation], to exhibit as what is to be known, the liberated Soul, i.e. absolute Soul in general; and in some other text, declaratory, for example, of creatorship, etc., proceeded by resolution [to create, is intended] to extol [and to purify the mind of the contemplator, by enabling him to take part in the extolling] the eternity, etc., of the familiarly known Brahma, Vishnu, Siva, or other *non*-eternal 'Lord'; since these, though possessed of the conceit [of individuality] etc., [and, in so far, liable to perish,] have immortality, etc., in a secondary sense; [seeing that the Soul, in *every* combination, is immortal, though the combination itself is not so]. (Ballantyne 1889: Bk. 1 aph. 95)

The aphorisms (with commentary) which follow immediately on the ones quoted go on to argue that neither the Soul (*paruṣa*) generally conceived, nor the soul (*paruṣa*) individually conceived exercise what might be termed governorship by resolve. The Sāṃkhya view is that *paruṣa* acts on nature as the loadstone acts on iron – by proximity (Kapila, Ballantyne 1885: aph. 96 and 97). The whole development of Nature is, therefore, for the Sāṃkhya system, impersonal.[25] Only the individual soul, which Sāṃkhya (as we have seen in the summary of its major tenents quoted earlier) distinguishes from mind and body – both of which are thought of as part of physical nature – is free to realize its essential distinction from natural processes, rather like Immanuel Kant's noumenal self. For Sāṃkhya, however, the soul is a spectator not an actor (cf. *Sāṃkhya-Kārīka* of Īśvara Kṛṣṇa 19, 59 and 60 [Śāstri 1935]).

The aim of the original system would appear to have been liberation through knowledge – knowledge of the fundamental distinction of the soul from nature; although Sāṃkhya's interest in natural processes goes far beyond what would have been necessary for this aim and betrays an interest in nature in and for itself.[26] In this Sāṃkhya might properly be compared with early Greek naturalism. Ethical interests are only evident in the later commentaries. For Sāṃkhya there are three sources of knowledge; perception, inference and authoritative statement (*aptavacana*).

> Perception, Inference and Authoritative Statement are the three kinds of approved proof, for they comprise every mode of demonstration.
>
> Perception is the mental apprehension of particular objects; Inference, which is by means of a mark and the marked, is declared to be three-fold; authoritative statement is true revelation. (*Sāṃkhya-Kārīka* 4 and 5; in Īśvara Kṛṣṇa, *Sāṃkhya-Kārīka* [Śāstri 1935])

At a later stage yogic perception was added as a fourth mode of knowledge. But it is the acceptance of the original third mode – authoritative statement – that has troubled those who believe that the Sāṃkhya system is at bottom naturalistic. For most commentators it is held to mean *śruti* – the supernatural revelation contained in the *Vedas* – though some add that this is included in the system only as a matter of policy, as a concession to orthodoxy. There were, however, those within the Sāṃkhya school – notably Vacaspati in the tenth century – who offered, from our point of view, a rather more interesting interpretation. For them *aptavacana* [authoritative utterance] was oral instruction which was found to be true on grounds either of perception or inference – authoritative, therefore, not because someone has said so, but because it has survived the test of reason, a position which begins to emerge in Europe during the eleventh century AD with regard to the 'authorities' within the Christian tradition.

Vacaspati, for instance, rejects the supposed revelations of certain teachers within the Sāṃkhya tradition on the ground that their 'revelations' are unproven.

> Though there is nothing prescribed, yet what is unreasonable cannot be accepted, else we should sink to the level of children, lunatics and the like. (*Sāṃkhya-Sūttras* i. 20, in Banerjee 1909: 47)

For many Sāṃkhya teachers this is also the case with regard to the sacred scriptures (*śruti*). These are not regarded as self-authenticating, but to be tested and proven by a criterion other than intuition or self-evidence. This is the task of reason. The *Tattvakaumudī*, for instance, says that the invalidity of certain revelations:

> ... is due to their making unreasonable assertions, to the lack of sufficient support, to their making statements opposed to the canons of logic, to their acceptance ... by low classes. (*Tattvakaumudī*, 5. [Jha 1934])

And according to the fifteenth century commentator Aniruddha:

> Huge giants [or Gods] do not drop from heaven simply because a sacred verse [apta], or competent person, says so. Only sayings which are supported by reason should be accepted by me and others like yourselves. (*Sāṃkhya Sūtra Vṛtti*, 1.26 [Sinha 1915])

And on the whole, Aniruddha holds that testimony must be consistent with perception and inference. He, like many others, is sufficiently aware that within the accepted orthodox schools the *Vedas* were capable of many differing interpretations.

As Radakhrishnan has pointed out, Sāṃkhya never actually opposes the *Vedas*, but adopts, as he says, 'the more deadly process of sapping their foundations', and he instances the Sāṃkhya saying that 'those who have attained "release" do not need the *Vedas*, whilst those who have not are not competent to understand them (Radakhrishnan 1948: 302).

Sāṃkhya, therefore, would thus seem to be very close epistemologically to the Cārvāka system, particularly as that system was modified by the later teacher Purandara, in the seventh century AD, who admitted a limited validity to inference. As Sir Arthur Keith says:

> The absence of any attempt to examine more closely the nature of perception and of inference and their mutual relations is striking, and indicates how firmly fixed was the view of the system that perception gave immediate knowledge of reality, and that inference gave mediate knowledge. (Keith 1918: 88-89)

But although Sāṃkhya betrays strongly naturalistic tendencies, both in its epistemological theory and in its metaphysics, as well as in its cosmology, it later acquires, as we have seen, supernaturalistic elements, for not only does it evoke *Paruṣa* to explain [initial] movement in nature – when the natural world already contained such a principle of motion in *rajas* [energy] – but its notion of *paruṣa* migrating according to the law of *karma* is also non-naturalistic. As time went by this school became more and more orthodox and, as Sāṃkhya-Yoga, has exerted an influence on Indian religious thinking second only to Vedanta. A similar pattern of development can be observed within the Vaiśeṣika school.

As was the case with the Sāṃkhya school the origins of Vaiśeṣika are hard to determine, but it would seem almost certain that the school is later than Sāṃkhya and probably post-Buddhist, although attempts have been made to date it earlier (Roy 1951: 83) and certainly many of the views which it contains can be found in pre-Buddhist times. Its legendary founder is Kaṇāda – the name is a nickname and means 'feeder on atoms' – but nothing is known of him. In the philosophical tradition the school is linked with the Nyāya school, and it may be that Vaiśeṣika is simply a development of that school, adding a metaphysical dimension to interests that were previously almost exclusively epistemological and logical (cf. Raju 1971: 143).

Our chief sources for knowledge of the schools are the *Vaiśeṣika Sūtra* of Kaṇāda, with the gloss on it by Praśastapāda – known as the *Padārtha-dharma-Śaṇgraha* – written in the fifth century AD, and the *Nyāya Sūtra* of Gautama, which is of uncertain date and may be anytime between 400 BC and the third century AD.

The name itself is also difficult to determine but the most likely etymology is from *viśeṣas* which means 'particulars', and certainly the view of reality which this school puts forward is pluralistic.

In its later development the school was certainly theistic, but here again it would appear that we have an originally atheistic and naturalistic school becoming, over a period of time, gradually more and more orthodox. It is difficult to determine whether the original interests of the school were exclusively academic – concerned with how we know what we know and the elements of what we know as they are represented in objects – and not at all with 'liberation', as Faddegon has maintained (1918: 12), and certainly there is little concern in the system with ethics and much with the workings of the world, which are known to us according to this school by a mode of knowledge which we in the West would designate as naively realistic.

The *Vaiśeṣika Sūtra* of Kaṇāda postulates seven categories or *Padarthas.* These are (1) substance (*dravya*); (2) quality or property (*guṇa*); (3) activity (*karma*); (4) generality (*samanya*); (5) particularity or individuality (*viśeṣa*); (6) coherence or perpetuate intimate relation (*samavaya*); and (7) non-existence or negation of existence (*abhāva*). Nine substances are postulated: earth, water, fire, air, ether, time, space, soul (*ātman*) and mind (*manas*). Of these substances the first five are called elements (*bhūtas*) and constitute the material world of the five senses. The first four, which are perceivable, (ether must be inferred) are held to be atomic (as is mind) and are said to be eternal and non-eternal, non-eternal in their various compounds, eternal in their ultimate atoms (*aṇus*) to which they must be traced back. Time and space are two independent eternal, indivisible, and all-pervading substances. The *ātman*, or soul, is also an eternal, all pervading substance and is the substratum of the quality of consciousness. However, as in the Sāṃkhya system, consciousness is not an essential and inseparable quality of the *ātman*, for it is only incidental. The *ātmans* – as in Jainism – constitute an infinite plurality.

It would take us far beyond the scope of this book to elaborate on the details of the Vaiśeṣika system. Suffice it to say that whilst most scolars are agreed that originally the Vaiśeṣika system was atheistic and probably naturalistic as well, Vaiśeṣika moved early in a theistic direction. However, whilst Vaiśeṣika postulates God as the all-knowing Being who disposes the atoms so as to bring about the world as we know it, such a God is little more than a demiurge working with pre-existing material. He does not create the atoms, for they, like him, are eternal. He acts to the world as an efficient cause. In arguing for the existence of a God, Nyāya-Vaiśeṣika puts forward versions of both the cosmological and the teleological arguments, as well as relying on the authority of the *Vedas*.

Salvation or liberation in the Nyāya-Vaiśeṣika system comes from striving to realise the *ātman*'s original nature – by withdrawing from the world of action, which contains both pleasure and pain. In its original nature the *ātman* is not only devoid of pleasure and pain, but of consciousness as well. When liberated from contact with nature (which, as we have seen, includes, as it did for the Sāṃkhya, from mind also) the *ātman* is likened to a stone – in that it is devoid of all consciousness and all capacity for feeling pleasure or pain. Not, perhaps, a very attractive goal for those wedded to a Western view of human personality.

2.9 JAIN AND BUDDHIST NATURALISM

Both Jainism and Buddhism were originally atheistic religions, but whilst Jainism has remained atheistic to this day, Buddhism, at least in its Mahāyāna form, has developed both theistic and more overtly supernaturalistic tendencies.

Both religions arose in the sixth century BC, but both have their roots in much earlier traditions. Both were probably influenced by the heterodox, non-Vedic speculation which, as we have seen, was current from at least the eighth century.

Although the roots of Jainism go back to early Vedic times, the man who must be regarded, if not as the actual founder, at least as the resuscitator of Jainism, Vardhamāna, who was accorded the titles Jina, which means Conqueror (of all passions) and Māhavīra, [the Great Hero], was an older contemporary of Siddhartha Gautama, the Buddha. Attempts were made soon after the death of Vardhamāna to compile his teachings, but the first systematic treatise that we possess is the *Tattvārthadhigama-sūtras* [Aphorisms for Understanding the Nature of the Categories] of Umāsvāmim, which dates from about the third century AD.

Although accepting the Hindu doctrines of *karma* and *samsāra*, and the desirability of release from bondage to this world, Jainism rejects both the authority of the *Vedas* and the notion of a transcendent creator-God. The cosmos, according to Jainism, is everlasting and uncreated. In it there are two kinds of entities – souls (*jīva*) and non-living matter (*ajīva*). Souls are infinite in number and, when unattached to matter, are omniscient and in a state of bliss. Being attached, as things now are to matter, through *karma*, the aim of the Jain system is to free the soul from such attachment so that it may regain its previous 'unfallen' state.

It is interesting that both souls and their *karma* are thought of in Jainism almost materialistically, despite the absolute ontological distinction which Jainism draws between souls and the material universe – a fact which shows how near early Jainism came to an almost totally materialistic theory of the universe. Souls possess varying sizes, expanding and contracting to 'fit' the bodies they successively possess. Whilst involved in *samsāra* 'they exist in combination with karmic matter' (Kundakunda, *Pañchāstīkaya-gatha* v. 27 [Jaini]), which literally weighs them down – though their intrinsic direction of motion is upwards towards the summit of the universe, a notion that brings us very close to Gnostic ideas as these developed in the West during the early centuries of the Christian era.

Whilst Jainism is fundamentally atheistic, the great Jain teachers, who are known as *Tīrthaṃkara*, – the Ford-Makers who have shown the way across the stream of rebirth to the other side – and who are twenty-four in number (Vardhamāna being the last), early become the focus, as the religion developed, of a temple cult.[27] It would be a mistake, however, to regard the Tīrthaṃkara as gods analogous to the gods of the Hindu pantheon – despite superficial resemblances between Jain and Hindu worship – for it follows from the Jain belief in the motionlessness of the liberated soul that the *Tīrthaṃkara* are beyond any kind of transaction with the rest of the universe. They are not, therefore, beings who exercise any sort of creative activity or who have the capacity or ability to intervene in answer to prayers. Hence, as Ninian Smart has said:

> The cult of Jainism still leaves its essential character unaffected – namely an atheistic system which allows the Indian gods a place in the hierarchy of intra-cosmic heavens.
> Both Buddhism and Jainism, [he says] transcend polytheism, by exalting above the gods the idea of a liberation which has nothing to do with God or gods. Both can therefore be dubbed 'transpolytheistic atheism'. (Smart 1964: 64)

Reacting to criticism from orthodox Brahmannical Hinduism, Jainism went beyond simple ignoring, as irrelevant, the question of the existence or non-existence of a Creator of the universe and developed arguments designed to prove the non-existence of such a Being. It opposed in particular the theistic teachings of the Nyāya philosophy. From the vast literature of Jainism, which contains many attacks on the theistic position, the following, taken from *The Great Legend* (*Mahāpurāṇa*), a lengthy poem in Sanskrit composed by the Jain teacher Jinasena, written in the ninth century of the Christian Era, is typical:

> Some foolish men declare that Creator made the world.
> The doctrine that the world was created is all-advised,
> and should be rejected.
>
> If God created the world, where was he before creation?
> If you say he was transcendent then, and needed no support,
> where is he now?

No single being had the skill to make this world –
For how can an immaterial god create that which is material?[28]

How could God have made this world without any raw
material?
If you say that he made this first, and then the world
you are faced with an endless regression.

If you declare that this raw material arose naturally you fall
into another fallacy,
For the whole universe might thus have been its own creator,
and have arisen quite naturally.

If God created the world by an act of his own will,
without any raw material,
Then it is just his will and nothing else – and who will believe
this silly nonsense?

If he is ever perfect and complete how could the will to create
have arisen in him?
If, on the other hand, he is not perfect, he could no more
create the universe than a potter could.

If he is formless, actionless, and all-embracing, how could
he have created the world?
Such a soul, devoid of all morality, would have no desire
to create anything.[29]

If he is perfect, he does not strive for the three aims of man,[30]
So what advantage would he gain by creating the universe?

If you say that he created to no purpose, because it was his
nature to do so, then God is pointless.
If he created in some kind of sport,[31] it was the sport of a
foolish child, leading to trouble.

If he created because of the karma of embodied beings
[acquired in a previous creation]
He is not the Almighty Lord, but subordinate to something
else ....

If out of love for living beings[32] and need of them he made
the world,
Why did he not take creation wholly blissful, free from
misfortune?

If he were transcendent he would not create, for he would
be free:
Nor if involved in transmigration, for then he would not be
almighty.

Thus the doctrine that the world was created by God
Makes no sense at all.

And God commits great sin in slaying the children whom he
himself created.
If you say that he slays only to destroy evil beings, why did he
create such beings in the first place ...?

Good men should combat the believer in divine creation,
maddened by an evil doctrine.
Know that the world is uncreated, as time itself is, without
beginning or end,

And is based on the principles, life and rest.
Uncreated and indestructible, it endures under the compulsion
of its own nature.
(*Mahāpurāṇa*, 4.16-31, 38-40, in Bary 1960: 75-76)

Buddhism, at least in its early period, is far less of a speculative philosophy than any system we have considered so far and indeed the Buddha himself is held to have warned his disciples against the dangers of philosophic speculation,[33] on the grounds that not only does speculation detract from the following of the 'Eightfold Path' that leads to salvation from involvement in the world of suffering but also on the grounds that such speculation is at bottom wrongly conceived.

But although early Buddhism was essentially a pragmatic philosophy of life, designed to offer human beings a diagnosis of their condition and a practical way of liberation from attachment to a world which brought nothing but suffering and death and rebirth, nevertheless the cure for the human condition was thought out against the background of a view of the cosmos and of the nature of the human being. It is not, therefore, surprising that the first rung of the ladder of the eight-fold path that leads to the attainment of *nirvana* is 'right-view'.

But before looking at early Buddhist cosmology, metaphysics and anthropology it will be necessary to look briefly at the history of Buddhism, so greatly has that religion diversified in the course of its development.

As a historic religion Buddhism originated in the teachings (known as the *dhamma*) of Siddhartha Gautama – the Buddha or Enlightened One. Siddhartha Gautama was born about the year 563 BC into the kingly family of the Sakya tribe in N.E. India in the foothills of the Himalayas. Abandoning the princely role which was his birthright he sought enlightenment about the meaning and purpose of existence – which he would appear early to have diagnosed as being characterised by suffering, disease and death – first in traditional Yogic fashion by means of a severe ascetic discipline, but later, more passively, by awaiting such enlightenment as might intuitively dawn upon him. In about his thirty-fifth year he believed that such enlightenment had come to him and for the next forty-five years he preached his *dhamma* of the four noble truths and the eightfold-path that leads to the attainment of *nirvāṇa*, before dying at the age of about eighty in 483 BC of a gastric ailment. According to tradition he exhorted his followers, shortly before his death, not to accept his teachings simply on his own authority but to test their truth for themselves.

Such, now greatly overlaid by a hagiographical tradition, would appear to be the main outline of the life of the historic Buddha.

The Four Noble Truths are essentially a diagnosis and a suggested cure of the business of life in this world. The human situation is analysed as one of suffering (*dukka*) caused by craving or attachment to this world – including, perhaps, individual existence. The cure is the eradication of craving or desire by treading the Eightfold Path that leads to *nirvāṇa* – a state of being where suffering and mortality are overcome.

This doctrine was independent of any belief in a supreme Creator – God and of priestly rites and functions, although the Buddha did form his disciples into a semi-religious order known as the *sangha.*

From about the third century BC a split occurred within Buddhism and from about this time on we can see the emergence of Mahāyāna Buddhism or the Greater Vehicle. In this school the historic Buddha is regarded not simply as a man who has found a way of release from attachment to the world – and here we can perhaps detect the influence of Bhakti developments within Hinduism, which taught a way of salvation (Bhakti Yoga) based upon loving devotion to a personal Lord, who was thought of as periodically becoming incarnate (as an avatar) for the salvation of men – but as the incarnation of a supernatural Being or Eternal Buddha.

With these developments the Hināyāna, or Little Vehicle school as they were called by the Mahāyānas, and whose teachings survive today in the Theravāda school, will have nothing to do, and they claim in their scriptures, known as the Pali Canon, to preserve the teachings of the historic Buddha – a claim which, with some reservations, most scholars (and not a few Mahāyānas) are inclined to accept.

With the Mahāyāna school we will not be concerned as it is out and out supernaturalistic. From our point of view Theravāda Buddhism is much more interesting.

In this tradition, the Buddha, though surpassing ordinary men (and such gods as may exist) in achievement, is, theoretically at least, in no sense regarded as divine. Temples there certainly are, but the action of ordinary people in laying flowers and burning incense before statues of the Buddha is often no more than the paying of respect to a departed teacher.

In view of this attitude to the historic Buddha in the Theravāda tradition many have doubted whether in fact Buddhism of this variety ought to be called a religion at all. Much here depends on how narrowly we define religion. Certainly from a Western point of view the religious element in Theravāda Buddhism is minimal but looked at in the context of Indian religion Theravāda is certainly a religion in that it accepts what is the basic doctrine of all Indian religion, namely, the doctrine of *samsāra* and the desirability of release from it. Where it fundamentally departs from Hinduism (and Jainism) is in its rejection of the notion of a permanent self. In this respect the Buddha was close to some contemporary materialists. The rejection of a permanent 'self' underlying psychological and physical states means that persons are assimilated in one important respect (in Buddhist theory) to the rest of nature. Early Buddhism also taught the doctrine of *anicca* or *anitya* [impermanence], in which all entities were analysed into a succession of impermanent states. Only *nirvāṇa* can be said to be a permanent state. Rebirth, therefore, for the Buddha, was not the migration of a permanent self or soul from one organism to another. Rather, it was conceived, somewhat as David Hume conceived it, as a new set of psychological events being set up. The Buddha, therefore, rejected the materialist view that after death nothing of what had been a person remains. This is only so when *nirvāṇa* has been achieved. How *nirvāṇa* differs from annihilation – which the Buddha explicitly condemned – is of course a problem if no individual self nor no set of psychological events which might be termed an individual remains, and it is no wonder that many Western commentators have striven to rehabilitate within Buddhism a doctrine of the self – something which no Buddhist has yet dared to do: or at least not in those terms. The Buddha himself, whilst condemning materialistic forms of annihilation, placed the question, 'Does the Buddhist who has attained *nirvāṇa* continue to exist after death?' in the category of undetermined questions – and as his analoguous questions show he did so because he believed that the question was an improper one in that it admitted of no answer. It does look, however, as if the only point in Buddhism is escape from *samsāra*. Reject the whole notion of *samsāra* as the Cārvāka/Lokāyāta philosophers did – and apart from a way of living which it is hoped will minimise pain and suffering in this world, it is difficult to see how early Buddhism differs from the materialism which has obviously so heavily influenced it.

With regard to the question of the existence of the gods of the traditional Hindu pantheon, the Buddha would appear to have been completely agnostic – neither denying their existence nor giving any grounds of assurance that he believes them to exist. He is, for all practical purposes – and Buddhism is, as should now be evident, an essentially practical philosophy of life – an atheist. Man must depend on himself for his salvation and not upon the divine – a view which was however mitigated in the later Mahāyāna tradition. Thus although it rejects this world and sets before man a rather different goal – which despite prevarication can only be called annihilation – early Buddhism is essentially, if mistakenly, humanistic. It is, however – despite the fact that of late much has been made by its protagonists in the West of its compatibility with empirical science – essentially unscientific. Not only are its basic insights derived from intuition – this in itself would not make it unscientific – but it is totally lacking in curiosity about the natural world. As a historian of science has written:

> When I spoke of Buddha ... I suggested that the religion or wisdom which he explained was not incompatible with scientific research. Indeed no religion is nearer to the religion of science than the pure original Buddhism. Unfortunately, the true scientific spirit of Buddhism was made barren by excessive otherworldliness, by lack of curiosity. (Sarton 1931: ch. 2)

One other factor which would seem to militate against regarding early Buddhism as an essentially practical non-supernaturalistic philosophy of life is the tacit acceptance on the part of the Buddha of a cosmology which allows for heavens, hells and a variety of demi-gods and demons. Such, however, must be seen within the context of the Buddha's day and age which did not draw our fairly rigid distinction between the natural and the supernatural. Reading behind the Buddha's professed 'agnosticism' however, it is surely not an improper inference that the Buddha was in fact a practical atheist, for the question on which he – the Enlightened One – offers no guidance and upon which he urges his disciples not to speculate is no mean question. If he considers it superfluous for his disciples to think about this question it can only be because he himself does not believe in a God who is in any sense relevant to the life of man. Could one believe in God and yet consider his existence irrelevant to human destiny? His 'agnosticism' was, therefore, more likely than not directed against the traditional gods of the Hindu pantheon.

The question whether the Buddha was also a *theoretical* atheist is one over which historians of Buddhism differ. A.S. Geden, writing in the *Encyclopaedia of Religion and Ethics*, thinks not. He recognises, however, the essentially materialistic and naturalistic character of the Buddha's approach to the world. He writes:

> It is probably an erroneous view of the original teaching of the Gautama Buddha which explains his attitude as entirely and of set purpose atheistic; as construing the universe in a materialistic sense, and denying the existence of a God. That he interpreted the universe in the sense indicated is in all probability true; and his views in this respect were derived from the ancient doctrine of the Samkhya philosophy. The latter view, however, – that the founder of Buddhism intended to give expression to distinctly atheistic views – seems to be a mistaken inference from the response which he is recorded in the Buddhist books as having given to the questioning of his disciples ... and his refusal to offer any definite instruction on the spiritual and unseen, or to illuminate with any ray of light which he was competent to give, the uncertainty and darkness of the unknown realm that lay beyond the touch of sense .... The position which it was his purpose to adopt was neither atheistic, nor, in the strict sense of the term agnostic. But for his hearers it was immaterial whether the reply was in the affirmative or negative; and speculation on the subject was discouraged or forbidden, lest it should impair or destroy that firm spirit of self-reliance which it was his object to arouse ... he simply refuses to communicate to his disciples knowledge which he judges to be needless for practical life, and the consideration of which would only minister to a harmful curiosity anxious to speculate on matters beyond human ken. (Geden, in *E.R.E.*, VI: 270)

This seems to me to summarise admirably the attitude of the historic Buddha so far as this can be established. However, in Buddhist literature of a later period – and in the *Buddhacarita* of Aśvaghoṣa in particular, written in the first century AD – we do find a number of quite explicit anti-theistic arguments. These for the most part concentrate on what we in the West would call the problem of evil.

> If the world had been made by God, there should be no change or destruction, there should be no such thing as sorrow or calamity, as right or wrong, seeing that all things, pure and impure must come from Him. If sorrow and joy, love and hate, which spring up in all conscious beings, be the work of God, He Himself must be capable of sorrow and joy, love and hatred, and if he has these, how can he be said to be perfect?... But if sorrow and joy are attributed to another cause, then there would be something of which God is not the cause. Why, then, should not all that exists be uncaused too? Again, if God be the maker, He acts either with or without a purpose. If He acts with a purpose, He cannot be said to be all perfect, for a purpose necessarily implies satisfaction of a want. If He acts without a purpose, He must be like the lunatic or suckling babe. Besides, if God be the maker, why should not people reverently submit to Him, why should they offer supplications to Him when sorely pressed by necessity? And why should people adore more gods than one? Thus the idea of God is proved false by rational argument, and all such contradictory assertions should be exposed. (Radhakrishnan 1933: 456)

According to the *Buddhacarita* the Buddha also used the same line of argument to dispose of those who maintained the existence of an Absolute, an Unconditioned or an Unknowable behind the world of phenomena.

> Said the Blessed One to Anathapindika: 'If by the absolute is meant something out of relation to all known things, its existence cannot be established by any reasoning. How can we know that anything unrelated to other things exists at all? The whole universe, as we know it, is a system of relations: we know nothing that is, or can be, unrelated. How can that which depends on nothing and is related to nothing produce things which are related to one another and depend for their existence on one another? Again the absolute is one or many. If it be the only one, how can it be the cause of the

different things which originate, as we know from different causes? If there be as many different absolutes as there are things, how can the latter be related to one another? If the absolute pervades all things and fills all space, then it cannot also make them, for there is nothing to make. Further, if the absolute is devoid of all qualities, all things arising from it ought likewise to be devoid of qualities. But in reality all things in the world are circumscribed throughout by qualities. Hence the absolute cannot be their cause.

If the absolute be considered different from the qualities, how does it continually create the things possessing such qualities and manifest itself in them? Again if the absolute be unchangeable, all things should be unchangeable too, for the effect cannot differ in nature from the cause. But all things in the world undergo change and decay. How then can the absolute be unchangeable? Moreover if the absolute which pervades all is the cause of everything, why should we seek liberation? For we ourselves possess this as absolute and must patiently endure every suffering and sorrow incessantly created by the absolute.' (*Ibid.*)

The Buddha himself may have simply accepted this outlook as part of what we would call 'nature'. But, no matter, for such metaphysics play no part at all in the central concern of early Buddhism which is the quest for liberation from *samsāra* and all that it involves in the way of suffering.

We thus see that although the dominant approach to life in Indian culture has certainly been a religious one, scepticism, and even out and out naturalism are not unknown and whilst, from about 600 AD onwards, religious idealism becomes not only the dominant but well nigh exclusive Indian outlook on life, scepticism, rationalism and humanism do in fact eventually, towards the close of the nineteenth century, begin to re-assert themselves once again. That, however, is another story and we must now leave the Indian subcontinent and move further East to China.

3

China

3.1 EARLY CHINESE RELIGION

The earliest recorded evidence of religion in China comes from the period of the Shang dynasty; that is from the period 1765-1112 BC. Excavations of the capital Anyang in North Honan in Eastern China have revealed brass bowls with inscriptions indicative of their having been used in a cult surrounding the ancestors. From Anyang have also come a number of oracle bones – of ox and tortoise-shell – used in divination to elicit communication from various deities. From these finds we can deduce that the religion of China during this period was a fairly highly developed polytheism not dissimilar to that which characterised the early periods of Near Eastern and Indian cultures. Dr. A. C. Bouquet writes:

> Chinese religion from about 3000-1200 BC much resembles other Bronze-Age polytheism. If there is a high god, there are nature and fertility festivals, and in the harmonies of dance and song and the mating of men and women the rhythms of nature are believed to be expressed and embodied.... The ancient Chinese religious world was pluralistic. There were spirits of heaven and earth, spirits of the departed ancestors and daemons of storm and drought. The relations between Deity and humanity were on the level of '*do ut des*'. (Bouquet 1956: 178-179)

The Shang dynasty fell towards the end of the second millenium BC when a group of tribes known as the Chou came from the Western part of China and overthrew it. Now took place a fusion of religious ideas. The religion of the Chou was associated with the worship of *Hao-T'ien* – a supreme sky-god. The Shang people had called their high-god *Shang-Ti* and he was thought to have a personal relationship with the Shang rulers. The two conceptions became conflated and there developed the notion of the Chou as inheriting the 'Mandate of Heaven' – originally thought of rather anthropomorphically, but later as a self-existing moral law whose constant, reliant factor was 'virtue'. 'According to this doctrine', writes the Chinese historian of philosophy Wing-Tsit-Chan, 'Man's destiny – both mortal and immortal – depended, not upon the existence of a soul before or after death nor upon the whim of a spiritual force, but upon his own good words and good deeds' (Chan 1963: 3) – an idea that was to become fundamental for much subsequent Chinese thinking and which lies at the basis of the essentially humanistic approach to life that characterises Chinese thought.

The idea that the destiny of men and nations depended on 'virtue' rather than upon the whim of some supposed supernatural power marks a radical change indeed. During the Shang dynasty the influence of supernatural beings on men and events was considerable and nothing could be done without their approval. As the *Li Ki* (*Book of Rites*) says:

> The people of Yin [Shang] honour spiritual beings, serve them, and put them ahead of ceremonies... the people of Chou honour ceremonies and highly value the conferring of favours. They serve the spiritual beings and respect them, but keep them at a distance. They remain near to man and loyal to him. (Legge 1885: 342)

'Heaven' was not, it needs to be emphasised, thought of as a Creator, for the earliest idea was of a more or less spontaneous evolution out of the Self-Existent by the rhythms of *Yin* and *Yang* – the two complimentary Primary Modes or Creative Agents. The idea of creation, in fact, only comes into Chinese thought during the Ming dynasty – that is from about the fourteenth century AD.

It is during the Chou dynasty (i.e. from 112-249 BC) that the notion of 'Heaven' begins to undergo a progressive depersonalisation. As Bouquet notes:

> The earliest ideographic symbol for T'ien is , which is plainly anthropomorphic, and must surely denote 'the man in the sky'. Later the symbol becomes stylised, as , and today it is 天, which

> has been analysed as 一 = one, 大 = great thing. T'ien is really used in two senses, (a) sky and (b) god.... It may be supposed that the depersonalisation of the ideogram goes along with the depersonalisation of the idea, which we will have to record (1956: 177).

It is no coincidence that it is during the Chou dynasty that philosophical thinking begins to emerge in China and there is some evidence that from its inception it ran in a naturalistic and indeed humanistic direction.

3.2 THE BEGINNINGS OF RATIONALISM

It is during the Ch'un Ch'iu period (722-481 BC) – the Spring and Autumn period as it is commonly called – that we first meet with those who would appear to have lost their belief in supernatural beings and also in the 'Way of Heaven'. The *Tso Chuan*[1] records the sayings of several such men. For example, under the year 679 BC we read:

> Prince Li, having heard the story about the apparition of the two serpents, asked Shen Hsü about them, saying 'Do people still see apparitions of evil augury?' Shen Hsu replied, 'When a man fears something, his breath, escaping, attracts an apparition relating to that which he fears. These apparitions have their principle in men. When men are without fault, no ominous apparitions appear. But when men throw away the rules of constant behaviour, they appear. Such is the way in which they are caused. (Couvreur 1951: 160)

And for the year 662 BC we read:

> It is when a state is about to flourish that [its ruler] listens to his people; when it is about to perish then he listens to the spirits. (Legge 1872: 170)

And under the year 524 BC:

> The Way of Heaven is distant, while that of man is near. We cannot reach to the former; what means have we of knowing it? (*ibid.*, 671)

And under 509 BC:

> The state of Hsieh makes its appeal to men, while that of Sung makes its appeal to spirits. The offence of Sung is great. (*ibid.*, 744)

Though these statements do not absolutely deny the existence of a 'Way of Heaven', or of supernatural spirits, they are certainly evidence for scepticism with regard to such concepts.

More important is the fact that during this period an attempt is made to explain all phenomena through the theory of *yin* and *yang*, the two forces which originally represented the male and the female, darkness and light, inactivity and activity, but which now begin to take on a much more naturalistic flavour. An explanation of the phenomenal universe in this vein appears in the *Kuo-Yu* (*The Sayings of the States*) under the year 780 BC. Under the year 644 BC appears the record:

> Six fish-hawks flew backwards past the capital of Sung, which was caused by the wind.

Upon which a later historian of Chou comments:

> This is something pertaining to the *yin* and the *yang*, which are not the producers of good and bad fortune. It is from men themselves that good and bad fortune are produced. (Legge 1872: 171)

The *Kuo-Yu* records the following speech for the year 494 BC:

> It is only Earth which is able to embrace the ten thousand creatures, so as to make them one, unfailing in its affairs. It gives birth to the ten thousand creatures, and bears and nourishes,

> after which it accepts the fame [achieved by them] and combines their usefulness. Those that are beautiful and those that are ugly are both brought to maturity through its nourishing and life-giving. And until the proper time has arrived things cannot be forcibly be brought to completion....
> One must have that whereby one may know the eternal laws of Heaven and Earth, in order to enjoy Heaven and Earth's complete usefulness... one must make use of the regularities of *yin* and *yang*, and comply with the regularities of Heaven and Earth... (*Yueh Yu*, II, 1 [Fung, Yu-Lan 1952 vol. I 33])

As the greatest living historian of Chinese philosophy, Fung Yu-Lan comments:

> The attempt to explain the phenomena of the universe through the yin-yang theory, though still primitive, is a step forward compared with explanations based on a T'ien, a Ti [god] and a multitude of spirits. The 'heaven' described in the last quotation is a naturalistic one. (Fung 1952: Vol I, 33)

Fung Yu-Lan further sees in the above passages a foreshadowing of the Taoist approach to nature which we shall be considering shortly.

Further evidence of early rationalistic thinking can be found in the attempts made from the Ch'un Ch'iu period onwards to give a progressively more and more humanistic interpretation to laws and statutes, previously regarded as being of divine institution, but now regarded as having being established wholly by human beings for their own benefit and, therefore, capable of change, as well as to sacrificial rites, and to the office of the ruler.[2] One example must suffice. The *Shu Ching* (*Book of Documents*) – a very early work – states:

> Men must act for the work of Heaven! From Heaven come the relationships with their several duties....
>
> Heaven gave birth to the multitude of peoples, so that they had faculties and laws....
>
> Be in accordance with the pattern of God....

> Heaven having produced the people below, appointed for them rulers and teachers.... (Fung 1952: vol. I, 33-34)

In the Ch'un Ch'iu period such sentiments give way to a purely humanistic interpretation of such institutions, as in the following:

> The early kings deliberated on all circumstances [of each crime] to make their ruling on it, and did not make [general] laws of punishment, fearing lest this should give rise to a contentious spirit among the people. But still, as crimes could not be prevented, they set up for them the barrier of righteousness, sought to rectify them with government, set before them the practice of propriety and the maintenance of good faith, and cherished them with benevolence. They also instituted emoluments and [official] positions to encourage their allegiance, and strictly laid down punishments and penalities to awe them from excesses.... When the people know what the exact laws are, they do not stand in awe of their superiors.... etc. (Legge 1872: 609)

Many more passages exhibiting the same humanistic tone could be cited from this period, but it is time that we turned to look at the two philosophies which have dominated Chinese thinking for well over two and half thousand years – those of Confucius (the *Ju-Chia*) and of Lao-Tsu (the *Tao-Chia*).

3.3 CONFUCIUS

Confucius, as his name was Latinised in the West, was born in the small kingdom of Lu about the year 551 BC, probably of an aristocratic but impoverished family. He made his living as a minor government official. Having got himself an education he sought to regenerate Chinese society by opening a school for all comers in which he taught *Li* or ceremonial (in reality political theory). After a period of travel throughout China preaching his doctrines he retired back to his native kingdom to spend his retirement writing up his teachings before dying, about 479 BC, a disappointed man, believing that his efforts to reform Chinese society were a complete and utter failure.

Of late much argument has raged over Confucius' attitude to religion, some seeing him as one who felt himself called upon to fulfil a divine mission, others as a secular humanist. The truth of the matter is that Confucius was not primarily a religious thinker, nor even a philosopher, and his interest in religious and metaphysical questions was, therefore, minimal. As the *Analects*[3] state, 'The Master would not discuss prodigies, prowess, lawlessness nor supernatural beings.' (*Analects* VII, 20 [Legge 1861]).[4] Confucius was primarily a scholar, a transmitter of (Chou) culture and therefore, for the most part, inherently conservative, keeping off controversial ground save where absolutely necessary. However, Dr. Joseph Needham, in his monumental work *Science and Civilisation in China*, notes that whilst Confucius' concern was wholly centered upon man and society – Needham describes his doctrine as one of 'this worldly social-mindedness' – he saw men's needs and desires as embedded in the whole range of Nature so that goodness and social virtue among men 'were congruent with the will of the highest powers in the universe' which had 'by the time of Confucius, lost whatever personalisation they had anciently possessed, and were referred to by the awe-inspiring name of *T'ien* [Heaven].' (Needham 1956: 12). Confucius himself believed that Heaven 'knew' and 'approved' his activities.[5]

Whilst, however, recognising the existence of 'Heaven' and of Spirits, Confucius' attitude, certainly to the latter, is one of distance bordering on indifference. As is recorded:

> Fan [Tzu-] Chhih asked what constituted wisdom. The Master said, 'To give oneself earnestly to securing righteousness and justice among the people, and while respecting the gods and demons, to keep aloof from them, that may be called wisdom.' (*Analects* VI, 20 [Legge 1861])

and on another occasion:

> Chi-lu asked about serving ghosts and spirits. The Master said,

> 'While you are not yet able to serve men, how can you serve ghosts?' Chi-lu then ventured to ask a question about the dead. The Master said, 'You do not yet know about the living, how can you know about the dead?' (*Analects* XI, 11 [Legge])

Similarly, with regard to religious rituals, Confucius was far from holding an *ex opere operato* view of their efficacy. Whilst believing in the value of rituals for the participants, both Confucius himself and his school rejected their supposed magical power to affect either spirits, ancestors or local deities. As the *Analects* record: 'He sacrificed [to the ancestors] *as if* they were present. He sacrificed to the spirits *as if* the spirits were present.' (*Analects* III,12 [Legge]; italics mine). Human sacrifice Confucius condemned in no uncertain terms.[6]

Confucius also carried further the de-sacralising of the office of the ruler. Not only did he not refer to the ruler as the 'Son of Heaven' – his traditional title – but he made that office wholly dependent upon character, ability and education, without regard to birth, and on one occasion went so far as to assert that one of his disciples, who was not the heir to a ruling house, might properly occupy the ruling office (*Analects* VI, 1).

It should also be noted that Confucius, like Socrates, with whom in so many respects he might properly be compared, made no claim – as so many religious leaders have done – to possess ultimate truth. As he said on one occasion: one should

> hear much, leave on one side that which is doubtful, and speak with due caution concerning the remainder... see much, but leave to one side that of which the meaning is not clear, and act carefully with regard to the rest. (*Analects* II, 18 [Legge])

and on another occasion: 'To hear much, select what is good, and follow it; to see much and remember it; these are the steps by which understanding is gained.' (*Analects* VIII, 27 [Legge]) He also said that meditation of itself does not lead to wisdom (*Analects* XV, 30 [Legge]).

As Max Weber has pointed out, no other great thinker – with the possible exception of Bentham and the Utilitarians – can be said to have divorced ethics so completely from metaphysics as did Confucius. Weber writes:

> In the sense of the absence of all metaphysical and almost all residue of religious anchorage, Confucianism is rationalist to such a far-going extent that it stands at the extreme boundary of what one might call a 'religious' ethic. At the same time, Confucianism is more rationalistic and sober, in the sense of the absence and the rejection of all non-utilitarian yardsticks, than any other ethical system with the possible exception of J. Bentham's. (M. Weber 1964)

These humanistic and rationalistic tendencies were to continue in the school of Confucius even after that school became progressively more religious, as we shall see.

3.4 EARLY TAOISM

It was, however, in early Taoism that the mythological view of the world first gave way to that 'pantheistic naturalism'[7] which underlay the development of science and technology in China. In early Taoism Needham sees two originally separate developments coming together. (Needham 1956: 33f.) On the one hand the philosophy of the Warring States period (ca 480-222 BC) which had developed a *Tao* [or Way] of Nature rather than of society and which arose amongst those philosophers who withdrew into the forest to meditate upon the Order of Nature and to observe its manifestations – and whom Confucius thought totally irresponsible, if not indeed 'mad' (cf. *Analects*, XVIII, 5 and XVIII, 6). On the other hand, there were the ancient traditional rites of the shamans and magicians, who had long practised in China and who were extremely influential among the ordinary people (cf. early *Lokāyāta* in India). These sought not simply to observe but also to manipulate nature – bending it to their will.

Of the founder of Taoism, Lao Tzu, little is known and much dispute has raged over the dates of his life. Formerly he was regarded as an older contemporary of Confucius but of late Fung Yu-Lan has shown, well nigh conclusively, that the *Tao Te Ching* attributed to Lao Tzu is without doubt a document from the Warring States Period, which would place Lao Tzu somewhere between 480 and 222 BC (Fung 1952: Vol I, 170).

The naturalistic emphasis in early Taoism is evident from the way in which the Taoists regarded the *Tao* itself. As we read of the natural world in the *Tao Te Ching*:

> The Tao gave birth to it
> The Virtue [of the Tao] reared it
> Things [within] endowed it with form,
> Influences [without] brought it to its perfection.
> Therefore of the ten thousand things there is not one that does not worship the Tao and do homage to its Virtue. Yet the worshipping of the Tao, and the doing of homage to its Virtue, no mandate ever decreed.
> Always this [adoration] was free and spontaneous.
> Therefore [as] the Tao bore them, and the Virtue of the Tao reared them, made them grow, fostered them, harboured them, fermented them, nourished them and incubated them – [so one must]
> 'Rear them but not lay claim to them,
> Control them but never lean upon them,
> Be chief among them but not lord it over them;
> This is called the invisible virtue.'
> (Waley 1934: ch. 51)

It is obvious that the *Tao* referred to above is nothing more, (and nothing less) than the whole Order of Nature – originator and sustainer of all that is. That a quasi-religious and mystical attitude is adopted towards to the Tao need not blind us to the essentially naturalistic leitmotif of the passage, for this response, as the passage explicitly states, is not commanded by the *Tao*, but is a free and spontaneous one on the part of the creature towards Nature, and, moreover, one that can be paralleled among European naturalists from Epicurus onwards. What we find in the above and in similar passages, is what

Dr. Needham has termed 'a pantheistic naturalism which emphasises the unity and spontaneity of the operations of Nature' (Needham 1956: Vol 2, 58); a pantheism, however, which is far removed from the realm of the personal since, for the Taoist, as for the pre-Socratic thinkers Anaximander, Parmenides and Empedocles, necessity governs all.

Speculation concerning the ultimate origin and the ultimate end of Nature the Taoists actively discouraged – suffice it for them to contemplate the operations of Nature and in that contemplation find peace. As we read in the *Chuang Tzu*:

> Words can describe [the operations of nature] and knowledge can reach them – but not beyond the extreme limit of the natural world. Those who study the Tao [know that] they cannot follow these changes to the ultimate end, nor search out their first beginnings – this is the place at which discussion has to stop. (Legge 1801: 128)

The Taoists stressed, in fact, the eternity and uncreatedness of the *Tao*. We read, for instance, in the *Tao Te Ching*:

> [In the beginning] there was something undifferentiated [*hun*] and yet complete [*Ch'eng*]
> Before Heaven and Earth were produced,
> Silent and Empty!
> Sufficient unto itself! Unchanging!
> Revolving incessantly, never exhausted.
> Well might it be the mother of all things under heaven.
> I do not know its name.
> 'Tao' is the courtesy-name we give it.
> If I were forced to classify it, I should call it 'Great'.
> But being great means being penetrating [in space and time],
> And penetrating implies far-reaching,
> And far-reaching means coming back to the original point....
> The ways of men are conditioned by those of earth, the ways of earth by those of heaven, the ways of heaven by those of

> the Tao, and the Tao came into being by itself.
> (Waley 1934: ch. 25)

The important phrase is *tzu-jan* — by itself — and it is one which occurs frequently in Taoist writings and is indicative of the underlying naturalistic attitude to nature which we find there. Needham compares the above passage with that found in the Roman Epicurean philosopher Lucretius:

> Nature, delivered from every haughty lord
> And forthwith free, is seen to have done all things
> Herself, and through herself, of her own accord
> Rid of all gods....
> (Lucretius, *De Rerum Natura* II, 1090-2. Needham 1956: 50)

One might also compare it with the speculation concerning 'the One' which we came across in Indian thought as early as the period of the *Ṛg Veda* and which we shall encounter again when we come to look at early Greek speculation into the workings of the universe. It is indeed fundamental to any concerted systematic enquiry into the workings of the world, indicative as it is of a grasp of the fundamental unity of natural processes, as well as of their independence of supernatural interference. It is, of course, the gradual recovery of this outlook in Europe, from the time of the Renaissance onwards, that brings to fruition the near-consistent naturalism of our own time.

The *Chuang Tzu*, following the naturalistic attitude expressed earlier in the *Tao Te Ching*, offers a naturalistic account of wind noises — phenomena, as Needham says, 'most inviting to the ancients to postulate the activity of spirits etc.' (1956: 50) —:

> 'The breath of the universe', said Tzu-Ch'i, 'is called wind. At times it is inactive. But when it rises, then from a myriad apertures there issues its excited noise....'
> Tzu-Yu: 'The notes of earth then are simply those which come from its myriad apertures, and the notes of man may be com-

> pared to those which [issue from the tubes of] bamboo – allow me to ask about the notes of heaven?'
> Tzu-Chhi said, 'When [the wind] blows, and its cessation makes them stop *of themselves* [*tzu i*]. Both these things arise from themselves – what other agency could there be exciting them?' (Legge 1891: 177. Italics mine.)

In another passage the same work asserts what Needham describes as 'a veritable organic philosophy' (1956: 51) and, more interesting from our point of view, goes on to suggest, on the basis of the operation of the natural processes in an animal or human body uncontrolled by consciousness, that in the whole universe *Tao* needs no consciousness to bring about its effects.

> It might seem as if there were a real Governor [tsai] [says the *Chuang Tzu*] but we find no trace of his being. One might believe that he could act, but we do not see his form. He would have [to have] sensitivity without form. But now the hundred parts of the human body, with its nine orifices and six viscera, all are complete in their places. Which should one prefer? Do you like them all equally? Or do you like some more than others? Are they all servants? Are these servants unable to control each other, but need another as ruler? Or do they become rulers and servants in turn? Is there any true ruler other than themselves? (Fung 1952: Vol 1, 46)

The early Taoists, it would seem, held that neither for the microcosm nor for the macrocosm was there need to postulate a conscious Controller. In this Needham contrasts them with the Greeks whose organicism was vitiated time and time again by the idea of a demiurge (Needham 1956: 52).

The Taoists also sought – as did the Epicureans and the Stoics in Classical Antiquity – for that peace of mind which comes from contemplating the inexorable operations of Nature. Despite the fact that a more active concern with Nature and natural processes developed in Taoism, taking it more and more in the direction of alchemy and magic, from the evidence available it would appear that such was not the original motivation behind the Taoist contemplation of nature, but that this was the search for *ataraxy* or peace of mind called in Chinese *ching-hsin.*

There are many passages in the literature of early Taoism which refer to this. The *locus classicus* is as is to be expected, found in the *Tao Te Ching* and reads as follows:

> Push on to the Ultimate Emptiness
> Guard the unshakeable Calmness
> All the ten thousand things are moving and working
> [Yet] we can see [the void, whither they must] return
> All things howsoever they flourish
> Turn and go home to the root from whence they sprang.
> This reversion to the root is called Calmness
> It is the recognition of Necessity
> That which is called Unchanging
> [Now] knowing the Unchanging means Enlightenment
> Not knowing it means going blindly to disaster....
> (ch. 16 [Waley] 1934)

Similarly the *Chuang Tzu*:

> The ancients who regulated the Tao nourished their knowledge by their calmness and all through life refrained from employing their knowledge in action [contrary to Nature], moreover they may also be said to have nourished their calmness by their knowledge. (ch. 16 [Legge] 1891)

Chuang Tzu himself demonstrated this on the death of his wife.

> Chuang Tzu's wife died and Hui Tzu went to offer his condolence. He found Chuang Tzu squatting on the ground and singing.... He said, 'Someone has lived with you, raised children for you and now she has aged and died. Is it not enough that you should not shed any tear? But now you sing.... Is not this too

much?' 'No,' replied Chuang Tzu. 'When she died, how could I help being affected? But as I think the matter over, I realise that originally she had no life; and not only no life, she had no form; not only no form, she had no material force. In the limbo of existence and non-existence, there was transformation and the material force was evolved. The material force was transformed to be form, form was transformed to become life, and now birth has transformed to become death. This is like the rotation of the four seasons.... Now she lies asleep in the great house [the universe]. For me to go about weeping and wailing would be to show my ignorance of destiny. Therefore I desist'. (ch. 18 [Wing Tsit Chan] 1963)

That a strong religious sense pervades the early Taoist attitude to Nature and natural processes need not be doubted, but it is important to see that it is non-theistic.[8]

3.5 LATER CONFUCIAN NATURALISM AND SCEPTICISM: HSUN TSU AND OTHER SCEPTICS

Two minds dominated Chinese thought throughout the Han Period (206 BC-220 AD): Mencius (371-289 BC) and Hsun Tzu (298-238 BC). Both were followers of Confucius but diverged in their interpretation of his teachings; the former, Mencius, giving rise to what has been termed Idealistic Confucianism, the latter, Hsun Tzu to Naturalistic Confucianism. In his conception of Heaven (*T'ien*) Hsun Tzu comes close to the Taoist conception of the *Tao* and, as has been pointed out, 'Nature' is often, within the context of his writings, a much more accurate translation of *T'ien* than the more usual heaven (cf. Chan 1963: 117); for whereas for Confucius and Mencius *T'ien* is purposive and the source and ultimate controller of man's destiny, for Hsun Tzu it is simply the processes of Nature. This is evident in the following quotation from the *Hsun Tzu*:

Nature [*T'ien*] operates with constant regularity. It does not

> exist for the sake of [sage emperor] Yao nor does it cease to exist because of [wicked king] Chieh. Respond to it with peace and order, and good fortune will result. Respond to it with disorder, and disaster will follow. If the foundations of living [agriculture] are strengthened and are economically used, then Nature cannot bring impoverishment. If people's nourishment is sufficient and their labour in keeping with the seasons, then Nature cannot inflict sickness. If the Way is cultivated without deviation, then Nature cannot cause misfortune.... If the people violate the Way and act foolishly then Nature cannot give them good fortune.... This cannot be blamed on Heaven; this is how the Way works. (ch. 17 'On Nature' [Wing Tsit Chan] 1963)

There is much more in the *Hsun Tzu* in a similar vein. Traditional ceremonies are demythologised for instance: 'To accomplish without any action and to obtain without effort, this is what is meant by the office of Heaven' (*ibid.*).

Similarly, the influence of supernatural forces is completely ruled out by Hsun Tzu. What people attribute to spirits is for him but the outcome of natural processes.

> When people pray for rain, it rains. Why? I say: There is no need to ask why. It is the same when it rains when no one prays for it. When people try to save the sun or the moon from being eclipsed, or when they pray for rain in drought, or when they decide an important affair only after divination, they do so not because they believe that they will get what they are after, but to use them as an ornament to governmental measures. Hence the ruler intends them to be an ornament, but the common people think they are supernatural. It is good fortune to regard them as ornamental but it is evil fortune to regard them as supernatural. (*ibid.*)

But Hsun Tzu goes further and in a remarkable passage suggests the possibility of controlling Nature, of bending it to men's will – something which takes him beyond traditional Confucianism and Taoism which, as we have seen, simply suggest the idea of living in terms of the cosmic harmony. Hsun Tzu writes:

> Instead of regarding Heaven as great and admiring it,
> Why not foster it as a thing and regulate it?
> Instead of obeying Heaven and singing praises to it,
> Why not control the Mandate of Heaven and use it?
> Instead of looking on the seasons and waiting for them,
> Why not respond to them and make use of them?
> Instead of letting things multiply by themselves,
> Why not exercise your ability to transform [and increase] them?
>
> Instead of admiring how things came into being,
> Why not do something to bring them to full development.
> (*ibid.*)

This ethical and practical interest is evident in an earlier passage where he maintains that portents and presages mean very little compared with good or bad government. He wrote:

> When stars fall or a sacred tree groans the people of the whole state are afraid. We ask 'Why is it?' I answer: there is no [special] reason. It is due to an aberration of heaven and earth, to a mutation of the Ying and Yang. These are rare events. We may marvel at them but we should not fear them. For there is no age which has not experienced eclipses of the sun and moon, unseasonable rain or wind, or strange stars seen in groups. If the prince is illustrious and the government tranquil, although these events should all come together in one age it would do no harm ... but when human ominous signs come, then we should really be afraid. Using poor ploughs... spoiling a crop by inadequate hoeing and weeding ... these are what I mean by ominous human signs. (*ibid.*, ch. 17 [Dubs])

Further, a whole chapter is devoted to an attack upon the most prevalent superstition of the time – physiognomy.

Yet for all his sceptical rationalism Hsun Tzu is interesting in that he did little if anything to actually promote the furtherance of the practice of science. In fact he actively opposed the attempts of others to work out a scientific logic, insisting only on the practical application of technology, not on the exploration of its theoretical basis. He was also given, on occasions, to almost mystical rhapsody on the harmony of human society and the cosmos through *li* – rites and ceremonies – which he exalted to the status of a cosmic principle, a fact which, as Needham notes, brings him perilously close to pantheism (1956: 27).

A corollary of Hsun Tzu's naturalistic view of Heaven is his view of human virtue. Whereas Mencius, believing as he did in Heaven as a moral force suffusing the world, held that man was naturally virtuous, Hsun Tzu believed that morality is acquired and was under no illusion as to the difficulty of this task. It is in fact for his views on morality that he is chiefly remembered in later Confucian tradition – and none too favourably either!

Hsun Tzu is not the only sceptic, however, of this period. Han Fei Tzu stands within the same tradition. He wrote that 'If the ruler believes in date-selecting, worships gods and demons, puts faith in divination, and likes luxurious feasts, then ruin is probable' (*Han Fei Tzu* ch. 17 [Dubs]). And elsewhere he cites wars which ended in ruin because tortoise-shell and milfoil (two traditional methods of divination) rather than military strategy were employed (*ibid.* ch. 19).

Another sceptic is Huan T'an (40 BC-25 AD), who is recorded as having held that 'life is like the flame of a lamp, going out when the fuel is exhausted' and who is recorded as rebuking the Emperor Kuang Wu for his reliance on divination.

It is during the early Han period that Confucianism becomes established as the official state religion of China, but it must be noted that the Confucianism which becomes so established is neither the near-agnostic, social and humanistic Confucianism of Confucius himself, nor the atheistic, naturalistic Confucianism at which we have been looking, but a theistic form of Confucianism which had developed in the fourth and third centuries BC.

Similarly when Taoism emerges as a religion in the second century BC it is not the atheistic Taoism of the early period, but a theistic form which developed during the same period and under the same influences as theistic Confucianism 'together with a thousand superstitious features from the religion of the common people' (Needham 1956: 366).

That the sceptical tradition did not die out, but continued to challenge the superstitions of the time is evidenced by a passage in the *Hou Han Shu* – the history of the later Han Dynasty (25-220 AD) – dated 45 AD (ch. 109 A. p.5a in Needham 1956: 367). It tells of one Liu K'un, the prefect of the city of Chiangling who, when a fire was on the point of devastating his city, prostrated himself before it. At which point the fire went out. Similarly when he was prefect of Hung-nung, in an incident reminiscent of St. Patrick and the snakes in Ireland, he purged that city of the menace of tigers. The Emperor hearing of his doings sent for him and asked him by what virtue he had done these things. Liu Khun replied that it was all 'pure chance' – a remark which, contrary to the expectation of bystanders, did not go unrewarded, for the Emperor, recognising an honest man when he saw one, replied: 'This reply is worthy of a really superior man! Let the annalists record it.'

It is, however, in the philosophy of Wang Ch'ung that the sceptical tradition reaches its supreme expression in ancient China.

3.6 WANG CH'UNG

Wang Ch'ung has been called the Lucretius of China. He was born about the year 27 AD and died about the year 97 AD. In an age increasingly given over to superstition Wang Ch'ung, an independent thinker if ever there was one, upheld, in a series of critical essays, *Discourses Weighed in the Balance* (*Lun Hêng*), the pure light of reason. One phrase, as he himself said, covers all the chapters of this work, 'hatred of fictions and falsehoods' (ch. 61 [Fung Yu-Lan]). The list of those as he opposed is a long one. In his essays he maintains, contrary to the belief of his day and age, that 'Heaven' takes no action; that natural events, including prodigies, occur spontaneously, that there is no such thing as teleology in nature; that fortune and misfortune come by chance; and that a man does not become a ghost after death but disintegrates into nothingness.[9]

Making little use of the terms *li* or even *Tao*, Wang Ch'ung's attitude to natural processes, whilst allowing for chance, is thoroughly deterministic. The term which he himself uses to describe natural processes is *ming*, which means fate or destiny, but he uses this in a way highly reminiscent of the use of 'necessity' in early Greek philosophical writings. Like the Taoists, he denies both consciousness and motivation to Heaven and holds a naturalistic world-view in which 'spontaneity' is the key-word. Natural processes are explained in the traditional *yin-yang* terminology.

Also in accordance with his naturalism, Wang Ch'ung attacks the notion — prevalent in his day — that what happens in the world is the result of human merit or demerit. Much happens by chance or accident, he maintains. Similarly, he is led to deny purpose in the world. The world, for him, is not the creation of a divine Designer. In a passage reminiscent of Lucrecius (cf. Lucretius, *De Rerum Natura*, II 177-181; V 185-189), he writes:

> Tilling, weeding and sowing are designed acts, but whether the seed grows up and ripens or not depends upon chance and spontaneous action. How do we know? If Heaven had produced its creatures on purpose, it ought to have taught them to love each other and not to prey upon and destroy one another. (*Lun Hêng*, ch. 14 [Forke 1907: 104])

More important for the development of naturalism in China was Wang Ch'ung's attack upon anthropocentrism. Time and again he describes man's life upon earth as like that of lice living in the folds of a garment. Whilst recognising that man, (by reason of his intelligence), is the highest of all known beings on earth, man is still, as are lice, part of the natural order. How absurd, therefore, to imagine that either Heaven or earth can understand the words of man, or bother themselves about his wishes! As Needham says:

This position once gained, the whole weight of Wang Ch'ung's attack on superstition was deployed. Heaven, being incorporeal, and Earth inert, can on no account be said to speak or act; they cannot be affected by anything which man does; they do not listen to prayers; they do not reply to questions. Hence was swept away the whole basis of the systems of divination.[10]

What remained of superstition, once divination had been denied, Wang Ch'ung attacked, either by demonstrating the statistical absurdity of some beliefs (the thousands of debtors in the gaols, for example, cannot all have chosen unlucky days for their business), or the sheer unreasonableness of others (e.g. sacrifices to ghosts and spirits). Man's happiness is in his own hands and the spirits have nothing to do with it. In a passage reminiscent of Confucius he writes:

> The world places confidence in sacrifices, trusting that they procure happiness; and likewise it approves of exorcisms, fancying that these remove evil. The first ceremony performed at exorcism is the setting out of a sacrifice, which we may compare with the entertainment of guests among living men; but after savoury food has been hospitably set out for the spirits and they have eaten of it, they are chased away with swords and sticks. If the spirits were conscious of such treatment they would surely stand their ground, accept the fight, and refuse to go: and if they were susceptible of indignation, they would cause misfortune. But if they have no consciousness they cannot possibly effect any evil. Accordingly exorcising is lost labour, and no harm is caused by its omission.
>
> Besides, it is disputed whether spirits have a material form. If they have, it must be like that of living men. But anything with the form of living men must be capable of feeling indignation, and exorcism would therefore cause harm rather than good. And if they have no material form, driving them away is like [trying to] drive out vapour and clouds, which cannot be done. And since it cannot [even] be ascertained whether spirits have a material form, we are not at all in a position to guess their feelings. For what purpose do they gather in human dwellings anyway? If disposed to killing and injury, they will, when exorcised,

> simply abscond and hide, but return as soon as the chase is over. And if they occupy our homes without nefarious purposes, they will not be harmful, even though not expelled....
> Decaying generations cherish a belief in ghosts. Foolish men seek relief in exorcism. When the Chou dynasty rulers were going to ruin, sacrifice and exorcism were believed in, and peace of mind and spiritual assistance were thus sought. The foolish rulers, whose minds were misled, forgot about the importance of their own behaviour, and the fewer their good actions the more unstable their thrones became. The conclusion is that man has his happiness in his own hands, and that the spirits have nothing to do with it. It depends on his virtues and not on sacrifices. (*Lun Hêng* ch. 1 [Forke 1907: 532, 534])

A splendidly humanistic passage!

He also attacked the Taoist search for the elixir of life – although there is just a suggestion that at the end of his life he changed his mind on this. Overall, however, we can say that Wang Ch'ung remained the opponent of all forms of supernaturalism, combating the many and varied forms of the superstitions beliefs of his day and seeking, wherever possible, to offer a scientific explanation of phenomena.

His most concerted attack, however, was upon those Han Confucians who maintained that ethical irregularity caused cosmic irregularities – a view which was particularly prevalent during this period, and one that can be paralleled in both early Greek and Jewish culture.[11] Its most explicit statement in China can be found in Tung Chung-Shu's, *Ch'un Ch'iu Fan Lu* (*String of Pearls on the Spring and Autumn Annals*)[12] Tung Chung-Shu there holds that, for example, if the emperor and his advisors do not practice the correct ceremonial (*li*) in their conduct of affairs then there will be excessive gales and trees will not grow; that if the emperor's audiences fail to be discriminating, there will follow rains and floods. Even fault by minor governmental officials, he held, would produce cosmic irregularity.

Another aspect of popular belief was what Needham has called an 'inverted astrology' (1956: 379) – namely the belief that the perturbations of the planets' motions are also effected by governmental irregularities. In the *Fa Yen* of Yan Hsiung, written about 5 AD we read:

> Someone asked whether a sage could make divination. Yang Hsiung replied that a sage could certainly make divination about Heaven and Earth. If that is so, continued the questioner, what is the difference between the sage and the astrologer? Yang Hsiung replied, 'The astrologer foretells what the effects of heavenly phenomena will be on man; the sage foretells what the effects of man's actions will be on the heavens'. (Forke 1934: 95)

To this growing belief in the moral reactivity of Nature, Wang Ch'ung led the opposition. He brought forth argument after argument to urge that excessive heat or cold could not be dependent on the behaviour of the ruler; that plagues and grain-eating insects were not caused by the irregular behaviour of minor bureaucrats; that natural calamities were not manifestations of the anger of 'Heaven' etc. In the chapter of *Lun Hêng* in which he argues against such widespread superstitions he ends as follows:

> The heart of high Heaven is in the bosom of the sages. When Heaven reprimands it does so through the mouths of the sages. Yet people do not believe their words. They trust in the Chi of calamitous events, and try to make out Heaven's meaning therefrom. How far is this away from the truth! (Forke 1907: 129)

And turning the tables on such views, he goes on to assert in a later chapter that instead of natural calamities depending on human virtue, human virtue depends on natural calamities! For instance in times of famine, Wang Ch'ung asks:

> What are the causes of disorder? [and replies] Are they not the prevalence of robbery, fighting and bloodshed, the disregard of

> moral obligations by the people, and their rebellion against their rulers? All these difficulties arise from want of grain and other goods, for the people are unable to bear hunger and cold beyond a certain limit. When hunger and cold combine, there are few who will not violate the laws; but when they enjoy both warmth and food, there are few who will not behave properly. (Forke 1911: 12)

Wang Ch'ung's fundamental position is made clear in chapter 41 and it is that all the assumed coincidences were due to pure chance. He writes:

> The setting in of torrid and frigid weather does not depend on any governmental actions, but heat and cold may chance to be coincident with rewards and punishments, and it is for this reason that the phenomenalists falsely ascribe them as having such a connection. (Forke 1907: 281)

As we saw in our opening chapter on the mythological world-view the notion of chance – which lies at the heart of the naturalistic approach to life – is lacking in such an outlook. Wang Ch'ung's assertion of such places him firmly within the naturalistic tradition.

Wang Ch'ung's common-sense naturalism was not, however, effective and the *Ch'an-Wei-Shu* (*Treatises on Prognostications*), which enshrined the popular superstitions which he attached, continued to find favour even as late as the T'ang dynasty, that is until at least the ninth century AD, despite the fact that as one rebellion after another claimed justification from this and similar treatises, they began to be first frowned upon and ultimately supressed by the emperor Yang Ti in the seventh century AD.[13] It was not until the rationalist influence of the Neo-confucians of the Sung dynasty in the twelfth and thirteenth centuries that this particular form of superstition died out in Chinese culture.

Wang Ch'ung's positive teaching must be briefly mentioned, for we find in it a humanism which is rare, not only within Chinese culture, but within any other culture of this time. His conception of human destiny or fate (*T'ien ming*) was not that of an inexorable decree of 'Heaven', predetermined for each and every individual – the *νεῖμαρμηνη* of the Greeks [that which falls to one's lot] nor the *dira necessitas* [unalterable fate] of the Romans, nor the predestinations of the early Christian Fathers – but the more humanistic and rationalist conception of *Ching Shen*, which asserted that one's destiny depended solely upon a combination of temperament and chance.[14]

Ching Shen, or spiritual essence, signified, in the writings of Wang Ch'ung, not only mental capabilities but something very physical. 'The fact of individuals is inherent in their bodies, just as with birds the distinction between cocks and hens exists already within the egg-shell' (Forke 1907: 132) he wrote. This emphasis on genetic inheritance is extremely interesting, not least because, as Needham notes, it presages by almost two thousand years the determination problem so basic to modern experimental embryology (1956: 383). What interests us, however, is that Wang Ch'ung offers a naturalistic explanation for what the vast majority of his contemporaries would have explained in terms of supernatural causation.

His writings on chance betray a similar bias. As we have seen one of the fundamental ingredients in the mythico-religious outlook on the world is the lack of any conception of chance. Chance, Wang Ch'ung analyses naturalistically into the effects of time and contingency.

Wang Ch'ung died about 97 AD but his influence lived on, and whilst he did not found a school, we know that at least two later philosophers, Ts'ai Yung (133-192 AD) and Wang Lang (died 228 AD) both valued his writings highly. It is also likely that his writings inspired Hsun Yueh's vigorous opposition to the superstitions rife in popular Taoism during the latter half of the second century AD.

Han scepticism is also evident in Liu Shao's, *Jen Wu Chih* (*Study of Human Abilities*), a work on the psychology of character, written about 235 AD, which contains not a single reference to current views regarding physiogonomy, but is based wholly on a rationalistic observation of psychological traits and their effects in human affairs.

3.7 THE LATER SCEPTICAL TRADITION

'Throughout subsequent Chinese history the sceptical tradition runs on. Indeed, it stands out as one of the great achievements of that culture, when one compares it with the rabble of religious and magical writings dominant in some other civilizations' (Needham 1956: 386). Needham's judgement is amply substantiated. The ridicule of spirits becomes a common-place of Confucianism. Also, despite the growth of Buddhism in China, there were always Confucians at hand to oppose its teachings. The historical records for the year 484 AD tell of a debate before the Prince of Ching-Ling in which a certain Fan Chen attacked the doctrines of *samsara* and *karma* – i.e. the belief that a person is continually reincarnated; his present form of incarnation being determined by the quality of the deeds he performed in previous existences. We noted earlier that Wang Ch'ung attacked the prevalent belief of his time in immortality. Fan Chen now said that, 'The spirit is to the body what sharpness is to the knife. We have never heard that after the knife has been destroyed the sharpness can persist' (*Thung Chien Kang Mu* ch. 28 [Wieger]) – an analogical argument very like the one put forward by Uddālaka within the early Indian naturalistic tradition. Fan Cheng's views were written down in a treatise with the significant title, *On the Destructibility of the Soul* (*Shen Mieh Lun*) – a work which the Buddhists considered of such importance that they wrote no less than seventy refutations of it!

Further, Confucian attacks on Buddhism (and particularly on popular Buddhism) are recorded for the year 631 AD when the Confucian scholar Fu Li engaged Buddhist thaumaturgists in argument.[15] His contemporary, Lu Ts'ai, although complying with the order of the Emperor that he edit the existing works of divination (and of the *Yin-Yang* and five element theory) was careful to add sceptical prefaces to each. Although his actual works are now lost, fragments from them, which have been preserved in the *Disputations Concerning Doubtful Matters* (*Pien Huo Pien*) of Hsieh Ying-Fang of the mid fourteenth century AD, show that his position was very similar to that of Wang Ch'ung. He argues, for instance, that disasters in which innumerable people perish make nonsense of notions of individual destinies.

From about the seventh century AD onwards stories directed against superstition become increasingly prevalent. Needham cites one from the *Notes and Queries on Doubtful Matters* (*Pien I Chih*) of Lu Ch'ang-Yuan, written during the T'ang dynasty and dated about 770 AD, which tells of a temple, where it was believed that the body of a Taoist nun had remained undecomposed for centuries. A group of young men bursting into the temple after a riotous evening opened the coffin and found only mouldering bones! (Needham 1956: 387).

The year 819 AD is the year of the celebrated protest made by Han Yu against the official reception by the emperor of a relic of the Buddha.[16]

During the Sung dynasty (960-1279) Ch'u Yung in his *Discussions on the Dispersion of Doubts* (*Ch'u I Shuo Tsuan*) gave a subjectivist interpretation – along the lines of a placebo effect – of the effectiveness of Taoist charms and talismans.

An outright sceptic of the same dynasty, Shih Chieh (1005-1045), wrote in his *Lai Chi*:

> I believe that there are three illusory things in this world, immortals, the alchemical art, and Buddheity. These three things lead all men astray, and many would willingly give up their lives to obtain them. But I believe that there exists nothing of the sort, and I have good grounds for saying so. If there were any one man in the world who had obtained them, no one would be more honoured than he. Then no one would strive without accomplishment or pray without response.... Ch'in Shih wished to become immortal, Han Wu Ti wished to make gold, and Liang Wu Ti wished to become a Buddha, and they spent themselves in these aims. But Chhin Shih Huang Ti died on a long journey, Liang Wu Ti starved himself to death, and Han Wu Ti never obtained any gold. (Forke 1938: 48)

This, moreover is not an isolated cry, for the entire Neo-Confucian school, which comes to the fore during the Sung Dynasty, is characterised by a sceptical and indeed by a naturalistic spirit.

To estimate its significance it will be necessary, briefly, to outline the religious situation out of which it arose, and in particular we should notice the rise to pre-eminence during the previous centuries of Buddhism, which from about the beginning of the Christian era had become the single most important religious factor in the cultural development of China. Political and socio-economic factors are also important in accounting for both Buddhism's rise to pre-eminence and its eventual decline.

The impact of Buddhism on Chinese culture was far reaching. Until the incursion of this new outlook on life, Chinese culture had been extremely introverted and for the most part unspeculative, concerning itself primarily with problems relating to man and society. Buddhism, China's first contact with an alien approach to life, meant for those who accepted it a complete reorientation to the whole business of living and, even for those who rejected it, it meant that, henceforth, an alternative way of looking at the world was presented to them. Buddhism was to perform this function within Chinese culture for well over a thousand years. The basic beliefs of Buddhism have already been outlined.

The earliest form of Buddhism to reach China – probably about the beginning of the Christian Era – was Hināyāna, a form of Buddhism that had much in common with early Taoist notions of the value of inaction. It was, however, Mahāyāna Buddhism with its veneration of the bodhisāttva's and its highly speculative metaphysics that was ultimately to have the great influence on Chinese culture.

In achieving the position which it eventually did in Chinese society, Buddhism was aided by the political and social upheavals of the later Han period (second century AD), which resulted in China being divided into three states, followed by the barbarian invasions. In such turbulent times many sought refuge in Buddhism, nihilism or Taoist mysticism. Confucianism virtually died out – but not quite; for, impregnated as it had indeed become during late Han times with Taoist metaphysics, and although inherently conservative, it never quite lost its role as the champion of the common people. Confucian scholars through the troubled second, third, fourth, fifth and sixth centuries continued the study of the Confucian classics and when finally China once more became a united nation under the T'ang dynasty (618-906 AD) the officials of government were recruited from their ranks. This was the beginning of a resurgence of Confucianism which was eventually to supercede the imported religion of Buddhism.

In this it was aided by the fact that the very success of Buddhism had caused that religion to become identified with all the political and social abuses of the time. Confucianism was thereby strategically placed to become the religion of those favouring reform.

One should also note that however successful Buddhism in China became, it would seem that it never fully accommodated itself to the Chinese mind which, as Creel has pointed out, 'is normally practical, a bit sceptical, and eminently this-worldly' (Creel 1953: 203). Creel constructs the reply that Confucius, had he heard the Buddha teaching, might well have given as follows:

> What you say is interesting and may be true. But your doctrine of reincarnation would require a great deal of proof, which I do not see how you could provide. A part of your ethics is admirable, but taken as a whole your programme offers little or nothing to remedy the grave political, social, and economic problems by which men are oppressed. On the contrary it would probably make them worse. (*ibid.*, 207-208)

This is an admirable insight into the whole Confucian approach to religion.

However, by the time of the Sung dynasty (960-1279 AD) speculative metaphysics had made such inroads into Chinese culture that a more vigorous frontal attack was needed. Neo-Confucianism initially sought to provide this by seeking to show that it could match everything offered by Buddhism in the way of cosmology, metaphysics and ethics, and at the same time justify social and political activity, and so vindicate man's hope of finding happiness in the everyday pursuits of life. This it did by drawing heavily on the *Book of Changes* – a fortune-teller's manual wholly alien to the thought of Confucius himself, despite its claim to represent his thought.

With Chu Hsi (1131-1200 AD) – perhaps the greatest single and certainly the most influential thinker in the millenium in China before the advent of Mao Tse-Tung – the situation changes radically, for the picture of the world which he puts forward is, almost without exception, thoroughly naturalistic.[17]

For Chu Hsi the universe is an organism, and its process of operation is that of *ch'i* or substance working in accordance with *li* or principle. Chu Hsi's universe is an ordered whole and the principles of its operation are without birth and indestructible, nor do they change in any way. They are all ultimately part of one great *li*, which Chu Hsi more often than not equates with the *Tao*. *Ch'i* and *li* alone are responsible for producing the universe and its ongoing process.

Human nature too has its *li* and this is the same in all men, however, differ in their *ch'i*, thus giving rise to the differences which we find among individuals.

The Yuan dynasty (1280-1367) witnesses the appearance of a truly scientific mind in the person of Liu Chi (1311-1375 AD), yet another thinker who seeks throughout his writings for purely natural explanations of phenomena. For example, taking up Wang Ch'ung's arguments about lightning he argues against the idea that death by lightning is anything other than pure chance. In his book, the *Yu Li Tzu*, he likens dying to the pouring back of a tumbler of water into the sea – the *ch'i* [matter] returning to universal matter. Though he did write a treatise on geomancy, the tone of his approach is throughout scientific even though we today would perhaps dispute his premises and his conclusions.

Also interesting is a contemporary of his, Hsieh Ying-Fan, who made a collection of the attacks by Confucian scholars, in a work entitled, *Disputations on Doubtful Matters*, (*Pien Huo Pien*), on such popular superstitions as praying for long life, burning paper money for the dead, Buddhist conceptions of immortality and of hell, reincarnation, divination, astrology, lucky and unlucky days, geomancy, physiognomy, etc. He also quotes, with approval, passages from such earlier Confucian scholars as Hsun Ch'ing and Hsi men Pao, as well as Confucian texts advocating the abolition of Buddhist temples. He also attacks those who claimed that 'Heaven' had not favoured those dynasties which had supported Buddhism.

The most outstanding sceptic of the early Ming dynasty (1368-1644 AD) was Ts'ao Tuan (1376-1434 AD), a great admirer of the *Pien Huo Pien*, who wrote his own sceptical work, *The Candle in the Night* (*Yeh Hsing Chu*) for his father who was a Buddhist.

In the late Ming a materialist outlook can be found in Wang Ch'uan-Shan (1619-1692 AD) – in Needham's opinion, the last great indigenous naturalist.

Wang Ch'uan-Shan served the Ming dynasty as an extremely competent administrator for as long as it remained. At its fall he retired into the mountains near Hengyang to study and to write.[18] His position as we have it in his commentary on the *Book of Changes* (*I Ching*) – the *Chou I Wai Chuan* – and in such smaller works as his *Record of Thoughts and Questionings* (*Ssu Wen Lu*) and the *Wait and Analyse* (*Ssu Chieh*) is not only sceptical but out and out materialistic as well, and he combatted not only current forms of Idealism but also popular superstitions, attacking both astrology and phenomenalism. Although identifying himself with Neo-Confucianism he positively refused to go along with Neo-Confucian ideas of cosmic cycles and, in fact, he was inclined to dismiss all cosmogonic speculation as being outwith what could be observed and therefore sensibly discussed (cf. *Ssu Wen Lu*, 25a; quoted Needham 1956: 511). In this he might fairly be said to be returning to the original Confucian position.

For Wang Ch'uan-Shan reality consists of matter in continuous motion and he picked up and emphasised the materialistic side of Chu Hsi's philosophy, asserting that *li* – the principle of order in the universe – had exactly the same status as *Ch'i* – matter. 'Apart from phenomena' he wrote, 'there is no Tao' (quoted Needham *ibid.*, 511-512). His naturalistic philosophy – the actual details of which are too complicated to be dealt with here – is known as the *Theory of the Generative Power of Nature* (*Yin Yun Seng Hua Lun*); an apt designation of his approach to the world.

Nature and its workings were not the only phenomena that interested Wang's fertile mind, and it is, in fact, his approach to historical questions that best exhibits his naturalistic and materialistic philosophy, and it is with some justification that contemporary Marxist-

Leninist philosophers regard him as a forerunner of their own approach to history.[19]

The materialistic movement of the Ming period – for such it can indeed be called – was not confined to one man: many other materialists might be cited, among them two contemporaries of Wang Ch'uan-Shan, Yen Yuan (1635-1704 AD) and Li Kung (1659-1733 AD). The group that they founded became known as the 'Yen-Li School' or more popularly the 'Back to the Han School' (*Han Hsueh P'ai*) in that they sought, in opposition to the Neo-Confucians, to return to the ideas of the scholars of the Han period. In so doing they prepared the way for Wang Ch'uan-Shan's eighteenth century successor, Tai Chen (1724-1777 AD), the greatest scholar of the Ch'ing dynasty (1644-1911).

Yen Yuan and Li Kung showed in their writings just how impregnated with Taoist and Buddhist notions Sung Neo-Confucianism had become. Building on this, Tai Chen formulated a system of nature devoid of all extraneous Taoist and Buddhist metaphysics. Rejecting the entire conception of *li* [principle or form] as a power outwith nature, Tai Chen sought to account for the process of nature, man included, entirely in term of *Ch'i* or matter. He thus, as Needham has pointed out, returned to the older and more fundamental conception of the Tao as simply the 'order of nature' as exhibited by the *Yin-Yang* and the five element theory (Needham 1956: 514). Whereas under the influence of Buddhist (and possibly Christian) metaphysics *li* had taken on an almost supernatural significance, for Tai Chen *li* was simply the order or pattern observable in nature – a function of *Ch'i* – something which Chu Hsi, as we have seen, sought to attribute to it.

Politically too, the materialistic school, in the person of Tai Chen, opposed the existing social structure, which, as so often in religious cultures, sought to justify itself in terms of its exhibiting in the microcosm the unalterable order of the macrocosm. Neo-Confucianism, like the Buddhism which preceded it, had become the tool of political and social privilege – its universal pattern-principle interpretation of *li* being understood as a universal law justifying law-abidingness, and the maintenance of the *status quo* at all costs. Tai Chen broke completely with this interpretation and severed all connection between law as pattern, organisation and structure, and laws as laid down to be obeyed.

The principles of the operation of nature, for Tai Chen, were not derivable from intuition or meditation, but were to be arrived at only on the basis of observation of actual natural processes, or as a contemporary Chinese philosopher Fang Chao Ying puts it, 'by wide learning, careful investigation, exact thinking, clear reasoning and sincere conduct.' 'Reason' he claimed, 'was not something superimposed by Heaven on man's physical nature; it is exemplified in every manifestation of his being, even in the so-called baser emotions' (Hummel 1944) – a remark that one might put alongside David Hume's that 'Reason is and ought to be the Slave of the Passions' (*Treatise on Human Nature* Bk II). Neo-Confucianism had become Buddhicised to the extent that it regarded all man's emotions and desires as inherently evil and therefore to be eradicated. In Tai Chen's ideal society all desires and feelings could be expressed freely, provided that they did not harm others – his only criterion of the rightness or wrongness of actions. Virtue for, Tai Chen, would not be, as it was for the Buddhists (and one might add for many Hindus, and Christians), the suppression of desire, but its orderly expression and fulfilment. As Needham comments, 'Tai Chen, though a contemporary of Rousseau and almost of Blake, would have found himself at home in a post-Freudian world at least as much as they' (Needham 1956: 517).

We have now reached a point in our survey of Chinese naturalism where Western post-Renaissance science – mediated, oddly enough, in the first place, by Jesuit missionaries – begins to make inroads into Chinese culture, and where, consequently, Chinese naturalistic thinking merges with the world-wide unity of modern science – the consequences of which are not exclusive to Chinese culture and which fall, therefore, outside the scope of this present study.

4

Greece

4.1 INTRODUCTION

Within Western culture during the last half-century or so the breakdown of the mythico-religious approach to the world has become well-nigh complete. Whereas, we have seen, strong naturalistic strains can be found in both Indian and Chinese culture, it is only within Western culture – and in other contemporary cultures in so far as they have come under the influence of Western culture – that the naturalistic approach comes to systematic fruition and supercedes the hitherto dominant religious outlook on life.

The origins of this development, within Western culture, began in the Greece of the sixth century BC where, as is now generally agreed, the decisive step forward was taken which was to lead human thinking about the world away from mythology, and eventually from religion also. The great classicist and historian of ideas F. M. Cornford put it as follows:

> At that moment a new spirit of rational inquiry asserted its claim to pronounce upon ultimate things which had hitherto been the objects of traditional belief (1957: v),

although as he went on to show, the advent of this spirit did not represent a sudden and complete breach with older approaches to the world but was rather an organic development from them. He maintained:

> There is real continuity, between the earliest rational speculations and the religious representations that lay behind them.... Philosophy inherits from religion certain great conceptions – for instance, the ideas of 'God', 'Soul', 'Destiny', 'Law' – which continue to circumscribe the movements of rational thought and to determine their main directions.
>
> Religion expresses itself in poetic symbols and in terms of mythi-

> cal personalities; Philosophy prefers the language of dry abstraction, and speaks of substance, cause, matter, and so forth. But the outward difference only disguises an inward and substantial affinity between these two successive products of the same consciousness. The modes of thought and action that attain to clear definition and explicit statement in philosophy were already implicit in the unreasoned intuitions of mythology (1957: v).

This is not, of course, to say that there were not important differences between these two approaches nor that, in the last resort, we may have to choose between them; it is only to assert continuity where others, before Cornford's seminal study, had seen but a clear-cut break.

However, granted that early Greek, like early Indian speculation concerning the ultimate nature of the world-stuff (*φύσις*) out of which the world as we apprehend it came, and of the process by which this occurred and continues, has its roots deep in mythology, the rationalistic tendency in Greek thinking, which first asserts itself in Ionia in the sixth century BC initiated an ongoing movement in Western thinking which has continued, though with interruptions, to our own day. But before turning to look at the beginnings of this tradition a word is called for about the religious background out of which it arose.

4.2 EARLY GREEK RELIGION

The earliest recorded evidence for the religion of the Greeks[1] is found in the Homeric poems and dates from about 800 BC, although the Homeric corpus includes orally transmitted material from a much earlier period.

The religion of the Heroic period there recorded differs but little from that of the Aryan invaders of India whom we considered at the outset of our study – which is to be expected as the Greeks were of the same Indo-European stock.

But, as happened in India, the religion of the (Aryan) invaders of Greece – invaders who first came to that country from about

1300 BC — took into itself much of the earlier culture, that is, of the Mycenean/Minoan culture which they overthrew, including, of course, much of Mycenean religion.

We thus find two elements in early Greek religion; an originally polytheistic cultus centering upon the Olympian deities with the sky-god Zeus at their head — the upholder although not the creator of the cosmos — and elements derived from the agricultural rituals of the earlier Myceanean/Minoan civilization centering on the worship of the mother-goddess. Both are, however, thoroughly mythological. The primitive Greek thought of his gods very much as did other primitive peoples — life is subject to external supernatural personal powers that cannot be controlled; best therefore to keep on good terms with them and in rite and ritual strive to create a harmonious relationship with them.

Similarly with regard to inner life, where forces and passions occur which seem also to be beyond control. These too in ancient Greek religion become externalised as powers outwith man, who, from time to time, take possession of him and decree his activity — an onslaught of love, for example, is the work of Aphrodite, poetic inspiration the work of the Muses. As Maurice Bowra has written:

> The Greeks, like other peoples needed gods to explain what is otherwise inexplicable. To the prescientific consciousness, nature, both human and physical, is encompassed with mysteries which cry out to be penetrated and mastered. The Greeks solved the matter to their own satisfaction by believing in gods who not only rule the visible world but are at work in the fortunes and hearts of men. Just as it was natural to explain by divine agency thunder or storms or earthquakes or the growth of the crops, so it was equally natural to attribute to gods the inspiring thoughts or qualms of conscience or onslaughts of passion which assail human beings. Both classes of phenomena were outside control or prediction — (The Greeks) were indeed proud of their own powers, but they recognised that much lay beyond their own summons and all this belonged to the gods. It was therefore important to form relations with them and to solicit the utmost help from them, not merely because otherwise the order of physical nature might be reversed

> and the earth cease to yield her fruits, but because the very springs of human action depend upon unpredictable moments of inspired thought or accesses of energy which man cannot evoke at will. (1959: 56)

Fr. Copleston too notes the dark, rather frightening side to the Greek view of life. He writes:

> It is a great mistake to suppose that the Greeks were happy and careless children of the sun ... they were very conscious of the dark side of our existence on this planet, for against the background of sun and joy they saw the uncertainty and insecurity of man's life, the certainty of death, and the darkness of the future. (1962: 33)

Something which was to be one of the main motivating factors behind both divination and the later search for immortality through deification.

But underlying the mythico-religious outlook of ancient Greece, we find a conception not unlike that of *Ṛta* in ancient India and of *Tao* in ancient China, and this is the conception of Μοῖρα (*Moira*) or fate which as early as the time of Homer and Hesiod appears as a law to which both gods and men are subject; a regular rhythm of the universe which gods and men may strain but never break – a conception which, as we shall see, contains the germs of both a revised theism and of philosophic naturalism.

But before looking at this extremely important conception a word must be said about the development of the mythological outlook outwith the naturalistic tradition in ancient Greece.

Two things stand out. The first is that, as in Vedic religion, the myths of the earlier period undergo a gradual process of rationalisation. The second is a growing moral criticism of the behaviour of the supernatural beings who are the subject of the earliest myths. To take the latter development first.

Plato (428/7-347 BC), in the tenth book of his *Republic* (X, 607B), having banished poets from the ideal city that he is describing, refers to the long standing quarrel between poetry and philosophy, a quarrel which it is not difficult to document from the side of philosophy for, at bottom, it is a quarrel centering on the poetic/mythological accounts of the doings of the gods and the philosophical criticism of them. Xenophanes of Colophon, writing in the sixth century BC says:

> Homer and Hesiod have attributed to the gods
> everything that is a shame and reproach
> among men, stealing and committing adultery
> and deceiving each other.
> (Kirk and Raven 1957: Frag. 11)

Heraclitus too, writing about the same time, says of the type of religion represented in Homer and Hesiod:

> They vainly purify themselves with blood
> when they are defiled with blood, as though
> one who had stepped into mud were to wash
> with mud; he would seem to be mad if any of
> men saw him doing this. Further, they pray to
> these statues, as if one were to carry on a
> conversation with houses, not recognising
> the true nature of gods and demi-gods.
> (*Ibid.*, Frag. 169)

Heraclitus' criticism, whilst basically a moral one, also calls into question the anthropomorphism of the early mythology. Xenophanes in celebrated fragments did the same.

> Men believe that the gods are clothed and
> shaped and speak like themselves
> (*Ibid.*, Frag. 14)

and more bitingly,

> If oxen and horses and lions could draw
> and paint, they would delineate the gods
> in their own image
> (*Ibid.*, Frag. 15)

similarly,

> The Negroes believe that their gods are flat nosed and black; the Thracians that their gods have blue eyes and red hair (*Ibid.*, Frag. 16).

Xenophanes, like Heraclitus, is not however irreligious, for he puts forward in place of the older religious representations a revised conception of divinity.

> One god is the highest among gods and men; in neither his form or his thought is he like unto mortals. He sees as a whole, perceives as a whole, hears as a whole

and again,

> Always he remains in the same place, not moving at all, nor indeed does it benefit him to go here and there at different times; but without toil he makes all things shiver by the impulse of his mind. (*Ibid.*, Frag. 23 & 24)

This is revisionary theism or 'adevism' (to use Müller's term), already referred to with reference to developments within Vedic religion, rather than irreligion – so much so that Werner Jaeger sees in Xenophanes the first beginnings of what was later to become known as theology (Jaeger 1948). Xenophanes, an adherent of what Diogenes Laertius, writing the history of Greek philosophy in the third century of the Christian era, was to designate the Italian school, belongs to that mystical side of Greek philosophy which, beginning with Pythagoras, was to find its fullest expression in the ancient world in Plato and the tradition which stems from him – a tradition which still has influence today as one polarity of the human search for understanding; the other pole being the naturalistic tradition. In accord with his programme of revisionary theism Xenophanes also critised divination.

We thus see that philosophy early enters into the debate regarding mythology and religion but that it does so, not initially to banish religion, but to revise it and to set it upon a more rational footing. The same will be seen to be so when we come to look at the earliest philosophers in what was eventually to become the naturalistic tradition.

Myth did not, however, disappear under the criticism of its immorrality and anthropomorphism, for it was to be taken up by the artists and philosophers within the Italian, mystical tradition and used creatively. It was also, as we shall see, to be reinterpreted, rather than abandoned, by the philosophers of the Ionian naturalistic tradition.

Pindar, Aeschylus, Sophocles and Euripides all used myth creatively as a medium with which to wrestle with the religious, moral and philosophical problems of their time. To take but one example: Euripides, writing in the fifth century BC, and retelling the myth of Medea in his tragedy of that name, makes Medea, who had been betrayed by her husband Jason, murder not only Jason's new Corinthian wife, but also her own and Jason's children. The central incident here, the murder of the children by their mother, is pure invention on the part of Euripides for in the traditional version they were killed by the people of Corinth. Euripides completely alters the myth, whilst yet retaining the mythological form, not to create a part for a star tragic actress, nor yet to write a rather improbable psychological study, but to show how devastating both to the immediate sufferer herself, and to society at large, is passion uncontrolled by reason (Kitto 1951: 202). Many other examples of the creative use of myth might be cited, not least from Plato, but it is time we turned to that other development within Greek mythology, the rationalisation of myth.

Whereas the tragic poets were to use myth creatively, other more philosophical minds, as in ancient India, were to attempt, first, to rationalise the chaotic plurality of the mythological universe and then to reinterpret it. And we should perhaps note that in doing this the Greeks were to differ profoundly from their Latin kinsmen, among whom the divine powers remained both multitudinous and anonymous in the same way as the ritual surrounding them was to remain a matter of observing, with the most legalistic exactitude, ancient formulae whose very meaning had become well nigh forgotten. There was a barely imagined *numen* which concerned almost every action of a man's life from the cradle to the grave and if the rites were observed in the exact form little else mattered. Not so among the Greeks.

In the first place the impulse towards order and unity, so characteristic of the Greek mind at its best, obliged them to reduce the number of the gods and to rationalise their functions; a process which we can observe as early as Hesiod's *Theogony*, written about the year 700 BC. This work, whilst remaining firmly in the world of myth, seeks to account for the origin and order both of the gods and of the world. Homer, a century previously, had, in the words of Herodotus 'first fixed for the Greeks the genealogy of the gods, given the gods their titles, divided among them their functions, and defined their images' (Herodotus II, 53), and there is some truth in the statement, for Homer does indeed show a distaste for that darker side of traditional Greek religion – snake-gods, fertility rites, and orgiastic ceremonies; for the frenzied Dionysian side of religion – though it is more likely that Homer is unconscious of this and is simply recording the traditional mythology of the Aryan invaders and not those aspects of Greek religion which, as we have said, came from the earlier pre-Aryan civilization. It is the poet Hesiod, however, who produces what is in fact the first fully fledged theogony or rationalisation of mythology in Greek thought.

His cosmogony begins with the coming into being of Χάος (*Chaos*), Γαῖα (*Earth*) and Ἔρως (*Eros*); then out of Χάος arose Darkness and Night, of which were born blazing Fire and Daylight. Then follows the division of the world into its three parts – Earth, Sky and Sea.

> Earth [Γαῖα] first of all gave being to one

equal to herself, the starry Heaven [Οὐρανός],
that he might enfold her all round, that there
might be for the blessed gods a seat secure
forever. And she brought forth the high mountains
wherein the gods delight to inhabit. And she gave
birth also to the waste Ocean, swelling with rage,
the Sea [Πόντος].
(Hesiod, *Theogony*, 1. 124 in Wender, 1973)

These three provinces are ascribed respectively to Hades, Zeus and Poseidon. The point to be noticed is that, according to Hesiod, the triple division into Sky, the dry Earth and Sea takes place 'without love or attraction of desire' (*Ibid.* 1. 132). It was not an act of marriage and consequent birth of division, repulsion, strife. Only afterwards were the sundered Sky and Earth united in marriage by Eros; the marriage of which the eldest gods were born. Thus Hesiod, by making the triple division older in time than the gods – cosmogony older than theogony – acknowledges the supremacy of Μοῖρα – the dimly personified principle of that division – over the gods. To the conception of Μοῖρα, therefore, we now turn.

The origins of this concept, as F.M. Cornford has shown, were religious and moral. He wrote:

> Besides the notions of God and the Soul, we shall find that philosophy also inherits from religion the governing conception of a certain order of Nature, variously regarded as a dominion of Destiny, of Justice, or of Law.... It will soon appear that the reign of Necessity is also and equally a moral rule, a kingdom of Justice. (Cornford 1957: 5)

– and he cites Hesiod in support of this; since, for Hesiod, the course of Nature is anything but careless of right and wrong. Hesiod tells us that when men do justice, and do not go aside from the straight path of right, their city flourishes and they are free from war and famine. Hesiod is clear that there is a sympathetic relation between human conduct and the behaviour of Nature – a belief that we have observed to have been widespread in China also. As the notion of Μοῖρα becomes more and more depersonalised this belief disappears.

But for the Ionian philosophers of Nature of the seventh and sixth centuries BC. Nature, and the Law which Nature obeyed, was, we shall see, anything but impersonal. Just as those early thinkers in India and China whom we have already considered speculated on the 'One' out of whom the plurality which we now observe in the world came and on the process by which it came, so these great Ionian thinkers sought to understand not man or the nature of human society but the nature (*φύσις*) of the universe. As Aristotle, our most important authority for the history of early Greek speculation tells us, the characteristic feature of Ionian speculation was their asking the question, 'What is Nature?' – a question which they at once converted into the question, 'What are things made of?' or, 'What is the original, unchanging substance which underlies all the changes of the natural world with which we are acquainted?'

4.3 IONIAN NATURALISM

Ionian naturalism which was to reach its culmination in the atomism of Leucippus and Democritus in the latter part of the fifth century BC, began in Miletus, a Greek colony on the coast of Asia Minor in the early sixth century BC. The city-states of Ionia, of which Miletus was by far the most important, were among the wealthiest and most civilized in the whole of the Greek-speaking world. They would also appear to have been characterised by an attitude of worldly detachment from religion bordering on indifference. W. K. C. Guthrie has described the culture of Miletus as one which

> may be broadly described as humanistic and materialistic in tendency. Its high standard of living was too obviously the product of human energy, resource and initiative for it to acknowledge any great debt to the gods. The poetry of the Ionian Mimnermus was an appropriate expression of its spirit in the late seventh century. To him it seemed that, if there were gods, they must have more sense than to trouble their heads about human affairs. 'From the gods we know neither good nor evil'. The poet looked inward, at human life itself. He extolled the enjoyment of momentary pleasures

> and the gathering of roses while they lasted, mourned the swift passing of youth and the misery and feebleness of old age. The philosopher of the same period and society looked outward to the world of nature, and matched his human wits against its secrets. Both are intelligible products of the same material culture, and the same secular spirit. (Guthrie 1962: 30)[2]

Iona was also the country of the Homeric poems in whose dealings with the gods religious awe was reduced to a minimum. The indebtedness of the Ionian natural philosophers to the Homeric tradition in which, as we have seen, the notion of Μοῖρα or destiny was fundamental, may well have been considerable.

The Ionian philosophers, of whom the most well known are the Milesian Thales, Anaximenes, Xenophanes of Colon and Heraclitus of Ephesus, were all, with the exception of Xenophanes, interested primarily in nature and natural processes. When Western speculation began in sixth century Ionia nature was not considered, however, as something dead and inert but as something living and therefore divine – a conception which derives ultimately, as we have seen, from mythology. When Thales and his successors sought, as had Indian philosophers some centuries previously, to get behind the multiplicity of the observable phenomenal world to the One underlying all plurality, to the primary 'stuff' out of which the world as we now observe it came, they were, therefore, returning to what F. M. Cornford has called, 'that original representation out of which Mythology itself gathered shape,' and which I sought to characterise in an earlier chapter. Cornford goes on to explain:

> If we now call it 'metaphysical' rather than 'supernatural', the thing itself has not essentially changed its character. What has changed is, rather, man's attitude to it, which from being active and emotional, has now become intellectual and speculative. His earlier, emotional reaction gave birth to the symbols of myth, to objects of faith; his new procedure of critical analysis dissects it into concepts, from which it deduces various types of systematic theory. (1957: ix-x)

A. H. Armstrong emphasises this latter point. He writes:

> Yet there are important differences between mythology and Mile-

> sian philosophy. The Milesians do not put forward their stories about the universe as handed down from immemorial antiquity or told by inspired poets, but as their own conclusions. Their first principle does not, like Hesiod's, mysteriously come to be but exists eternally [a most important change]. Instead of the personifications of the old myths we have descriptions of the various entities of the cosmic process in common-sense terms derived from everyday observation, and the process itself is conceived impersonally and in terms of natural and necessary movements. (1965: 5)

Armstrong adds, however, that this does not make them 'scientific thinkers' as we now understand that occupation – something that older historians of pre-Socratic philosophy such as John Burnet and Benjamin Farrington were inclined to read into them. Their method of producing elaborately sweeping accounts of the world and of its mode of coming into being on the basis of a few unsystematically observed facts makes them more akin to the myth-makers than some have realised. They are, perhaps, best thought of as not dissimilar to the ordinary men and women of today – unreligious without being anti-religious, interested and expert in technical skills without being theoretically scientific minded, curious about natural phenomena, deeply influenced, without knowing it, by traditional ideas and inclined to sweeping generalisations without sufficient evidence, on the whole, to back them up.

While Thales of Miletus is traditionally hailed as the first philosopher in the Western Tradition – a position ascribed to him as early as Aristotle – most things concerning him are matters of dispute.[3] The one certain fact is that in all the ancient histories of thought Thales has a place as one of the Seven Sages of the ancient world. Herodotus and others speak of his knowledge of Astronomy and it is the mention of his having successfully predicted the eclipse of the sun during the war between the Medes and the Lydians which enables us to fix, roughly, the time at which he lived, for the eclipse took place in the year 585 BC. Extrapolating from the tradition surrounding him we can say that Thales was probably born about 630-620 BC and that he lived until the fall of Sardis in 546/35 BC.

Whether or not his prediction of the eclipse of the sun in 585 BC meant that he understood what an eclipse actually is is open to doubt. Tradition speaks of his having spent some time in Egypt where he learned geometry from the priests and brought it to Greece. Connected with this is the tradition that Thales measured the height of the pyramids by their shadows and also put forward (a naturalistic) theory to account for the annual flooding of the Nile. From the time of Herodotus the Greeks tended to speak glowingly of the wisdom of the East – of Egypt and Babylon. Aristotle also bears witness to this at the beginning of his *Metaphysics.* Connecting the rise of wisdom with leisure he writes: 'Hence it was in Egypt that the mathematical arts were first developed, for there the priestly class was set apart as a leisured one' (Aristotle, *Metaphysics*, 981B, 23-25). However, what we know of Egyptian and Babylonian mathematics gives little support to the view that that science as it developed in Greece could have owed much to them.[4] The renown of Thales as a geometer is based entirely on his having computed the heights of the pyramids and measured the distance of ships from the shore – computations which do not require any large degree of geometrical science. Similarly Thales' prediction of an eclipse could have been made without his knowing the cause of an eclipse, and as the knowledge of this was unknown to his immediate predecessors it would appear extremely unlikely that so important a piece of knowledge could have been lost so soon. The priests of Babylon had compiled records of eclipses for religious purposes and could have gained thereby a knowledge of a cycle of solstices within which eclipses could be predicted at certain internals. Thales, who appears to have travelled a great deal, may well have had access to this knowledge.

This is, perhaps, the place to mention that the Greeks, unlike the Babylonians and the Egyptians, were singularly lacking in astrological interests – at least until a much later stage in their culture when influences from without brought such interests into prominence. As Cumont wrote:

> The universal curiosity of the Hellenes by no means ignored astrology, but their sober understanding rejected its adventurous doctrines. Their acute critical sense knew well how to distinguish between the scientific observations of the Chaldeans and their

erroneous inferences. It remains their everlasting glory that they discovered and made use of the serious, scientific elements in the confused and complex mass of exact observations and superstitious ideas, which constituted the priestly wisdom of the East, and threw all the fantastic rubbish on one side.[5] (Quoted by Burnet 1914: 7-8)

The motivation behind Thales' prediction of the eclipse of 587 is now unknown, but that he was seeking to import Eastern astrology into Greece would appear highly unlikely.

Thales is better known as the first philosopher of the Western Tradition, not for his supposed geometric or astronomical knowledge but for the answers which he gave to the question regarding the origin of the world process and, most important of all, for the way in which he answered it.

For these answers we are indebted almost exclusively to Aristotle who records Thales' views as follows:

> Thales, the founder of this kind of philosophy, says that the principle is water [and therefore declared the earth to be on water] perhaps taking the supposition from the fact that the nutriment of all things is moist and that heat comes to be and is sustained by the moist, that from which they come to be is the principle of things.... He also noticed that the seeds of everything have a moist nature and that water is the beginning of the growth of moist things.... Thales at any rate is said to have explained the principles and origins of things in this way. (*Metaphysics*, I, 3 983B20-984A19 [Ross])[6]

> Thales seems also, from what they say, to have supposed that soul was something moving, if he said that the stone possesses soul because it moves iron. (*De Anima*, I, 2, 405A19)

> And some say that soul pervades everything, for which reason, perhaps, Thales thought that all things are full of gods. (*De Anima*, I, 5, 411A7)

Thales, therefore, would appear to have maintained three things; (1) that 'water' is the ultimate original of all things; (2) that all things have soul in them, and (3) that the all is divine. He would also, as the first quotation from Aristotle suggests, appear to have thought that the earth itself floats on water, an opinion Aristotle amplifies upon in his *De Caelo* where, criticising this opinion, he writes:

> Others say the earth rests on water. For this is the most ancient account, which they say was given by Thales of Miletus, that it stays in place by floating like a log or some such thing ... as though the same argument did not apply to the water supporting the earth as to the earth itself. (*De Caelo*, II, 13, 249A28)

The primacy of water, as in ancient India, Babylon and Egypt had, as Aristotle reminds us, a long history in mythology prior to Thales.

> Some think that those ancients who, long before the present generation, were the first to theologise, had a similar idea of nature, because they presented Ocean and Tethys as the parents of becoming and water as that by which the gods swore, which these people styled the Styx. (*Metaphysics*, I, 3, 983B27-32)

But not only had Thales' notion of water as primary a long history in mythological speculation, his notion that soul pervades everything, making it divine, is also derived from or, perhaps better, is the last remains of a primitive mythological animism, a point often overlooked by those who would read into Thales' speculations the workings of the mind of a mechanico-materialistically-minded physicist. I shall have more to say on this point shortly. For the moment let us look at some of the other Ionian naturalists.

The next generation of the Milesian school, if such we may call it, is represented by Anaximander. Born about the year 611 BC he was not a great deal younger than Thales of whom, in the doxographical tradition, he was the student and successor. He died shortly after the year 546 BC.

Anaximander was the first person known to the Greeks to have embarked upon a written account of Nature – and the title of his work was thought to have been just that, *On Nature.* Although it was common for the later tradition to attribute a work with this title to all whom Aristotle designated 'physical philosophers', it would appear from a quotation preserved by Simplicius in his commentary on Aristotle's *Physics* and perhaps derived from Aristotle's pupil Theophrastus, who compiled the first history of philosophical opinions, that Anaximander did indeed commit some, at least, of his thoughts to writing. The quotation from Simplicius, as reconstructed by Kahn, reads as follows:

> Anaximander... said that the principle and element of things is the Boundless [τό ἄπειρον], having been the first to introduce this term 'principle'; he says that it is neither water nor any other of the so-called elements, but some different, boundless nature, from which all the heavens arise and the world within them; out of those things whence is the generation for existing things, into these things again does their destruction come to be, according to necessity [ἀναγκή]; for they make amends and make reparation to one another for their offence, according to the disposition of time speaking of them thus in rather poetical terms. It is clear that, having observed the change of the four elements into one another, he did not think fit to make any one of these the material substratum, but something else beside these. (Kahn 1960: 166)

The first point to notice about Anaximander's view of the origin of the world is that he eschews completely making of any of the elements within nature the cause of all things. At the end of the quotation from Anaximander, Simplicius gives as the reason for Anaximander's choice of the 'boundless' the fact that the elements change into one another and he suggests that Anaximander no doubt concluded from this observation that no single one of them, therefore, could be the cause of the others. Aristotle had made a similar point in a passage which most commentators take to have been written with Anaximander in mind. He wrote:

> But yet, nor can the infinite body be one and simple, whether it be, as some say, that which is beside the elements, from which they generate the elements, or whether it be expressed simply. For there are some people who make what is beside the elements the infinite substance; for the elements are opposed to each other [for example, air is cold, water moist, fire hot], and if one of these were infinite the rest would already have been destroyed. But, as it is, they say that the infinite is different from these, and that they come into being from it. (*Physica*, III, 5, 204b22 ff)

Leaving aside the introduction by Aristotle of his own understanding of ἄπειρον as 'infinite', what he takes Anaximander to be saying is that the elements themselves cannot be the cause of the world process because of what was later to be known as the theory of 'primary opposites'. At a later stage in the Greek understanding of natural processes, that is after the notions of substance and attribute had been clearly defined by Plato and Aristotle, the standard view — which was to hold its place in European thought until the seventeenth century AD — was that the now clearly distinguished four elements of earth, air, fire and water, were characterised by one or more of a set of contrary qualities and because of this they were always in a state of conflict. Fire and water, for example are in a state of conflict in as much as water can put fire out or alternatively, be converted by fire into steam.

Anaximander did not have the vocabulary to express his opinions quite like this — he thought, for instance, of the opposites as things rather than qualities and spoke, therefore, of 'the hot', 'the cold' etc., as he was to speak also of 'the boundless', but the central idea is there all the same. Though expressed, as Cornford has pointed out (1957: 7 ff), in mythological language — 'They make just recompense to one another for their injustice according to the ordinance of time' — what Anaximander is driving at is that, because of the 'strife' which exists amongst the elements, no single element can itself be primary, for in a universe where the elements are ultimately derivable from one of their number no other element could ever have come into being. For water to turn into fire (via the transitional stage of steam) requires fire to have already existed as well as water – a fact Anaximander was to amplify when he came to speculate upon the evolution of the natural order. It was this 'strife' among the constituents of nature that for Anaximander keeps the world-process going; victory never being finally granted to any of them. If the world had evolved from a single element alone then there must have existed enough of this substance to make the whole world; but if any single element has so existed then it would have enjoyed a permanent victory over its rivals and so none of them could ever have come into existence. Anaximander's conclusion is that the world must have originated from some substance outwith the elements and this he called *τό ἄπειρον* (*to apeiron*) – 'the boundless' – a substance which, however, he is unlikely to have thought of as strictly 'infinite', which is a much later conception, but more likely as simply of an indefinite quantity large enough to be a reservoir for everything else.

It is important also to notice that Anaximander is interested not only in the *ἀρχή* (*arche*) or origin of the world but in the actual process of its evolution as well, and this process, for Anaximander, is thought of in terms of natural causes, despite the overtones of mythological language discernable in his mode of expression. As Guthrie has written with particular reference to Anaximander:

> The 'new understanding of the world' consisted in the substitution of natural for mythological causes, that is, of internal development for external compulsion. This, as Pohlenz says, is well expressed by the generalised use of *φύσις* (*physis*) which is something essentially internal and intrinsic to the world, the principle of its growth and present organization, identified at this early stage with its material constituent. The primary assumption is not simply that it consists of a single material substance, but that the diversity of its present order is not from eternity, but has evolved from something radically simpler at a particular point in time. (1965: 83)

The process by which the world as we now observe it evolved from the original *ἀρχή* is described by Anaximander as one of 'separating-off'. The actual details of this process as conceived by Anaximander need not concern us since they have been adequately dealt with elsewhere (cf. Guthrie 1965: 83 ff) and are in any case properly the concern of the history of science. We should, however, notice two things. Firstly the mythological undertones in Anaximander's language and secondly, that Anaximander himself, though he calls his 'boundless' divine, conceives of the process as an essentially naturalistic one, in the sense that no supernatural factor outwith this process is evoked to explain it. Such divinity as there is resides within the world-process.

Anaximenes, the third philosopher of the Ionian school, the friend and associate — as Theophrastus describes him — of Anaximander, abandoned the notion of *ἄπειρον* — the boundless — and, in the small fragment of his work *On Nature* which has survived, assigns a determinate element as the original world-substance — namely, Air. It would appear that this was suggested to him by the fact that air is the principle of life in man and animals. They live only so long as they breathe, and he draws an interesting parallel between man and nature. He writes:

> Just as our soul being air, hold us together so do breath and air encompass the whole world. (Kirk and Raven 1957: Frag. 2)

And he is reported as concluding:

> Air, then, is the primary stuff of the world,
> from which the things that are and have been
> and shall be, the gods and things divine, arose,
> while other things come from its offspring.
> (Hippolitus, Ref., i, 7 in Diels, 12A10)

Anaximenes account of the evolution of the world from air — into which he introduces the notions of condensation and rarefaction — is thoroughly naturalistic, and whilst he admits, as the above quotations show, the existence of gods, these are at bottom simply powerful beings created by the same world process as produces human beings also.

With the fall of Miletus in 494 BC the Milesian school comes to an end. The main philosophical importance of the philosophers of the school lies more in the questions which they asked concerning the ultimate nature of things than in the answers which they gave. Their contribution to the development of unbelief lies in their postulating the eternity of matter. As Fr. Copleston writes: 'The idea of an absolute beginning of this material world does not enter their heads. Indeed for them this world is the only world' (1962: 43).

Their work reaches fruition in the Atomism of the next century. But before turning to the Atomists mention must be made of Anaxagoras, a thinker who did much to further a naturalistic approach to the world.

Anaxagoras was born at Clazamenae in Asia Minor about 500 BC and although a Greek was probably originally of Persian extraction. He arrived in Athens in the year 480/479 BC, probably as a soldier in the Persian army, and was the first philosopher that we know of to settle in that city. From Plato (*Phaedrus*, 270A) we learn that Pericles was his pupil. Thirty years later he was to be tried for impiety and banished from Athens.

The charge of impiety against Anaxagoras was based, Plato tells us, on his having taught that the sun is simply a red hot stone in the sky, thereby denying its divinity. The moon, he further maintained, was made of the same substance as the earth (*Apology*, 26D).

With the other pre-Socratics Anaxagoras holds to the eternity of the world. 'The Hellenes' he writes, 'do not rightly understand coming into being and passing away, for nothing comes into being or passes away, but there is an intermingling and a separation of things which are' (Kirk and Raven 1957: Frag. 17) – a process which he goes on to explain in his own unique way. When, however, he comes to the question of the power or force that is responsible for the formation of the world and its ongoing process we arrive at Anaxagoras' own peculiar contribution to philosophy. A contemporary of his, Empedocles, had attributed change in the world to the twin physical forces of love and strife but Anaxagoras introduces the notion of *νοῦς* (*nous*) or Mind. However, as Socrates informs us in that little piece of autobiography recorded in Plato's *Phaedo*, where he tells of the hope with which he turned to Anaxagoras' writings for a solution to his difficulties, although Anaxagoras introduces Mind as the principle behind or undergirding change in the universe he makes singularly little use of it. Socrates' criticism is that although Anaxagoras holds Mind to direct the process of change in the universe he tells us nothing of the end or purpose of the universe. Thus for all practical purposes the universe might just as well be mindless. Anaxagoras is interesting, however, in illustrating that a naturalist need not be a crude mechanico-materialist. The notion of immanent Mind is one which later philosophers within the Western tradition will pick up and develop in a pantheistic direction.

4.4 ATOMISM

The founder of the Atomistic school – which brings to fruition the naturalistic side of early Greek philosophising, just as Plato was to bring to fruition the mystical religious philosophising of Pythagoras and the Italian school – was Leucippus of Miletus. Of him we know little and it is impossible to fix his life with any precision. The *Great Diakosmos*, which was incorporated into the works of his successor Democritus, a contemporary of Socrates, is undoubtedly his, although, as Burnet has suggested, the Democritean corpus is probably like the Hippocratean and no single work in it can be ascribed to any single author (1914: 331). Thus in considering the Atomistic philosophy we are dealing with the work of a school.

Atomism is the logical development of the philosophy of Empedocles, who had tried to reconcile Parmenides' denial of the passage of being into non-being and vice versa with the evident fact of change, by postulating four elements which, mixed together in various proportions, form the objects of our experience. Empedocles did not, however, fully work out his doctrine of particles nor carry his quantitative explanation of qualitative differences to its logical conclusion. His philosophy, therefore, marks a transitional stage to the explanation of all qualitative differences by a mechanical juxtaposition of material particles in various patterns. Moreover, Empedocles' forces of love and strife were – for the most part – metaphorical powers which would have to be eliminated in a through-going mechanical philosophy. The final step to complete mechanism was made by the Atomists.

Being, for the Atomists, does not come to be or perish. It simply is. But it is not one but many, indeed it is infinite in number. What truly is are quite small particles, so small as to be invisible. If these are the things to which being properly applies, there is as well the void, empty space, not-being, in which the particles move. Clusters of them form visible bodies and the things which we mistakenly regard as beings – these come to be and perish, not what truly is, namely the small invisible particles. Thus being and space are the elements of explanation (cf. Aristotle, *Metaphysics*, I, 4, 985b4). Further, the atoms, as these small particles are called, just happen to be the shape they individually are and they just happen to move around, so that the bodies we perceive and the world they compose are reducible to chance. The movement of the atoms the Democritean school attributed to their weight. Simplicius, quoting from a now lost work of Aristotle, *On Democritus*, gives us the following account of the world-process:

> As they move they collide and become entangled in such a way as to cling in close contact to one another, but not so far as to form one substance of them in reality of any kind whatever; for it is very simple-minded to suppose that two or more could ever become one. The reason he gives for atoms staying together for a while is the intertwining and mutal hold of the primary bodies; for some of them are angular, some hooked, some concave, some convex and indeed with countless other differences; so he thinks they cling to one another and stay together until such a time as some stronger necessity comes along from the surrounding and shakes and scatters them apart. (Kirk and Raven 1957: n581, 418-419)

The following account of the formation of the world is attributed to Leucippus by Diogenes Laertius.

> He declares the All to be unlimited ... but of the All part is full and part is empty, and these he calls elements. Out of them arise the world unlimited in number and into them they are dissolved. This is how the worlds are formed. In a given section many atoms of all manner of shapes are carried from the unlimited into the vast empty space. These collect together and form a single vortex, in which they jostle against each other and, circling round in every possible way, separate off, by like atoms joining like. And, the atoms being so numerous that they can no longer revolve in equilibrium, the light ones pass into the empty space outside, as if they were being winnowed; the remainder keep together and, becoming entangled, go on their circuit together, and form a primarily spherical system. This parts off like a shell, enclosing within it atoms of all kinds; and, as these are whirled round by virtue of the resistance of the centre, the enclosing shell becomes thinner, the adjacent atoms continually combining when they touch the vortex, adds to itself whatever atoms it touches. And of these some portions are locked together and form a mass, at first damp and airy, but, when they have dried and revolve with the universal vortex, they afterwards take fire and form the substance of the stars. (*Lives of the Philosophers* in Hicks 1925: IX, 31-32)

The whirling vortex, which is the first stage in the formation of the world, occurs in Anaxagoras but that philosopher, as we have seen, attributes its beginning to Mind. For the Atomists it just happens, given atoms and their motion, and what is more it can happen many times simultaneously since there is no dearth of atoms and we have no reason to think that all the atoms there are have gone into the formation of our world.

That the atomists held that worlds, including our world, occurred purely by chance working according to necessity – a perfectly proper notion to the Greeks (cf. Guthrie 1965: 414-419) – should be clear enough. The actual details of the development of the world-process need not detain us but we should note that for the Democritean school the soul too is composed of atoms – albeit of extremely subtle ones at the extremes of fineness and thinness. Sensation and thought involve the movement of the atoms of percipient and thinker in response to impingement from without. The soul is spread throughout the body, although what we call the mind is a concentration of atoms in the bosom. Death is the escape of the soul atoms – an escape which is gradual rather than instantaneous.

Now it will be obvious that this account of the world and the world-process leaves no room for divinity or the supernatural as ordinarily conceived. Democritus, did, however seek to account for the belief which men have in the gods. Sextus Empiricus, reviewing theories which had been put forward concerning the origin of the belief in divine powers ascribes two such theories to Democritus which at first sight do not seem entirely consistent. One is that the belief arose from awesome natural phenomena which men in their terror ascribed to the activity of gods. The second theory which Sextus ascribes to Democritus is more individual. He says:

> Democritus says that certain images come to men, some of which are beneficient and others maleficent [whence he desired to meet with 'propitious images']. ... hence the ancients, receiving a presentation of just these images, supposed that there is a god, though there is no everlasting god apart from them. (Sextus, *Math.*, 9.24 and 19)

Confronted with the actual fact of belief in the gods, Democritus could not on his own principles do other than suppose that they were the effect of material images or atomic films, since without the impact of such films no impression can be made on the mind or senses. A consequence of this view, as Clement of Alexandria pointed out in the fourth century AD, is that animals as well as men are aware of the gods! (Clement of Alexandria, *Strom.* 2.383.25)

For Democritus these images – which he terms εἰδωλα – are more than lifeless and ineffectual appearances from which men have constructed a false belief in beings powerful enough to harm or benefit mankind. The atomists cannot admit of wholly hallucinatory experiences. Whilst rejecting the notion that awe-inspiring natural phenomena are divinely caused and whilst rejecting the belief that the gods are immortal, since, like all compounds of atoms, they will eventually dissolve, Democritus admits not only the existence of gods but allows them also – or at least their appearances – a role in the moral life of mankind. They can reveal the future and it is important that those appearances with which we come into contact should be beneficient. Democritus interpreted prayer as a wish that this might be so – a view which anticipates to some extent the account of the nature of religious belief put forward by the contemporary Cambridge philosopher R. B. Braithwaite in his 1955 Eddington Memorial Lecture, *An Empiricist's View of the Nature of Religious Belief.*

It is doubtful, however, whether, as has sometimes been maintained, Democritus believed in the efficacy of prayer to these beings in any other sense than this. Fragment 30 of his literary remains suggests that he did not. There he says:

> Some few of the cultured men raised their hands to the place where now we Greeks speak of air, and said, "Zeus ponders all things, knows, gives and takes away all things, and is king of all". (From Clement of Alexandria, *Protr.* 1.52.16)

In Fragment 234 Democritus complains that men pray to the gods for health but fail to realise that it is in their own power – they throw away their health through their own intemperance and lusts. Democritus' view of the mainsprings of morality is thoroughly humanistic – moral improvement rests entirely upon a man's own initiative (cf. *Stob.* IV.5.46 [Democritus 264, 173, 217 etc.]).

There is some doubt whether the 'images' or 'appearances' of which Democritus speaks are themselves gods or whether they are given off by distant bodies as are the objects of sight and hearing. The critic of Atomism in Cicero's *De Natura Deorum* asserts that Democritus maintains both of these doctrines at different times but, as his references to other philosophical theories shows, he is a most unreliable source for ancient philosophies with which he disagrees. Clement of Alexandria certainly took Democritus to hold that the 'images' which some men have of the gods are images 'of the divine substance'. On the other hand Sextus says unequivocally that there are no gods, for Democritus, apart from the 'images'. Consistency within Democritus' epistemology would imply that the impressions which some have of the gods come, like our experiences of sight and hearing, by way of the impact upon us of films thrown off by bodies external to us. However, it must also be stated firmly that the events Democritus is describing when he talks of 'images' of the gods take place within our world. There is no trace in Democritus himself of the later doctrine, which we find in Epicurus, that the gods enjoy a life of bliss and immortality somewhere in intermundia. The gods or spirits that break into our experience of the world are indeed active and personal but just like men they are subject to such laws as govern atomic activity within the world and are therefore just as liable as men are to ultimate decay and dissolution.

We thus see that although Atomism might in many respects be said to represent the high point of religious unbelief in the ancient world it does not do so unqualifiedly. Consistent naturalist that he was, Democritus yet strives to placate, as far as he can, the religious beliefs of his time. His conservatism is perhaps to be properly compared to that of the Sceptics whom we shall be considering shortly. Far more radical in their rejection of religious beliefs are the Sophists to whom we now turn.

4.5 THE SOPHISTS

We now enter upon the golden age of Greek philosophising – the age of Socrates, Plato, Aristotle, and of the Sophists. Whereas Socrates and Plato are undoubtedly religious philosophers – despite their searching criticism of much in the popular religion of their day – the Sophists, by and large, are theoretical unbelievers. With the Sophists interest shifts in Greek thinking away from the object of knowledge to its subject, away from the external world to the life of man in society, and religion, morality and society itself are each subjected to radical criticism.

The Sophists took up and answered a question which had been the subject of debate before their time but which they raised with a new intensity. Contact with other cultures had made the Greeks acutely aware that their own culture – its religion and its morality, its political and social organisation – was not unique, even though to them it might appear superior to the cultures with which they were now in contact. Reflecting on the diversity of beliefs in the world they were led to ask whether religion, morality and social structure were part of the nature of things so that there was one true form of them, or whether they were simply the outcome of custom and therefore relative and subject to continual change. As they themselves put it – were these things of nature or of law? The Sophists chose the latter alternative. Religion, morality and society itself were, for them, a matter of man-made customs. Whether or not the opprobrium heaped upon the Sophists by Plato is justified by the actual teachings of such men as Gorgias, Protagoras and Prodicus of Ceos may well be doubted, but that the Sophists irritated their contemporaries by subjecting the foundations of society, religion and morality to searching criticism is beyond dispute. On the whole their teaching, which consisted for the most part of rhetoric, was designed to enable men to succeed in public life. Armstrong has described their beliefs as those of 'a humanistic agnosticism' (1965: 23) and this would appear justified by the relativistic position which they took up with regard to religion and morality. Protagoras expresses their outlook succinctly when he says that 'man is the measure of all things, of the reality of those which are, and of the unreality of those which are not' (Kirk and Raven, 1957: Frag. 1) – a saying by which humanists have stood ever since.

Protagoras was born, according to most ancient authors, about 481 BC in Abdera in Thrace, and seems to have come to Athens about the middle of the century. He was favoured by Pericles and was entrusted by him to draw up the constitution for the Panhellenic colony of Thurii founded in 444 BC. He was certainly in Athens at the outbreak of the Peloponnesian War in 431 BC and during the great plague of 430 BC. Diogenes Laertius tells us that he was indicted for blasphemy on account of his book on the gods but that he escaped before his trial and was drowned whilst trying to cross the sea to Sicily, probably about 411 BC.[8]

There is considerable uncertainty as regards the interpretation of the famous aphorism quoted above and scholars are divided over the question as to whether it should be understood to refer to individual men, which would give us a highly relativist theory of truth, or whether Protagoras means to refer questions of truth to the judgement of mankind as a whole. In the *Theaetetus* Plato takes it to refer to man as an individual so far as sense-perception is concerned. In the *Protagoras*, on the other hand, Plato does not take Protagoras as extending his relativistic doctrine to matters of ethics. However, a strict interpretation of Protagoras' statement that man is the measure of all things would imply that ethical values and religious opinions were not exempt from the vagaries of individual judgement. In the *Theaetetus* such relativity applies only to the collective judgement of different nations or states, and certainly there is no good reason why Protagoras could not maintain at one and the same time the absolute realitivity of sense-perception and a modified relativity with regard to ethical judgement. This in my view is his actual position. The position which emerges from the *Theaetetus* appears to be as follows. Protagoras is there depicted as holding that 'whatever practices seem right and laudable to any particular state are so for that state, so long as it holds by them,' and that the wise man should attempt to substitute sound practices for unsound – which is to say that there is no question of one ethical view being true and another false, only of one being sounder than the other in terms of expediency. 'In this way', Protagoras is depicted as arguing, 'it is true that some men are wiser than others and that no one thinks falsely.' Plato also depicts the Sophist in the *Protagoras* as holding that *αἰδώς* [a sense of shame] and *δίκη* [a sense of justice] have been bestowed on all men by the gods 'because cities could not exist if, as in the case of other arts, few men only were partakers of them.' I take it that what Protagoras means is this: Law is founded on certain innate tendencies in men but individual variations as found in different states are relative, the law in one state, without being truer, being perhaps more sound, in the sense of being more expedient.

As an upholder of tradition, Protagoras stresses, in the dialogue, the importance of moral education by which the young are imbued with the ethical norms of the state into which they are born and grow up – though he admits that the mature man may reform the laws of his particular state to make them more useful. But overall the individual should cleave to tradition – all the more so if one tradition is no truer than any other; an instance of conservative scepticism such as we shall meet with later within the Greek tradition. The position maintained by Protagoras in Plato's dialogue of that name, far from leading to revolution leads instead to arch-conservatism!

With regard to the gods Protagoras is reported to have said, in a work entitled *Concerning the Gods* that:

> I cannot feel certain either that they are or that they are not, nor what they are like in figure; for there are many things that hinder certain knowledge, the obscurity of the subject and the shortness of life. (Kirk and Raven 1957: Frag. 4)

– a view which many of us will, I feel sure, heartily echo! Unfortunately this is the only fragment of this work which has come down to us, and it would be unwise to build too much on it. Plato is far from portraying Protagoras as an out-and-out sceptic or as a destructive thinker who turned his critical powers against all religion and ethics. The most likely conclusion with regard to Protagoras' position – taking account of this – is that his position is that in view of the uncertainty surrounding religious matters, the only position a man can take is to acquiesce in the religious traditions of the state into which he has been born or in which he finds himself living. As in ethics, so in religion, scepticism is far more often than not the mother not of revolutionary innovation but of conservatism.

Prodicus of Ceos is more outspoken. Born on the Aegean island of Ceos he flourished towards the close of the fifth century BC, coming frequently to Athens on business and teaching there at the same time. Socrates himself is said to have paid to listen to him. Judging from the frequent references to him in Plato his major concern would appear to have been with correct and precise terminology and he is reported to have written on this subject and to have produced a book entitled either *On Nature*, or alternatively, *On the Nature of Man*, which seems a more likely title.

The gods he utterly rejected and he went so far as to offer a naturalistic explanation of their origin (Kirk and Raven 1957: Frag. 5). They arose he said out of those things which were necessary and beneficial to men. Thus bread became Demeter, wine Dionysius, water Poseidon, and so on – a theory that was developed by other thinkers within the Greek tradition. Prodicus gives as an example to support his theory the cult of the Nile in ancient Egypt. His view is also evolutionary, for he postulates a later stage in the development of religion in which the inventors of the various arts – agriculture, metal work and so on – were also elevated to divine status and became the objects of the various cults devoted to them. This being the true origin of religion Prodicus went on to maintain that prayer to the 'gods' was superfluous – a view on account of which he seems to have run foul of the civic authorities of Athens.

Little else is known about him but in the pseudo-Platonic dialogue *Axiochus* he is credited with holding that death is desirable in order to escape the miseries of life. Fear of death, the dialogue represents him as saying, is irrational, since, death should concern neither the living nor the dead – the former because they are still living and the latter because they are not living any more.

Prodicus' primary interest for us is his theory of the natural origin of religion and it is significant that many such theories begin to emerge in Greece at about this time, for theories of the natural origin of religion are only put forward when the overt claims of religion are doubted. We have mentioned already the theory put forward by the Democritean school. Another such theory is that put forward by one of the younger Sophists, the cynical and nihilistic Critias in his now lost drama, *Sisyphus*. The gods, he says, were invented to stop lawlessness. Laws, as we have seen, were for the Sophists the creation of the will of rulers, and some of the Sophists, such as Thrasymachus, contrasted law with natural justice in which right resided in the will of the stronger. It was thus held that men would naturally act differently in the absence of any possibility of detection — a situation discussed by Plato in the story of Gyges' ring (a ring which would make its wearer invisible) in *The Republic* (II. 359-360). Critias' view was that the gods were invented as hidden witnesses to acts done in private in order to provide the necessary coercian for civic morality.

This is how Sextus Empiricus records his words:

A time there was when anarchy did rule
The lives of men, which then were like the beasts',
Enslaved to force; nor was there then reward
For good men, nor for the wicked punishment.
Next, as I deem, did men establish laws
For punishment, that Justice might be lord
Of all mankind, and Insolence enchain'd;
And whosoe'er did sin was penalised.
Next, as the laws did hold men back from deeds
Of open violence, but still such deeds
Were done in secret, — then, as I maintain,
Some shrewd man first, a man in counsel wise,
Discovered unto men the fear of Gods,
Thereby to frighten sinners should they sin
E'en secretly in deed, or word, or thought.
Hence was it that they brought in Deity,
Telling how God enjoys an endless life,
Hears with his mind and sees, and taketh thought
And hears things, and his nature is divine,
So that he hearkens to men's every word
And has the power to see men's every act.
E'en if you plan in silence some evil deed,
The Gods will surely mark it..
So, speaking words like these,
Most cunning doctrine did he introduce,
The truth concealing under speech untrue.
[...]
Such were the fears wherewith he hedged men round,

And so to God he gave a fitting home,
By this his speech, and in a fitting place,
And thus extinguished lawlessness by laws. –
[...]
Thus first did some man, as I deem, persuade
Men to suppose a race of Gods existed.
(Sextus Empiricus, *Against the Physicists*, 1, 54 [Bury])

This is our very first recorded account of the theory – developed by Polybius at Rome and revived in Germany in the eighteenth century – that religion was a political invention to ensure good behaviour. It also, of course, reverses the growing criticism of the immorality of the gods.

This brings us to the end of those who offered naturalistic accounts of the origin of belief in the gods in the fifth century BC. A number of minor figures of the time were dubbed 'atheists' by their contemporaries, such as Hippon, but of their views we know nothing. It is however hard to believe that others who upheld nature φύσις (*physis*) against law νόμος (*nomos*), such as Callicles and Antiphon, held, in fact, any religious beliefs. Plato in his *Laws* mentions two types of atheist – those who held that the gods did not in fact exist and those who held that the gods did exist but were oblivious of the affairs of men, and Callicles and Antiphon could, of course, fall into either of these categories, since there is not much difference between gods who are totally ineffective and no gods at all. Plato admits, however, that disbelief in the gods need not lead to immorality and he recognises a man who in many respects resembles the ethical humanist of our own day. He writes:

For though a man should be a complete unbeliever in the being of gods; if he also has a native uprightness of temper, such persons will detest evil in men; their repugnance to wrong disinclines them to commit wrongful acts; they shun the unrighteous and are drawn to the upright. But those in whom the conviction that the world has no place in it for gods is conjoined with incontinence of pleasure and pain and the possession of a vigorous memory and a keen intelligence share the malady of atheism with the other sort, but are sure to work more harm, where the former do less, in the way of mischief to their fellows. The first man may probably be free-spoken enough about the gods, sacrifices, and oaths, and perhaps if he does not meet with his deserts, his mockery may make converts of others. But the second, who holds the same creed as the other, but is what is popularly known as 'a man of parts', a fellow of plentiful subtlety and guile – that is the type which furnishes our swarms of diviners and fanatics for all kinds of imposture; on occasion it also produces dictators, demagogues, generals, contrivers of private Mysteries, and the arts and tricks of the so-called 'sophist'. Thus there are numerous types of atheist, but two which legislation must take into account; the hypocritical, whose crimes deserve more than one death, or even two, and the others, who call for the combination of admonition with confinement. (*Laws*, 908 b-e [Taylor])

But to return to such men as Antiphon and Callicles. Antiphon, with his advice to heed *νόμος* (*nomos*) before witnesses, but to disregard it when one can get away with it unobserved, exhibits exactly the attitude that Critias imagines to have existed before the gods were invented. Such irreligion must have been common among the intelligentsia of fifth century Greece. The profanation of the mysteries and the mutilation of the Hermae that we read about were not the work of believers. The orator Lysias names one, Cinesias – whom the comic poets satirise – as forming what Guthrie calls 'a kind of Hell-fire club' with three other like-minded people. These deliberately chose forbidden or unlucky days on which to dine together and mock the gods and the laws of Athens. In the *Frogs* of Aristophanes Cinesias is also said to have defiled the statue of Hecate. This, however, is a new brand of irreligion and does not necessarily imply unbelief. The logic of blasphemy, as T. S. Eliot pointed out, demands that what is blasphemed be also believed to exist. That is as may be, but when taken in conjunction with the naturalism and rationalism of the physical philosophers and the Sophists, Cinesias' blasphemy contributed to the atmosphere in which Plato grew up and which moved him to use all his intellectual powers to combat.

4.6 THE CLASSICAL PERIOD OF GREEK THOUGHT

It is in the fifth century that criticism of religion comes to a head. The Presocratic philosophers, though retaining belief in the divinity of nature, had promulgated conceptions of religion far removed from the traditional beliefs of their time. Here they may be compared to the late Vedic and early Upanisadic thinkers in India whom they resemble in so many respects. As enlightment grows it shows itself in Greece, as it did in Europe after the Renaissance, under two main aspects (cf. Guthrie 1965: 226). On the one hand there is a determination to believe only what is reasonable with 'what is reasonable' assuming an increasingly positivistic aspect and becoming assimilated to what is in accord with the most advanced scientific opinions. On the other hand there is an increasing concern with morality, where morality becomes more and more utilitarian, concerned with the amelioration of human life in the here and now. This is often coupled with recognition of the fact that a deontological ethic, undergirded by supernatural sanctions, has, in the past, led to intolerance and cruelty. The Greek gods were extremely vulnerable in both these respects and as soon as more thoughtful attitudes to traditional opinions began to show themselves scepticism and disapproval of traditional religion increases. Some of this we have already traced.

As W. K. C. Guthrie has noted (1965: 227) the attack on religion in fifth century Greece was closely bound up with the *νόμος—φύσις* (law—nature) antithesis. Plato complains in his *Laws* (889e) of people who claim that:

> The gods are human contrivances, they do not exist in nature but only in custom and law, which moreover differ from place to place according to the agreement made by each group when they laid down their laws.

Such opinions, as we have seen in our review of the Sophists, were widespread. We will also see how Aristophanes refers to those who – like some of the thinkers referred to in the *Upaniṣads* – reject the gods in favour of 'time' and 'necessity'. Euripides too has Hecuba call νόμος (*nomos*) superior to the gods because it is by νόμος (*nomos*) that we in fact believe in them as well as in standards of right and wrong (*Hecuba*, 799 f). There is abundant evidence, in fact, that the hold of religion over men's minds was weakening in the ferment of the Periclean age, and also for the fact that the Athenian establishment was nervous about this, believing that the cult of the gods was integral to the fabric of both civic and private morality. We thus read of impiety trials and of a decree of Diopeithes against both atheism and cosmic speculation. Plutarch tells us that the Athenian rulers

> did not tolerate the natural philosophers and chatterers about things in the sky, as they called them, dissolving divinity into irrational causes, blind forces and necessary properties. Protagoras was banished, Anaxagoras put under restraint ... and Socrates, though in fact he had no concern with such matters, lost his life through his devotion to philosophy. (*Nicias*, 23)

He also tells us in his *Life of Pericles* that

> about this time [that is just before the outbreak of the Peloponnesian War] Aspasia was prosecuted for impiety ... and Diopeithes introduced a bill for the impeachment of those who denied the gods or taught about celestial phenomena.... (*Life of Pericles*, ch. 32)

The latter part of the fifth century, in fact, witnesses the highlighting of the conflict between the implications of the newly developed natural philosophy and religion in Greece. The best evidence for this conflict and the issues which it raises comes from Plato who bent all his energies to combatting the irreligious implications, as he saw them, of the new philosophy. We can also get some insight into what was one of the great debates of the time from the dramatic writers of the period and more especially from the comic playwright Aristophanes who took this debate as the theme for his drama *The Clouds.*

There is also evidence in the dramatists of this period for the growing moral criticism of the traditional religion. We have seen the beginnings of this line of criticism a century earlier in Xenophanes and Heraclitus. In the dramas of Euripides and Sophocles it emerges once again – if, indeed it had ever been suppressed. In passage after passage of these two dramatists the doings of the gods as recorded in Homer are the subject of moral disapproval. Indeed G. Lowes Dickinson once wrote of Euripides that his attitude to popular religion was so frankly critical that it would appear that 'the main object in the construction of his dramas was to discredit the myths he selected for his theme' (1941: 48).

Euripides gives full rein to popular moral criticism of the gods throughout his works. This can take many forms, ranging from reproach of the gods for their behaviour, through declarations that although gods exist they do not in fact behave as the popular mythology says that they do, to outright assertion of the fact that since these are what the gods are like, they either do not exist, or, if they do, they are unworthy of worship. In the *Ion,* for example, we witness the disillusionment of a pious young acolyte who learns that the god he has served has stopped to seduce a mortal woman. The *Heracles* contains a vehement denial that the gods could behave so wickedly. Complete disbelief in the gods based upon the prosperity of the wicked and the sufferings of the just is voiced in a passionate outburst in the *Bellerophon*: There are no gods in heaven. To believe such is to believe old wives' tales and is stupid. You have only to look around you. Tyrants rob, murder, cheat and ravage, and are happier than the pious and peaceful. Small god-fearing states are overwhelmed by the military might of those larger and more wicked. That one could appeal to the gods to excuse one's actions is also pointed out by Euripides. Phaedra's old nurse in *The Trojan Women,* for instance, condones her illicit love by pointing out that Zeus misbehaved with Eos. The same point is made by Aristophanes in *The Clouds.*

> Suppose you are caught in adultery, [says Unjust Argument] you will argue that you have done nothing wrong, and point to Zeus, who never could resist love or women. How, you will say, could you, a mortal, show greater strength than a god?

In Aeschylus we meet with the beginnings of the tradition of defiance rather than the theoretical denial of the gods. Although a god himself Prometheus, who was to become in the later western tradition the symbol of man's self-sufficiency, declares in Aeschylus' drama *Prometheus Bound*:

> In sooth all gods I hate,

and again:

> I shall never exchange my fetters for slavish servility. 'Tis better to be chained to the rock than bound to the service of Zeus

– two statements quoted with approval by the young Karl Marx in the foreword to his doctoral dissertation.

The reverse side of this can be seen in Sophocles and Aeschylus where we can discern developments towards ethical monotheism. A passage from Sophocles' *King Oedipus* will illustrate this. The Chorus is speaking:

> May destiny ever find me
> pious in word and deed
> prescribed by the laws that live on high:
> laws begotten in the clear air of heaven,
> whose only father is Olympus:
> no mortal nature brought them to birth,
> no forgetfulness shall lull them to sleep;
> for God is great in them and grows not old.
> (*King Oedipus*, 865)

Let us now turn to the conflict between naturalism and traditional mythological religion as this is presented by Aristophanes. In the following passage, taken from *The Clouds*, the materialistic understanding of nature is the main butt of his humour. It is something of an anachronism, of course, that Socrates is cast in the role of advocate for the naturalistic mode of explanation but this should not deter us from seeing the point at issue in the debate which follows, for philosophers other than Socrates certainly held to the position that Aristophanes is criticising. The passage opens with the Chorus – the clouds – themselves new divinities of the natural philosophers, – welcoming 'Socrates' their protagonist. The dialogue which follows is between Strepsiades and Socrates and it goes thus:

> *Strepsiades*: Oh earth! what a sound, how august and profound! it fills me with wonder and awe.
> *Socrates*: [referring to the Clouds] These, these then alone, for true deities own, the rest are all god-ships of straw.
> *Streps*: Let Zeus be left out: He's a God beyond doubt; come, that you can scarcely deny.
> *Socr*: Zeus indeed! there's no Zeus: don't you be so obtuse.
> *Streps*: No Zeus up above in the sky?
> Then you must first explain who it is sends the rain; or I really must think you are wrong.
> *Socr*: Well then, be it known, these send it along; I can prove it by argument strong.
> Was there ever a shower seen to fall in an hour when the sky was all cloudless and blue?
> Yet on a fine day, when the clouds are away, he might send one according to you.
> *Streps*: Well, it must be confessed, that chimes in with the rest: your words I am forced to believe.
> Yet before I had dreamed that the rain water streamed from Zeus and his chamber-pot sieve.
> But whence then, my friend, does the thunder descend? that it makes us quake with affright!
> *Socr*: Why, 'tis they I declare, as they roll through the air.
> *Streps*: What the clouds? did I hear you aright?

> *Socr*: Ay: for when to the brim filled with water they swim, by Necessity carried along,
> They are hung up on high in the vault of the sky, and do by Necessity strong
> In the midst of their course, they clash with great force, and thunder away without end.
> *Streps*: But is it not He who compels this to be? does not Zeus this Necessity send?
> *Socr*: No Zeus have we there, but a vortex of air.
> *Streps*: What! Vortex? that's something I own.
> I knew not before, that Zeus was no more, but Vortex was placed on his throne.
> (*The Clouds*, 358 [B. B. Rogers])

And so the debate continues through a naturalistic explanation of other events in nature and the suggestion is made that the atheist who dares to offer this kind of explanation is both immoral and anti-social. The above passage brings out well, comedy aside, the kind of explanation in terms of physical causation operating according to 'necessity' which the new philosophy of nature was putting forward in contradistinction to the explanations found in traditional religious mythology.

It is just such explanations with which Socrates professes himself dissatisfied in that little piece of intellectual autobiography which we find in Plato's dialogue, *Phaedo* :

> When I was a young man [he says] I was wonderfully desirous of that wisdom which they call history of nature: for it appeared to me to be a very sublime thing to know the causes of every thing, why each thing is generated, why it perishes and why it exists.

The works of Anaxagoras particularly seemed to offer what he was looking for, for here was a philosopher who

> said that it was intelligence that sets in order the cause of things.

> I was delighted, Socrates continues, with this cause and it appeared to me in a manner to be well that intelligence should be the cause of all things.

His delight was short lived, however, and he tells us the story of his growing disillusionment.

> From this wonderful hope ... I was speedily thrown down, when, as I advanced and read over his works, I met with a man who makes no use of intelligence, nor assigns any causes for the ordering of all things, but makes the cause to consist of air, ether, water and many other things equally absurd.

Socrates illustrates what he means by reference to his own actions, for Anaxagoras appears to him to be the sort of person who would explain Socrates' remaining in Athens to face imprisonment and death, not by saying that he chose and had good reasons for choosing so to remain, but by reference to his physiological constitution. To call an explanation in such terms an explanation at all is, says Socrates, manifestly absurd, though as he recognises:

> If anyone should say that without possessing such things as bones and sinews, and whatever else I have, I could not do as I pleased, he would speak the truth.
> (*Phaedo*, 96-99 [Lindsay])

The position that Socrates takes here, taken together with his view that a purely causal explanation, as offered by the physical philosophers, is, at best, a limited one, which does nothing at all to satisfy those like himself who are asking for other kinds of explanation, is one side of an argument which reoccurs again in Western Europe in the seventeenth century, when the postulating of final causes to account for events within the world begins to fade and explanations of events not dissimilar to those offered by the naturalistically-minded philosophers of Greece begin to reappear.

Further evidence that the empirical and naturalistic way of explaining events was widespread in the middle of the fifth century in Greece is provided by the medical writers of the period and in particular by those writings which have come down to us under the name of Hippocrates. Of the importance of these writings for the development of naturalism F. M. Cornford and others have made us aware.[9] In one of the best known treatises of this school, *On the Nature of the Sacred Disease*, i.e. epilepsy, the empirically, naturalistically-minded author inquires into the traditionally held belief of the divine origin of this disease and in the course of his enquiry raises some important questions about the nature of the divine and of the mode of its operation. He disposes quickly of the idea that epilepsy is the direct result of divine, supernatural activity and seeks rather to account for it as being the result of the same kind of natural causes as cause other diseases.

> The so called sacred disease [the author says] arises from the same causes as any other; from the things that enter the body and those that leave it: from cold and sunshine, and winds, which are always changing and are never still. These things are divine; and so there is no need of setting this disease apart and considering it more divine than the others; they are all divine and they are all human. (Hippocrates, *On the Nature of the Sacred Disease*, ch. 21 [Jones 1923-31: Vol. 2])

Deus sive Natura – God or Nature: we are reminded of Spinoza.

It is interesting to compare this sober minded empirical approach to medical causation with the writing of history as we find it in Thucydides – active also about this time. If we compare Thucydides' account of the Peloponnesian War with accounts of similar happenings in Homer and Herodotus we can see how far explanations of historical events have come since the time of the earlier 'historical' writers. Whereas in both Homer and Herodotus natural and supernatural causation operate side by side, we find nothing of this in Thucydides who eliminates the supernatural element altogether and gives us an account of the war in thoroughly naturalistic terms. As Drachmann says:

> Not only did he throughout ignore omens and divinations, except in so far as they played a part as a purely psychological factor, but he completely omitted a reference to gods in his narrative. Such a procedure was at this time unprecedented. (1922: 28)

This is an approach to the writing of history which has only really established itself in our own day. During the Christian age of our civilization historical writers were extremely prone to see the providential hand of God in historical events – even to the point of direct divine intervention.

It is during this period of Western Civilization that the two great philosophies which have dominated Western thinking since their time were formulated – that is the philosophies of Plato and Aristotle. Plato fathers a tradition in European thinking which reaches its zenith in the neo-Platonism of the fourth century AD and which then comes to influence the Christian tradition and so, for good or ill, the whole of European culture until at least the nineteenth century – if not beyond, up to and including the present day. The impetus behind Plato's approach to the world and to life is throughout religious and mystical and so was his influence on Western Europe. Aristotle's influence on the other hand has been ambiguous. Felt certainly as a threat to the religious understanding and the religious life in the West – particularly during the early Middle Ages – certain aspects of his thinking were picked up and developed, supremely by St. Thomas Aquinas and his philosophical successors, and so made to serve a religious understanding of the world. But despite this, Aristotle's influence has, on the whole, worked against religion. Writing of his influence on the early Middle Ages, David Knowles of Cambridge University has said, that

> the introduction of the whole canon of Aristotle to the West ... presented Europe with a philosopher who regarded human life from a purely naturalistic this-world point of view. Taken as a whole the translations of Aristotle gave Western Thinkers, for the first time, matter on which to construct a full and mature system, but the atmosphere, the presuppositions of this great body of thought were not Mediaeval and Christian, but ancient Greek and non-religious, not to say rationalistic in character. (1962: 192)

Knowles' judgement on Aristotle is far more apposite than the judgement of those who see Aristotle as simply undergirding a religious understanding of the world, for although Aristotle evokes 'God' in his metaphysical scheme of things to initiate motion or change in the world, he plays no further role for Aristotle other than that of First Mover or Uncaused Cause. From beginning to end his philosophy, and particularly his ethical and social philosophy, is wholeheartedly naturalistic and this worldy — and this ultimately was to be his legacy to the West.

4.7 THE HELLENISTIC AGE

The Hellenistic age, in which the culture and civilization of Greece, following in the wake of Alexander of Macedon's conquests, breaks out of the confines of its native environment to dominate the thinking of the whole Mediterranean world, sees the rise of four great schools of philosophy which more or less successfully challenge the Platonic and Aristotelian schools. These are the Stoic, the Cynic, the Epicurean and the Sceptical schools. Of these, the Stoic was for the most part pantheistic and gradually, and in the Roman world in particular, where Stoic morality freed itself from its original theological substructure, it came to dominate the whole ethical field, influencing, thereby some of the best minds of late Antiquity. The Cynic philosophy, founded by Diogenes of Sinope, a contemporary of Aristotle, was primarily a way of life founded upon the doctrine that virtue, which Diogenes interpreted as life lived according to nature, is the one thing that matters and that all else is τυφώς (*tuphos*) or wind. Of Diogenes it is reported that he did not take part in the worship of the gods because the gods were in need of nothing, but any further theological opinions that he might have expressed have not come down to us. On the whole the Cynic attitude to religion is best described as one of indifference and as such can be said to be practically atheistic though probably theoretically agnostic.

The philosophies of Epicureanism and Scepticism are much more interesting for the study of irreligion; the former in that many have looked back to it as one of the great secular and humanistic philosophies of Classical Antiquity; the latter because, taken in conjunction with the scepticism of the Middle Academy, it is the precursor of a scepticism which was revived during the European Renaissance to become one of the dominating approaches to the world of our own day.

4.8 EPICUREANISM

Lucretius, writing in the first century before the Christian era, looks back to Epicurus, the founder of the school which bore his name and who had died over a century previously in 270 BC, and hails him as the great liberator of the human spirit from the yoke of the superstitions of religion. In his classic work *De Rerum Natura* he writes:

> When human life lay grovelling in all men's sight,
> crushed to the earth under the dead weight of
> superstition whose grim features loured menacingly
> upon mortals from the four quarters of the sky, a
> man of Greece was the first to raise mortal eyes
> in defiance, first to stand erect and brave the
> challenge. Fables of the gods did not crush him, nor
> the lightning flash and the growing menace of the
> sky. Rather they quickened his manhood, so that he,
> first of all men, longed to smash the constraining
> locks of nature's doors. The vital vigour of his
> mind prevailed. He ventured far out beyond the
> flaming ramparts of the world and voyaged in mind
> through infinity. Returning victorious, he proclaimed
> to us what can be and what cannot: how a limit is
> fixed to the power of everything and an immovable
> frontier post. Therefore, superstition in its turn
> lies crushed beneath his feet, and we by his triumph
> are lifted level with the skies.
> (Latham 1951: 29)

Epicurus was born on the island of Samos in 341 BC. He was an Athenian citizen since Samos was in league with Athens and as a consequence of this he went, in the year 323 BC, to Athens for his two year military service. In 321 BC, upon his discharge, he joined his family who had in the meantime moved to Colophon. There he remained for ten years, moving at the age of thirty to Mytilene where he set himself up as a teacher of philosophy. The following year he moved again, this time to Lampsacus where he taught for four years, before moving in 306 BC to Athens with the small school which had gathered around him. Here he taught for the remainder of his life in the garden of the house which he had bought in Athens, though we are told of several visits made to the family house in Lampsacus.

Epicurus and the philosophy which he taught have been subject to misunderstanding and vituperation from ancient times to our own. Of old this was due, in part, to the cavalier way in which he dismissed all other philosophies, as well as to popular misconceptions of his actual teachings. Diogenes Laertius, in his *Lives of Eminent Philosophers*, mentions some of the charges levelled against Epicurus — that he was a dullard, an ingrate, a scorner of culture, a sensualist and an atheist, but he goes on to defend him in the following words:

> But these people are stark made. For our philosopher has abundance of witnesses to attest to his unsurpassed goodwill to all men — his native land, which honoured him with statues in bronze; his friends, so many in number that they could hardly be counted by whole cities, and indeed all who knew him held fast as they were by the siren-charms of his doctrine....
> (*Lives* X, 7-9 [Hicks 1925: 537])

Recent studies of Epicurus by De Witt and J.M. Rist have done much of late to confirm Diogenes' opinion.

Epicurus' concern, like those of the Stoics, was primarily moral and, like them, he sought for a way of living which would, amidst the troubled times in which he lived, produce ἀταραξία (*ataraxia*) — peace of mind. With this moral interest he combined the old Ionian interest in nature and made this latter, as it had been developed in the theories of the Atomists, subserve the former. Believing as he did that what most militated against tranquility were the superstitious beliefs of religion – fear of the gods and of what might await men after death – he found in the Atomism of Democritus just the philosophy to exclude such sources of trouble. Embracing the materialistic philosophy of Democritus – though modifying it in certain important respects – Epicurus believed that a wise man would draw from the picture of the world advanced in this philosophy peace and self-reliance.

However, Epicurus was no atheist: for him the gods most assuredly existed and he in fact put forward a number of arguments to show that this was the case. He also commended right religion. This said, however, we are probably correct in regarding him, with some modification, as a practical atheist, for reasons which will be stated below.

In the eulogy to Epicurus at the opening of book three of his *De Rerum Natura*, to which we have referred, Lucretius proclaims that as soon as reason begins to reveal to us the true nature of the universe, the terrors which have hitherto haunted the mind disappear and the awe-inspiring nature of the gods is manifested. They are seen to live an immortal and untroubled life in the intermundia, the spaces between the cosmic systems. Lucretius derives this Epicurean view of the gods from the first of Epicurus' *Basic Doctrines*, where Epicurus states that that which is blessed and immortal neither has troubles of its own nor does it trouble others. It is constrained neither by anger nor favour, for such emotions belong only to that which is weak. The consequences of this view of the gods for the lives of men are important, for the view that the gods do not concern themselves with human affairs is a basic tenet of the Epicurean approach to life, and it could well be, as J. M. Rist suggests, that the extraordinary hostility displayed by Epicurus to his Atomistic predecessors (mentioned by Diogenes Laertius) is due to the fact that they failed to utilise their theory to free men from fear of the gods and from the control of 'necessity' (ἀναγκή) – treating their enquiries simply as a piece of pure research which led in practice to absolute physical determinism (1972: 146). As Epicurus is reported to have said, 'Vain is the word of the philosopher which does not heal any suffering of man' (Porphyry, *Ad Marc.* 31) – an aphorism echoed by Karl Marx, possibly under Epicurean influence, in the eleventh of his *Theses on Feuerbach.* Both Lucretius and Plutarch – in his treatise *On Superstition* – tell us just how important a role fear of the gods, and of divine intervention, played in the lives of ordinary men and women in the ancient world. In Epicurus' fourfold remedy for the ills of mankind, fearlessness before the gods is given pride of place, ahead of not fearing death and the assertion that it is easy to possess the good and to endure the unpleasant. The reason for not fearing the gods is quite simply because the gods do not concern themselves at all with the affairs of men. Showing neither anger nor favour, the gods neither punish nor reward the deeds of men. Should the gods be troubled about human behaviour they would not enjoy untroubled repose.

Epicurus, however, goes further than simply denying that the gods are concerned with the affairs of men and he draws the conclusion from his physics that the gods are in fact themselves subordinate, as are mortals, to the primary constituents of the cosmos – atoms and the void. Epicurean physics precludes any possibility that the world is created by the gods, though we can also be assured that this is so from our own experience of life, for if the world had been created by the gods it would not contain the troubles that it does. It would not be, in Lucretius' phrase, *tanta praedita culpa* (*De Rerum Natura*, 5.199). Further, the notion that the gods created the world is shown to be impossible from the fact that it would involve the gods in having had a concept of the world before any world was formed – something which contradicts Epicurean epistemology in which all concepts derive from the evidence of the senses and the mind when the senses and the mind are directed to existing objects. When nothing existed, no concept could have been formed (*De Rerum Natura*, 5.181-186).

To summarise. For Epicureanism the world is not made by the gods and human behaviour is not judged by the gods. The gods, content in their perfect happiness, have no cause to concern themselves with such things, for the trouble involved in so concerning themselves would detract from their happiness. There is, for Epicureanism, no such thing as divine providence, no teleology in the world; such order as exists derives from the chance union of atoms. There is no divine retribution.

In the ancient world it was Epicurus' denial of providence that caused the greatest offence to be taken to his philosophy (cf. Usener 1887: 367-369). From Diogenes Laertius we can deduce that this denial of providence was originally directed both at popular religious ideas and at the natural philosophers who would have us bound by 'necessity'. Further, Plato and Aristotle, in arguing for the divinity of the heavenly bodies, had introduced new terrors, and both Epicurus' letter to Pythocles and Lucretius' poem go to considerable lengths to exclude all suggestions of divine activity from the operations of the heavenly bodies. What was originally a counterblast to Plato and Aristotle could, however, be utilised by a later generation against the astral speculations of the Stoics and their associated notions of fate. Velleius – the Epicurean protagonist in Cicero's dialogue, *De Natura Deorum* – attacks both Plato's demiurge and Stoic notions of divine providence in the same breath (*De Natura Deorum*, 1.18).

But what of what Epicurus has to say about 'right religion'? From what Epicurus says about the benefits which the gods are able to bestow on each other he appears to draw the conclusion that they can bestow the same benefits on men. As the gods show no concern for the affairs of men, petitionary prayer to the gods is obviously, for an Epicurean, of no avail; and, indeed, as Epicurus says in his *Vatican Sayings* 65, it is pointless to pray for happiness which a man can provide for himself. If the gods paid attention to human prayers the human race would long since have become extinct since men are continually praying for calamities to fall upon their enemies (Usener 1887: 388). Yet Epicurus recommends prayer, on the grounds that it is a natural act and that one should also participate in the religious life of one's country, and it seems that he himself, led the way by taking part, and urging his followers to take part, in the sacrifices to the gods, without worrying too much about popular superstitious beliefs. Even in antiquity, and certainly, later many have seen Epicurus' actions as those of a hypocrite concerned only for his own popularity and perhaps also for his personal safety. That Epicurus advised obedience to the laws and customs of one's own country as a means of living an untroubled life we know, but there is more to his participation in religious activities than this. The contemplation of the gods, for one thing, is a source of pleasure, filling the mind with delight and the spirit with hope at the thought of these immortal, happy beings. The sage in fact draws near and hopes himself to gain something of the tranquillity, though not of course of the immortality, of the gods. A quotation from Epicurus preserved for us by Philodemus, states that 'every wise man has pure and holy opinions about the divine and has understood that this nature is great and holy,' and a letter from the Epicurean school says that a proper understanding of the gods is itself blessed and that we should stand amazed at it and reverence the divine experience. The wise have kinship with the gods. Here the Epicurean – as Epicurus consciously held – is every whit the equal of the Platonic philosopher.

It is, however, the ethical doctrines of Epicurus that represent the great humanistic achievement of antiquity. Greek ethics are, on the whole, what are termed eudaimonian – that is they are concerned with the varieties of happiness and with the ways to achieve happiness. Epicurus takes up the problem of happiness or pleasure where it had been left by Aristippus, Eudoxus, Plato and Aristotle, and in the judgement of De Witt handled it 'with such superior precision that this line of inquiry, so far as antiquity is concerned, became exhausted' (De Witt 1954: 216).

That happiness or pleasure is, in fact, the end or τέλος (*telos*) of man Epicurus deduced from empirical observation of the behaviour of new-born infants. Such observations further established, for Epicurus, the unity of pleasure, and he thus opposed the distinction between pleasures which labelled some pleasures good and some bad and which exalted the pleasures of the mind over those of the body, which had been maintained by Plato and Aristotle.

Epicurus also draws out the logical consequences of his denial of immortality to the soul. As the soul was ultimately corporeal the conclusion that Epicurus drew was that in the pursuit of pleasure – the beginning and the end of the happy life – equal weighting must be given to body and soul. His ideal is thus that of *mens sano in corpore sano* – a sound mind in a sound body. Moreover, since the denial of immortality implied the forgoing of any notions of reward or fulfillment in a life beyond the grave, Epicurus insisted that immortality would not in fact increase pleasure and that the fullness of pleasure could be achieved in this life. He also took issue with Aristippus who had recognised only 'pleasures of excitement'. Whilst certainly recognising such pleasures, Epicurus went on to maintain the greater and more enduring value of static pleasures. For example, if the pleasure of escaping from violent death is great and momentarily exciting, how much greater is the static ongoing pleasure of possessing life. Such an approach to pleasure required a new way of thinking altogether than that which had chraracterised previous discussions of pleasure.

Also, as against his predecessors, Epicurus drew a distinction between 'the greatest good' – which he took to be life itself – and the end or τέλος (*telos*) of life. Those before him, who had defined the τέλος as that to which all other goods are referred whilst the τέλος itself was referred to nothing, he thought not only mistaken but illogical. Every good presupposes life. Life, therefore, must be the supreme good – not, as many have supposed Epicurus to have maintained, pleasure. Pleasure was, however, the end or purpose of life, and Epicurus sees life as occuring only between birth and death. Soul and body were born together and will perish together. As *Vatican Sayings* 30 asserts:

> The potion mixed at birth for all of us is a draught of death. (De Witt: 218)

For Epicurus there was not, as Plato had believed, a pre-existent life of the soul, nor, as the vast majority of his contemporaries believed, any life after death. *Vatican Sayings* 14 states that:

> We are born once and we cannot be born twice but to all eternity must be no more. (*Ibid.*)

The supreme values, therefore, must be sought between birth and death or not at all. That life itself is the supreme good Epicurus asserts in *Vatican Sayings* 42:

> The span of time includes both the beginning and the termination of the greatest good. (*Ibid.*, 219)

If we enquire in greater detail how Epicurus arrived at the view that the end or purpose of life is pleasure we must note first that the norm or criterion of truth in these matters was, for Epicurus, not reason but Nature. David Hume, the eighteenth century Scottish philosopher, was to follow him here. Eudoxus, some little time previous to Epicurus had also proclaimed pleasure to be the true end of man and had based his claim on the fact that all creatures – rational, irrational and a-rational – pursue it (so Aristotle *Nicomachean Ethics*, 1172b. 9-10). According to Aristotle's account of Eudoxus' opinion, Eudoxus would appear to have held that the pursuit of pleasure is analogous with the instincts of wild creatures in seeking for their proper food. Thus, in asserting that Nature was the criterion of the good for man, Epicurus was not original, but he was certainly the first to work out – as he did in his *Canon* – the full consequences of this view.

The question naturally arises whether, in admitting Nature to be the criterion of the end of man, Epicurus was not going back on his belief that Nature was non-teleological, devoid of purpose. The answer to this lies in the meaning which the term 'Nature' had for Epicurus. By 'Nature' Epicurus means us to understand 'human nature' – which for him, over against his atomistic predecessors, was, we must remember, to some extent a free human nature. (The details of his argument for human freedom – the famous doctrine of the swerve – we need not to go into.) Thus, when he writes, 'Nature is not to be coerced', he means 'human nature', as he does when he writes, 'It must be assumed that Nature was taught a multitude of lessons of all sorts by sheer experience.' By such phrases as 'the justice of Nature' and 'the limits of Nature' he means no more than that the intelligent man looks to the phenomenon of nature for those signs by which he can know the true nature of justice and the true limits of pleasures. In the same way he looks to the behaviour of the new born infant for the signs that will tell him about the identity of the end or purpose of living. In those passages where 'Nature' does not mean 'human nature' it signifies, without exception, the blind purposeless activity of the universe. That his later disciple Lucretius personifies 'Nature' is no more than poetic convention.

Epicurus' position is then that Nature is without purpose but that she brings into being a purposive creature who on account of his reason can conceive for himself an end.

Whilst the fact that the end of man is pleasure can be established by Nature, man must look to Nature also to determine what can be predicated of it. From Nature, Epicurus deduces that pleasure is one with normal human life – an essential ingredient and not something tacked on as an appendage to it. It is as normal to human life as pain and disease are abnormal. One is good and the other evil, as he states in *Vatican Sayings* 37:

> Human nature is vulnerable to evil, not to the good, because it is preserved by pleasures, destroyed by pains. (De Witt: 219)

Pleasure is the opposite of pain, not because all creatures pursue the one and avoid the other, but because they stand in the same relationship as health which preserves and disease which destroys.

Having established the association of pleasure with health the next step that Epicurus takes is to recognise that the good for man – pleasure – is of the soul and of the body – something which Epicurus further infers from his denial of immortality which confers a superior status on the soul. This is, of course his most well known and most influential doctrine.

The perfect condition for Epicurus, as was mentioned at the outset of our discussion, was ἀταραξία (*ataraxy*). This is often misrepresented. The Oxford English Dictionary, for example, defines 'ataraxy' as 'stoical indifference', which is to confuse *ataraxy* with ἀπάθεια (*apatheia*), or non-attachment, an ideal which is most unhumanistic but which has dominated not only Stoic and Christian ethics but

Hindu and Buddhist as well. The Epicurean sage, however, is not indifferent. It has even been said of him that 'he will be more disposed to feeling than other men' (Diogenes Laertius 10.117). The general objective of Epicurean ethics was not to attain immunity to feeling but to keep the emotions and feelings within natural bounds. *Vatican Sayings* 21 states that:

> Human nature is not to be coerced but persuaded and we shall persuade her by satisfying the necessary desires if they are not going to be injurious but, if they are going to injure, by relentlessly banning them. (*Ibid.*, 226)

The terme ἀταραξία is a metaphor derived from the sea and the weather. It means 'calm' and Epicurus compares the turmoils of the soul to storm and bad weather at sea. The main causes of turmoil in the soul are, as we have seen, fear of the gods and of what appertains after death. When a man has attained true knowledge concerning the groundlessness of these fears, and keeps his emotions within natural limits, he achieves peace. As Epicurus says in *Vatican Sayings* 78:

> The truly noble man busies himself chiefly with wisdom and friendship, of which the one is an understandable good but the other is immortal. (*Ibid.*)

By 'immortal' Epicurus means to assert that in friendship a man comes nearest to partaking in the life of the gods.

For true happiness we must also come to an understanding of the limits of pleasure as set by our human nature. We must also come to a full understanding of the unity of pleasure and of the fact that pleasure is continuous and not momentary. We should not allow ourselves to be stimulated by artificial pleasures – whipped up pleasures which satisfy artificial demands in our natures. We should seek to satisfy only the basic demands of our nature. To his youthful disciple Menoceceus, Epicurus writes:

> Plain-tasting foods bring a pleasure equal to that of luxurious diet when once the pain arising from need has been removed, and bread and water afford the very keenest pleasure when one in need of them brings them to his lips. (Usener 1887: 413; 21-25)

This is the fixed ceiling for pleasure which modern (and ancient) misrepresentations of Epicureanism fail to notice. This principle Epicurus extends to all our desires; for clothing, shelter etc. We should do away with what Epicurus calls 'embellishment', 'It is the ingratitude of the soul that makes the creature endlessly lickerish of embellishments' he says in *Vatican Sayings* 69 (De Witt: 228). Such embellishing of pleasures adds nothing to them and is superfluous.

In all the cultures of the world, but particularly in Western culture, we come across the cry that echoes so plaintively in the writings of such a one as Miguel de Unamuno (e.g. 1962), to the effect that if death ends all, then what pleasure can we take in life? Denying as he does that we live on in any sense after death Epicurus is obliged to say something in mitigation of this well-nigh universal response to death. We find his answer to this response in No. 19 of his *Authorised Doctrines*:

> Infinite time and finite time are characterised by equal pleasure, if one measures the limits of pleasure by reason. (*Ibid.*, 229)

and his answer has shocked the Christian tradition in the West every whit as much as it shocked the ancient world.

Epicurus also maintained, as we have seen, that there is a limit, a ceiling to all pleasures. When he states, therefore, as he does in the quotation just given, that the reasonable man will 'measure the limits of pleasure by reason', he is asking us to recognise the fact that the body, health and the continuation of health is the limit of pleasure and that the recognition of this limit emancipates the mind from fear of what may happen after death. The attainment of ἀταραξία is the summit of pleasure and pleasure is not increased any more than remaining on a mountain top, once scaled, increases the pleasure of having scaled the mountain and seen the view. We should be thankful for what we have and not pine for what cannot be. Hence the familiar story of the Epicurean sage taking leave of life as a satisfied guest leaving a banquet – the theme chosen by Lucretius for the grand finale of the third book of *De Rerum Natura*, where he personifies Nature and has her rebuke the complaining man because he cannot leave life as one who has had his fill. The wise man, on the contrary, is able to say at death – as Wittgenstein is reputed to have said (Malcolm 1958: 100) – *bene vixi*, I have lived a good life. This is the cry uttered by Diogenes of Oenoanda, an Epicurean of the second century of the Christian Era. It is worth quoting as one of the great humanistic statements of Antiquity.

> Facing the sunset of life because of my age and on the verge of taking my leave of life with a paean of victory because of the enjoyment of the fulness of all pleasures. (Frag. 2.2.7-3.1 [De Witt: 230])

This doctrine of the possibility of the fullness of pleasure in this, the only life that we have, is a supplementary one to the doctrine that after death there is nothing, but it helps, so Epicurus thought, to reconcile men to their fate. The possibility of having enjoyed the fullness of pleasure in the here and now counterbalances the having to abandon the enjoyment of eternal bliss. This is the 'true understanding' of which Epicurus speaks in the following passage preserved in Diogenes Laertius:

> Hence the true understanding of the fact that death is nothing to us renders enjoyable the mortality of existence, not by adding infinite time but by taking away the yearning for immortality. (10.124 [De Witt: 230])

What mitigates the yearning for immortality is the conviction that it is possible to taste all pleasures here in this mortal life. Having achieved this we should rest content.

The spread of Epicureanism, first eastwards and then back again to the West, during the period of the Roman Empire, and its widespread popular appeal, makes that philosophy not only the most missionary philosophy produced by the Greeks, but makes it also the great propagator of humanistic values in the ancient world. Its influence, often anonymous, was considerable, and is witnessed to by the number of attacks which it attracted from those who felt that its influence was subversive of their own. It survived until well into the fourth century of the Christian Era before going under before the rising tide of the newly established syncretistic religion of Christianity. Memories of this philosophy – often, however, inaccurate – lingered on to provide the memory of at least one great non-Christian philosophy during the Middle Ages, and in the seventeenth century, after having been ignored for the most part during the early Renaissance, it was revived in France by Gassendi and has continued to enjoy a limited influence since.

Of the wide popular appeal of this philosophy there can be no doubt. The evidence of friend and foe alike is unanimous. In the more conservative areas, such as the Peloponnesus and Crete, laws were passed against its adherents and persecution was not unknown. Its influence was also strong outside of Greece. In Antioch, at the time of Antiochus Epiphanes – that is about the middle of the second century BC – it enjoyed the status of a court philosophy. In Judea, at about the same time, its influence can be detected in the *Book of Ecclesiastes.* In Egypt it was known from the time of the first Ptolomy, and in the first century of the Christian era the Alexandrine Jew Philo shows more than a passing aquaintance with it. In the West evidence of its wide popular appeal exists in the form of an anonymous epitaph, *Non fui, fui, non sum, non curo* – 'I was not, I was, I am not, I am unconscious of it' – an epitaph which, with variations, has been found in Italy, Gaul and Africa. Its ubiquity is further shown by the number of works – in both East and West – written against it.

It was in Italy and Rome, however, that its influence was paramount. Unlike Stoicism, whose influence was restricted to the aristocracy and which was confined to Rome, Epicureanism was from its first incursion into Italy in the second century BC both a rural and a town philosophy, taking Italy by storm. Unlike Stoicism, it did not depend upon imported tutors and it was disseminated in Latin translations through reading circles. Abundant evidence survives, both of its ubiquity throughout Italy and of the fact that it appealed both to the high born and to the humble.[10] Its most famous exponent in the Roman world was, of course, the poet Lucretius who published his well known *De Rerum Natura* in 54 BC. Its chief opponents were the Stoics with their insistence on virtue and duty, and divine providence. The chief spokesman of the opposition at this time was Cicero, and we can get an insight into the debate in his dialogue, *De Natura Deorum*. Cicero's opposition was decisive and Epicureanism was discredited both socially and politically, and was forced to become anonymous – something which would have appealed in a way to Epicurus who urged men to 'live unknown and die unknown'. That Epicureanism survived is shown by the fact that Plutarch devoted a good part of his career to its refutation, and he is, in fact, one of our most important sources of evidence for the teachings of Epicureanism. In the early centuries of the Christian era, after the collapse of Stoicism, Epicureanism was left virtually alone to combat the rising Christian religion. Its greatest protagonist in this contest was Celsus, who was active towards the close of the second century, and who composed the most devastating attack on Christianity in all antiquity. Epicurean influences are also evident in the satirist Lucian, in Juvenal, and in the latter part of the second century in Galen, the last great medical writer of the ancient world.

The third and fourth centuries also witness to the influence of Epicureanism. As De Witt has remarked, the Christian writers Arnobius and Lactantius resemble each other 'in displaying a very deficient knowledge of Holy Scripture and a rather more abundant knowledge of Epicureanism (1954: 352). It has been suggested that both were, perhaps, Epicureans before their conversion to Christianity. So great, in fact, is the influence of Epicureanism that Lactantius sets down a long list of invidious reasons for the wide appeal of this philosophy. St. Augustine too shows himself not impervious to the influence of this philosophy and states that, were it not for its denial of immortality and divine judgement, he might well have been an Epicurean (*Confessions*, 6.16). His later writings, however, are evidence for the decline of Epicureanism.

But although Epicureanism is in decline by the beginning of the fifth century the memory of it is never quite lost. It was preserved, if nowhere else, in the writings of Cicero which were never lost to the West. Epicureanism also survived, not only in the writings of Classical writers, but also in the collections of the opinions of ancient philosophers which continued to be made from the fifth century onwards. As late as 1888 a collection of eighty-one such sayings – chiefly by Epicurus himself – were discovered in the Vatican Library and we have drawn on these in the account of Epicurean ethics given above.

It is during the Middle Ages that the stereotyped image of Epicurus as an out-and-out sensualist develops. In Jewish thinking too, his name is synonymous with unbeliever. Dante pays Epicureans the compliment of devising for them a unique form of torture.

Confused during the revival of Classical learning at the time of the Renaissance with Stoic ethics, Epicureanism was revived in seventeenth century France to exert a not inconsiderable influence upon the philosophical and scientific endeavours of the Enlightenment.

4.9 THE SCEPTICS

The Sceptical school – the last great school of Classical Antiquity – traces its origin back to thinkers who ante-date the rise of the Epicurean and Stoic schools of philosophy.

In fact at the very outset of Greek speculation as of Indian there is voiced the feeling that to understand the world, to wring knowledge from the void, is well-nigh impossible. This disconsolate note is sounded by Xenophanes, who is recorded as saying:

> The certain truth there is no man who knows, nor ever shall be, about the gods and all the things whereof I speak. Yea, even if a man should chance to say something utterly right, still he

himself knows it not: there is nothing anywhere but guessing. (Deils, Frag. 34)

And also by Empedocles:

> When they have but looked upon the little portion of their own life, they fly away in a moment, like smoke, persuaded each one of that particular thing only with which he has come into contact as they are driven hither and thither, and yet each one flatters himself that he has found the whole; so far are these things beyond the reach of men, not to be seen of the eye, or heard of the ear, or comprehended with the mind. (*Ibid.* Frag. 2)

The earliest avowed Sceptic is Pyrrho of Elis and it is from his name that the name by which Sceptics were invariably known both in the ancient world and in the Western tradition up to and including the nineteenth century, that is Pyrrhonism, is derived. Pyrrho, himself, alas, left no extant account of his views and it is from his disciple Timon of Phlius that his views have come down to us.

Pyrrho was born about 365 BC at Elis and came to philosophy after an unsuccessful career as a painter. He is reported to have studied philosophy under the Sophist Bryson, and with the Democritean philosopher Anaxarchus, whom he accompanied on one of Alexander the Great's campaigns. The variety of cultures, customs and beliefs to which this campaign exposed him are thought to have influenced the position which he was eventually to take up in philosophy. He opened a school in Elis about the year 330 BC and taught there until his death around 275 BC.

The great danger in endeavouring to establish Pyrrho's views is that, since he was hailed by later Sceptics as their founder, there was a tendency to read back into his sayings the positions adopted by the later school.

It was said that Pyrrho posed three questions – 'What are things in themselves? How should we be disposed towards them? What are the consequences of this disposition?' The answers he gave are bleak to say the least. Things do not differ from one another; they are equally uncertain and indiscernable. Our sensations and judgements can produce neither truth nor falsity, and consequently we should trust neither the senses nor reason but strive to be without opinions. No matter what is at issue we should neither affirm nor deny. The result is apathy — non-involvement, and this alone produces peace.

This latter point is important. Whatever Pyrrho's exact position there seems no reason to doubt that his primary concern was ethical and that his search was for ἀταραξία (*ataraxy*) — a notion which may have its origin in his teaching. There is a legend to the effect that Pyrrho's pupil Mauiphanes was the teacher of Epicurus. This is as may be, but there is no doubt that Pyrrho himself searched for ἀταραξία and it may well be, as had been suggested by Ralph McInerny, that:

> in times of incredible political upheaval, when there was such a proliferation of philosophical doctrines, represented by warring schools, Pyrrho, who had seen tyranny at first hand as well as the variety of cultures and customs and perhaps had been struck by the impassivity of Indian holy men, chose to find happiness in a despair of philosophy, with one being considered as good as another, and total indifference to the vicissitudes of life. (1963: 326)

Pyrrho's advice for such action as life necessitates is, as we might expect, conservative. If one has to act, then act in such a way as to follow the customs of one's time and place.

It will be obvious from what we have said earlier about the Sophists that, superficially, Pyrrho's iconoclasm has much in common with theirs. The difference, however, is that whereas the Sophists sought to have a practical influence, going about among men and charging for their services, Pyrrho appears to have withdrawn from the world, and preached resignation to it. Edwyn Bevan suggests that Pyrrho sums up the attitude of the ordinary man before the plurality of philosophies and the shifting political scene (1913).

Although Pyrrho's attitude to religion is not recorded we can surmise, from what appears to be his general position as outline above, that whilst he was no doubt theoretically agnostic about religious claims he followed in all things the religious customs of his time. His successors were to be far more outspoken.

Another source of Sceptical opinions in the ancient world derives from the Middle (Platonic) Academy and it is characterised by a more thoroughly destructive dialectic than that of Pyrrho. Whilst initially this was directed against the arguments of the Stoics – called by the Sceptics 'The Dogmatists' – as a weapon it was capable of being adapted for use against all forms of dogmaticism, philosophical and religious.

It was Arcesilaus who, towards the opening of the second century BC, introduced Sceptical doctrines into the Platonic Academy and so founded the second or Middle Academy as it is now known. It would appear that he was led from a criticism of Stoic criteria for truth to maintain that there could not be any criteria of truth and therefore no certainty with regard to anything whatever. The most we could hope for was probability – what he called *τά εὔλογα* (*ta euloga*) or the reasonable. Whether he was a sceptic with regard to religious claims is not recorded.

About the sceptical attitude towards religion of his successor, Carneades of Cyrene, we are in no doubt since both Cicero and Sextus Empiricus have made us well acquainted with his views.[11]

Carneades was born about 213 BC and is said to have lived to the age of eighty-five, dying about 129 BC. One certain date in his life is the year 156/155 BC when he visited Rome in the company of some other philosophers. It is recorded that on this occasion Carneades on one day put forward the arguments concerning justice of Plato, Aristotle, and the Stoa and on the next day refuted them all (cf. Cicero, *De Republica*). Although greatly influenced by the Stoic Chrysippus in his youth, Carneades joined the Platonic Academy and eventually became its head. He is regarded by many as the third founder of the Academy.

With regard to religious belief, as with everything else, there could, he maintained, be no certainty. But his critique of religion, and of theism in particular, went far deeper than this and in one respect he anticipates a discussion with regard to the concept of 'God' which is still very much alive in contemporary criticisms of theism.

Stoic theology was in many respects not dissimilar to Christian theology – which indeed it influenced. Integral to both is a teleological understanding of the universe based upon belief in a beneficent and providential God. It was this belief – in, of course, its Stoic formulation – that Carneades criticised.

Inquiring into the evidence offered for theism, Carneades begins by examining the evidence drawn from theism's supposed universality – the *argumentum e consensu gentium* so beloved of the Stoics and of many religious apologists from their time to our own! If, Carneades asked, belief in the gods is universal, why bother to try to base this belief on argument, thus suggesting that it might indeed by an open question? Whilst himself doubting the universality of theism, Carneades went on to ask what if anything would be proved by its universality? His answer was that all that would be established would be the fact that men believed in the gods – further argument would still be needed to prove that the gods existed. He argues further that questions of truth are not to be decided by plebiscite and he regards it as odd that the Stoics, who for the most part regarded the great mass of mankind as little better than fools, should commit such an important question to its judgement.[12]

Evidence drawn from 'appearances' of gods to men – which had so impressed Democritus and Epicurus – and from divination, Carneades dismisses as little better than old wives' tales. He also points to the arbitrariness of divinitation. If indeed it were a way of foretelling future events it would be possible to specify the principles on which it is based. As it is, it is little more than a hit or miss affair owing nothing to divine inspiration.

It would appear that Carneades himself believed that belief in the gods arose from the deification of awesome natural phenomena. But, however such a notion as that of a 'god' arose, Carneades holds that the notion as now held by the Stoics is not only false but meaningless, for it is self-contradictory or internally inconsistent. The import of his arguments is felt by many modern commentators to be wider than the Stoic concept of God which he attacked. As one of them, R. D. Hicks, has written:

This acute thinker used arguments which go much further than

> this and bring to light the fundamental difficulties in any conception of God, whether He be conceived as personal or impersonal, finite of infinite or veiled under some abstraction as the absolute or the unconditioned. (1910: 330)

From what Cicero and Sextus Empiricus tell us it would seem that Carneades argued that we cannot ascribe personal attributes to God without limiting his nature. The God of the Stoics — like the God of Jews, Christians and Muslims — is, however, thought of as both personal and unlimited and infinite. For example, the Stoics claimed that God was a rational being endowed with all excellence. Virtue, however, is incompatible with this, argued Carneades, for virtue presupposes imperfection overcome. To be courageous one must have been exposed to danger; to be temperate, pleasure must have been resisted. How then can God, as defined by the Stoics, exhibit virtue? How can a Being who, it is claimed, is omnipotent face danger and One who is passionless resist pleasure? Does God then lack the virtues of fortitude and temperance? If He does then he cannot be described as all-virtuous. Carneades attacked the notions of infinity and rationality in a similar vein. Carneades' attack on the Stoic notion of Divine Providence can also be construed as an attack on the argument from design, known also as the teleological argument, and in the arguments he brings forward against this he anticipates to a large extent the arguments which David Hume, the eighteenth century Scottish philosopher, puts forward against the argument from design in his *Dialogues Concerning Natural Religion.* The evidence for there being design in the world Carneades regards as inconclusive. He also points to those features of the world which seem to tell against its being the outcome of a designing Mind — poisonous snakes, destructive agencies on land and sea, diseases and so on. God's greatest gift to man, the Stoics held, was his reason. But why, Carneades asks, if God is providential, has this gift been so unevenly distributed? Is God guilty of partiality in His dealing with men?

His basic technique in argument would appear to have been the *σώριτης* (*sorites*) — which takes its name from the word for 'a heap' — *σωρός*; a term used to illustrate the difficulties of indicating precise differentiating characteristics. Suppose that someone is prepared to call a collection of thirty things 'a heap'; subtract one thing and then another and the question arises when does the heap cease to be a heap. It is clearly impossible to lay down precise quantitative criteria for designating 'heap' and yet 'heap' is a quantitative term. Applying this to theology Carneades sought to show that it is impossible to draw any hard and fast distinction regarding what is divine and what is not. A list of such sorites is given in both Cicero and Sextus Empiricus.[13] For example, from Cicero:

> If gods exist, are nymphs goddesses? If they are, are Pans and Satyrs also gods? Surely not. Then neither are nymphs. Yet they have public temples dedicated and devoted to them. So perhaps other beings who have temples dedicated to them may also not be gods. (Cicero, *De Natura Deorum* III, 43 [Latham])

If an opponent declines to accept a link in the chain then the sceptic asks what it is, say, about nymphs which marks them off from Pans and Satyrs given that both have temples dedicated to them. Cicero tells us that Carneades used such arguments, not to overthrow religion as such, but only to show the unconvincingness of polytheism, but Sextus makes no such qualification.

Carneades also exploited the differences of opinion between rival schools rather in the way a number of unbelievers have – from the middle of the sixteenth century[14] – exploited differences of opinion both between differing adherents of the Christian religion and between the adherents of differing religions. Epicurus, he points out, argued that the obvious imperfection of the world gives clear evidence that it is not cared for by the gods, whereas the Stoics argued quite the opposite – the world is manifestly the work of providence and even imperfection has its place; yet another example of the nice balance which exists between the arguments of those who affirm and those who deny the existence of the gods. The only sensible solution is to suspend judgement, and this the sceptic did – though for the most part observing the religious customs of his country.

Though not, so far as we know, a sceptic, one other figure must be mentioned before we leave the Hellenistic Age and pass to the world of Rome – Euhemerus, who lived towards the close of the third and the beginning of the second centuries BC. Euhemerus is well known for having propounded the naturalistic theory of the origin of the gods known as Euhemerism which holds that the gods are simply deified heroes from times past. His theory is not entirely original, for the Greek tradition had always held that the gods came into existence in time and lived in their own sphere a life not totally dissimilar to that lived by the heroes of old. Hecataeus had also held that excellent men became gods. Euhemerus' views, however, fell on fertile soil and it was destined to persist for some time to come. In the Roman world of the second century of the Christian era Diodorus seized upon it as the best explanation of religion and Thomas Carlyle in the last century also followed up this line of thought.[15]

5

Rome

5.1 INTRODUCTION

Such irreligion and unbelief as we find in the Roman world derives almost entirely from Greece. Roman religion, by the time we come across the emergence of irreligion, was not unlike Greek popular religion – polytheistic. It had not always been so. Rome began as a small city state in the eighth century BC and later became the political centre of the Mediterranean world, and its religion had changed accordingly often under foreign and more particularly under Greek influence. In its original form Roman religion was utilitarian, rather as the traditional religion of Africa, which it in no small measure resembles, is utilitarian to this day. It was concerned with the satisfaction of physical needs – food, and the prosperity of the family, and eventually of the state, in peace and war. The concept of the divine in ancient Rome lacked any really distinctive personification, being for the most part a matter of coming to terms with undifferentiated *numen* or sacred power. In contrast to Greek religion, Roman religion was distinctly poor in mythology and its rituals were little more than magical. Apart from certain priesthoods the chief officiant at traditional rites was the *paterfamilias* for the family and the magistrate for the state. This familial and civic aspect of Roman religion persisted to the time of the break-up of the Empire in the West and was one of the reasons why irreligion was held in far greater abhorrence in the Roman world than it ever was in the Greek.

The chief deities, Jupiter, Mars, Juno, Minerva and Venus, were of Italian or Etruscan origin. The cultus, such as it was, surrounding these deities was designed to make peace with them; their rights being meticulously defined and respected. This is why divination was held in such high regard, for it told the will of the gods, not, for the most part, for the individual, but for the state – except where a favoured individual's destiny and that of the state coincided. An individual's need for personal religion was met, from the third century BC onwards, by imported Greek and Oriental cults. In the period of the Empire the political side of Roman religion came to be focussed in the cult of the genius of the Emperor and the Roman state. Such Roman religion as survived into the third and fourth centuries of the Christian era was forcibly suppressed by Theodorus 1 in decrees issued in 391 and 399 AD.

Roman religion had no hard and fast dogma and a Roman was free to think almost what he liked about the gods, provided that he performed his religious duties. Thus there was no contradiction when Julius Caesar – *pontifex maximus*, head of the Roman State Religion and responsible thereby for several ceremonies designed to ensure the blessedness of the dead – publicly expressed the opinion, recorded for us by Sallust, that

> death is a relief from woes, not punishment; that it puts an end to all mortal ills and leaves no room either for sorrow of for joy. (*Catiline*, LI, 20 [Rolfe, 1921: 93])

Ancient Roman religion was tolerant and non-sectarian. Disputation was left to philosophy and it is after the introduction of philosophy into the Roman world that we first meet with truly irreligious opinions. The Romans, however, were no great philosophers and even in their irreligious opinions we hear the echo of ancient Greece. The three most important thinkers for the history of irreligion are Cicero, Lucretius and Pliny the Elder.

5.2 CICERO AND LUCRETIUS

Marcus Tullius Cicero was born in 106 BC at Arpinus, sixty miles south-east of Rome, on his father's rather well-to-do country estate. His father was a studious semi-invalid who set great store by the education of his children, taking a house in Rome in order that there they might be educated for a public career. To be qualified for a public career in Rome it was essential to read law and this Cicero did, reading rhetoric and philosophy as well. Thus Cicero, who had the good fortune to study under extremely gifted teachers, became acquainted with the three great philosophies of the Hellenistic period – Epicureanism, Scepticism and Stoicism, in that order. It was, however, the teaching of Philo, the leading exponent of the philosophy of the Academy, whom Cicero had met in 88 BC, which had the greatest influence on him, and Cicero remained faithful to the teachings of the Academy – which, as we have seen, proceeded by sceptical examination of all positions in order to find that opinion which was most probable – until his death, despite being attracted to Stoicism later in his somewhat troubled life.

The story of that life is not without interest for the student of irreligion, for it shows how a man might preserve his scepticism in the midst of high office and personal tragedy. Of the place of philosophy in his life three things need to be noted:[1] (1) that between the ages of seventeen and twenty-one Cicero had an extremely thorough philosophical training from the best expatriate Greek philosophical teachers; (2) that, throughout his life, Cicero kept alive his interest in philosophy by constant reading and discussion, as well as by writing; (3) that, to Cicero, philosophy was not a means of escape from life, but an integral element in all his varied activities as lawyer, orator, politician and writer.

In all these activities the Academic philosophy influenced his approach, so that he set out rival solutions to whatever problem he was engaged upon, then sought to determine where the balance of probability lay, before finally committing himself to action. In 84 BC Cicero began to practice as an advocate, but, after winning his first case, he retired to Athens where he resumed his philosophical studies, returning to Rome in 77 BC, where he soon established the reputation of being the best advocate at what we would call the Bar. He also showed great interest in poetry, writing verses himself and, later in his life, if we are to believe St. Jerome, although an implacable enemy of Epicureanism, he prepared Lucretius' poem *De Rerum Natura* for publication after that writer's suicide in 51 BC.

Having established his reputation as a lawyer, Cicero began to climb the official ladder, being elected to the Senate in 76 BC. After a brief period in Sicily spent, much against his will, supervising shipments of corn, he returned to Rome where he held various high offices – *aedile* in 69 BC and *praetor* in 66 BC. In 63 BC he was elected consul. As a result of his activities as consul – he nipped a rebellion in the bud – he had in 58 BC to flee Rome and seek refuge in Greece. He returned the following year, but never again did he hold high office. The two principals in Rome at this time were Caesar and Pompey, and Cicero spent the rest of his political life wavering between the two. In 53 BC he was appointed to the office of augur – the duties of which were to interpret the omens and so foretell the future. This office was, of course, very prestigious and Cicero valued it as such, though privately he doubted the whole business of divination. This, to some, might appear a gross failing in integrity, but this was not so in Rome, where, as we have said, practice rather than belief was what mattered. In the year 46 Cicero retired completely from public life and left Rome and in March 45 he began writing a series of philosophical books – the most important of which, from our point of view, was *De Natura Deorum*. He returned to Rome, however, in 43 BC after Caesar's assassination – of which he approved but in which he took no part – to deliver a series of powerful speeches against Antony. Failing to get the support from Caesar's great nephew, Octavianus, which he had been led to expect, he sought to escape from Italy, but Antony's agents caught up with him at Formiae in December 43 as he was about to board a ship. Realising that there was nothing left for him to do he calmly offered the centurion his neck. Studious to the very end, he was reading Euripides when his assassins found him.

But despite his, on the whole, succesful political career, Cicero was not really a politician but a scholar and a philosopher. As many have pointed out he had no other religion but philosophy – his only consolation and guide in the conduct of life. He himself wrote 'Philosophy is a physician of souls, takes away the load of empty troubles... banishes fears' (*Tusculans*, II, 4, ii), and 'Philosophy! without you, what would I ever have amounted to, and what would have become of all human life' (*Ibid.*, V. 2. 5). In a letter to his friend Atticus, written about the year 68 BC, when he was in the very midst of his public affairs, he wrote that 'Every day I find greater satisfaction in study, so far as my forensic labours permit (*Letters to Atticus* I. 20. 7 [Bailey 1965: 191]). And at every major crisis of his life – and there were many – he turned to philosophy and writing for outlet. For example, on his return from exile in 56 BC, the first thing he did was to resume his reading, and the year 55 BC was spent for the most part in Naples devouring the library of Faustus Sulla. He wrote to Atticus at that time that he would rather sit in the chair his friend had beneath the bust of Aristotle than in the ivory chair of office (*Ibid.*, IV. 10). The consolatory effect which philosophy had for him explains his literary output from March 45 BC. From that month he began to produce a series of books dealing not, as previously, with matters of state, but with such matters as immortality, the chief good, the importance of philosophy, the problem of pain, determinism, the possibility of divination and the concrete application of philosophy to the moral life. The explanation for this output Cicero himself mentions at the beginning of his treatise *De Natura Deorum*. After stating that he was at leisure and had nothing else to do and also that he wished to uphold the dignity and good name of his people by making a philosophical contribution to Latin literature, he says: 'I was also moved to these studies by my own sickness of mind and heart, crushed and shaken as I was by the great misfortune that I had to bear'. Cicero is here referring not to political disappointments, but to the tragic death of his beloved daughter Tullia – a blow made all the harder by the failure of his two marriages. When Tullia died in the Spring of the year, Cicero was inconsolable. All he could do was to grieve and to write. The completely unsympathetic attitude of his second wife Publilia to his loss compounded his woe and brought about their divorce.

H. A. K. Hunt, in his book *The Humanism of Cicero*, argues that Cicero's main objective in the writings of this period was not philosophical but ethical – his aim being to refute philosophical errors which he believed were injurious to morality. Believing as he did that certainty is impossible – whether about God, morality or the physical world – he yet wanted to give the ordinary citizen some probable guidelines for right conduct. Thus, before arriving at his culminating work, *On Duties*, he felt that he must first establish that man is a free moral agent and so refute the Stoic belief that human life is controlled either by fate or the gods. Hence the sequence of works, *The Ends of Good and Evil*, *The Tusculan Disputations*, *The Nature of the Gods*, and *Divination and Fate*. Whilst this thesis of Hunt's does much to explain the order of Cicero's writing, we must not forget the explicit personal reasons which Cicero himself gives us. Certainly, however, a humanistic concern is to the fore in Cicero's writings and he is, in fact, once of the great humanistic writers of antiquity.[2]

The Nature of the Gods was written, as we have said, during this most prolific period in Cicero's philosophic career. Beginning in his *Academics* with the chief problem in epistemology, whether we can ever have certain knowledge, he passed next, in *The Ends of Good and Evil*, to consider the chief problem of ethics – what is the highest good for man? Having discussed the immortality of the soul in the *Tusculan Disputations*, where he had argued that it is indeed probable that the soul lives on after death, he now, in *The Nature of the Gods*, turns his attention to the question of the relationship – if any – between the gods and the world. This question he regarded as an important one for ethics. He was himself convinced that morality ought to draw sustenance from religion – though his major ethical insights stand independently of this view and it is not something that Cicero himself took very seriously. In *The Nature of the Gods* he asks whether a reasonable, rational man can believe in the established religion. The chief topic for discussion, however, is the Stoic belief in providence, which raises the question – what effect, if any, the gods have on human affairs? This, as Cicero himself makes quite clear (in Section three of Book one), is the most important theological question for ethics.

Cicero sets about the task of discussing this important issue in an interesting way. As a follower of the Academic philosophy, he believed that it would be wrongheaded simply to state his own opinion and leave it at that. The right method in philosophy was to state and examine all the currently held positions and only then conclude by deciding which solution to the problem under discussion came nearest to the truth. He thus casts his discussion in the form of a dialogue – but a dialogue very different from the dialogues of Plato. Cicero lets each of his speakers have their say in full before subjecting them to critical examination. His work is, therefore, a mine of information for ancient views on theological questions. David Hume was to copy this method of discussing religious questions in his *Dialogues Concerning Natural Religion* but Cicero was, so far as we know, the originator of this method.

Three speakers take part in this imaginary dialogue – Velleius, an Epicurean; Balbus, a Stoic, and Cotta an Academic. Cicero himself will, as J. M. Ross has expressed it, 'out-Academic the Academics' (McGregor 1972: 27), by being sceptical even of scepticism, thus reserving his own judgement until the very end.

The dialogue must, of course, be read whole and no summary can do justice to it. It is eminently readable and as we read it we become aware of just how old are many of the arguments for and against theism which we meet again in the later theistic tradition in the West.

From the point of view of the student of irreligion, the section in which Cotta expounds the Academic critique of religion, and of Stoicism in particular, – that is Book III – provides as good a summary as any of the standard anti-religious arguments of the ancient world. Cotta himself is as good an example as we will find of the conservative sceptic – he was in fact a real person who had held the office of *pontifex* from 77 BC. As he says at one point in the dialogue,

> I am persuaded of this belief [the existence of the gods] by its traditional authority; but you have given me no reasons why I should believe it. (*De Natura Deorum* III. 7)[3]

This position he regards as quite rational for, as he has explained earlier:

> I am Cotta and a priest. By this you mean, I take it, that I ought

> to defend the beliefs which we have inherited from our ancestors about the immortal gods, with all their attendant ceremonies and sacred rituals. And I shall always defend them, as I have always defended them in the past. Nobody, be he learned or unlearned, shall ever argue me out of the views which I have received from my forebears about the worship of the gods. (*Ibid.*, III. 4-5)

However, Cotta, whilst, as the first quotation shows, holding in true Sceptical fashion to traditional religious ceremonies and beliefs, then proceeds to demolish Stoic natural theology in no uncertain terms. Many of the arguments which he uses are derived from Carneades. For instance, at the outset of his argument, he asks Balbus why he had argued at length about something which he had claimed needed no argument – the existence of the gods being obvious and generally agreed. He then proceeds to attack the second of Balbus's arguments, which was that when we look up at the heavens we immediately understand that there must be some divinity which governs them. As this argument is one which is repeated throughout the Western theistic tradition – Kant for instance was deeply impressed by it[4] – it will be worth our while looking at Cotta's reply. The essence of it is that it is a moot question whether the heavens do so declare the glory of god or whether, as indeed Vellieus and the Epicureans believed, the sun, moon, stars, etc. function in a purely impersonal manner. The 'appearances' of gods to men Cotta dismisses as old wives' tales. Divination – which he, however, accepts as part of tradition – is a mystery and no rational explanation of it is possible:

> And what was the origin of your art of divination? Who discovered the significance of a cleft in an animal's liver or interpreted the raven's cry? Or the way the lots fall? Not that I do not believe these things ... but how omens came to be understood is something I must learn from the philosophers, especially as the predictions of the sooth-sayers are often falsified by the event. But, you argue, doctors too are often wrong. There is however

> to my mind no comparison between medicine, which applies reasoning which I can understand, and the power of divination, the origin of which is a mystery to me. (*Ibid.*, III. 14-15)

Earlier, in his exposition of Stoic views, Balbus had given the four ways in which his Stoic predecessor Cleanthes had claimed that the ideas of the gods are formed in our minds. They were: (1) from premonitions of future events; (2) from the terror of storms and other natural disturbances; (3) from the usefulness and abundance of the commodities which we enjoy and (4) lastly, from the order of the stars and the harmony of the heavens. Cotta now turns his attention to these.

The first of these ways Cotta believes he has dispatched in his words about divination. With regard to the second argument Cotta says that, whilst one cannot deny that when natural disturbances on land or sea occur they do indeed strike terror into many people who attribute them to the power of the gods, the question of whether the gods do in fact exist is not the same as the question whether a number of people actually believe in their existence – an astute logical point, and one, which as we have seen, had been made by Carneades.

The latter argument Cotta defers until he comes to deal with Stoic notions of divine providence, although we have mentioned his preliminary reply. He also defers consideration of Chrysippus' argument, which Balbus had quoted, to the effect that, as nature shows phenomena which are beyond the capacity of men, there must be in the universe a power greater than man, as well as the argument from design – 'the harmony and common purpose of the whole of nature' as he calls it. Rather he takes up what Balbus had said about the nature of the gods – which he regards as showing that they do not in fact exist. He says:

> You pointed out how difficult it is for us to think otherwise than through visible images. Then you said that as there could be nothing more excellent than God, the universe itself must be God, as there was nothing more excellent than the whole

scheme of things. If we could only think of it as a conscious being, and see this truth with the eyes of the mind as we see other things with the eyes of the body! But when you say that there is nothing more perfect than the universe as a whole, what do you mean by perfect? If you mean 'beautiful', I agree. If you mean 'fitted to our needs', I agree again. But if you mean there is nothing wiser than the universe, then I do not agree at all. Not because I find it difficult to think otherwise than in visual images, but because the more I do the less I understand what you mean. There is nothing in nature, you say, superior to the universe itself. Well, I say there is nothing on earth superior to the city of Rome. Must I therefore imagine that the city of Rome thinks and reasons like an intelligent being? But since this is not so, do you consider that an ant, for example, is to be preferred to this beautiful city of ours? The city is not a conscious being, but the ant is not only conscious, but has powers of reason, thought and memory. So we have to decide, Balbus, just how much we can concede to you. You cannot merely assume whatever you like. (*Ibid.*, III. 20-23)

This is a very good example of the kind of difficulties which later theologians within the Christian tradition were to find in predicting certain attributes of their God. Cotta develops this point rather cleverly by reference to some syllogisms of Zeno, saying:

Zeno argues thus: 'Any being which reasons is superior to any being which does not. But there is nothing superior to the universe as a whole. Therefore the universe is a reasoning being.'

Balbus accepts this argument – indeed he has himself referred to it. But, Cotta continues:

If you accept this argument, then you will have a universe which is proficient in the art of reading books. Because if you follow in Zeno's footsteps, you will have to develop the argument as follows: 'A being which can read is superior to a being

> which cannot. But nothing is superior to the universe as a whole. Therefore the universe as a whole can read.' Then you will have to go on to say that the universe is a scholar, a mathematician, a musician, a master of all the arts and sciences. So you will end up by turning the universe itself into a philosopher. (*Ibid.*, III. 23-24)

Immanuel Kant was to develop this line of argument very effectively in the eighteenth century, when he pointed to the 'antinomies' which resulted when one sought to apply language which makes perfectly proper sense within the world to either the universe considered as a whole, or to that which lies beyond the universe. Wittgenstein was to make a similar criticism of religious language in his *Tractatus Logico Philosophicus*, and to conclude 'Whereof we cannot speak, thereof we must be silent.' It is interesting to trace this criticism to its source, though it is highly likely that Cicero is again making use of arguments developed originally by Carneades.

Passing next to the argument from the regular course of the heavenly bodies, Cotta suggests that it is equally, indeed more likely, that these have natural causes. Diseases such as the ague, he points out, follow a regular course but we do not immediately conclude that the ague is due to divine activity.

> No, he says, we must seek an intelligible cause for all these phenomena. The moment you [religious people] fail to find one, you run off to a god like a suppliant to an altar'. (*Ibid.*, III. 20-23)

How often has this been the case within the Western theistic tradition! Newton, for instance, endeavouring to apply his splendid discovery of the law of gravitation to as many different problems as possible and finding that although it would deal with the motion of the moon round the earth and the earth round the sun, but would not deal with the spinning of the earth around its own polar axis to give us night and day, concluded in a letter to the Master of Trinity College, Cambridge that 'the diurnal rotations of the planets could not be derived from gravity, but require a Divine Arm to impress it upon them' (Coulson 1958: 32-33).

Similarly, with regard to Chrysippus' saying that 'If anything happens which could not be brought about by man, it must be brought about by some power superior to man', Cotta points out that the superior to man need not be the gods but could be Nature, but unfortunately the argument he promises us, to show that this is in fact the case, does not appear in the text which has come down to us. Cotta then proceeds to assert that we must look for a natural explanation of many of the other things which Balbus has adduced as evidence of the divine in the world, including the existence of souls and the harmony of natural processes aforementioned.

> There is a natural explanation for all these things, [he says]. But this is not to be found in nature 'moving like a craftsman' [such as Zeno describes]; but in a nature which stirs up and keeps in motion all things by its own changing impulses. For this reason I was pleased with what you said about the harmony and interrelation of nature which you described as working together in a constant harmony. But I do not subscribe to your opinion that this could not happen unless the whole of nature was infused with one divine spirit. Nature persists and coheres by its own power without any help from the gods. There is indeed inherent in it a kind of harmony or 'sympathy' as the Greeks call it. But the greater it is in its own right, the less need it be regarded as the work of some divine power. (*Ibid.*, III. 28-30)

Such a passage might have come straight out of David Hume, but it was in fact written eighteen hundred years before.

Carneades' arguments against the immortality of the soul are adduced next — though the precise bearing of this on the question of the existence of the gods is a little obscure. The two are linked historically in most of the world's religions — with the possible exception of Judaism and Christianity, which, so some have argued, teaches rather the resurrection from the dead — but there is, of course, no logical connection, for there is no contradiction in holding to the immortality of the soul and yet denying the existence of God or the Gods. Conversely, with early Judaism, one could hold to the existence of God and deny that man lives after death.

After criticising the Stoic conception of 'fire' as the vital principle of all things, Cotta returns to his attack on the Stoic conception of God, but now it is the moral attributes of God which come under attack, and once again arguments from Carneades are employed. As we have dealt with these criticisms in our discussion of Carneades we need not go over them again.

This is followed up by an attack on polytheism and on the fantastic gods worshipped by both the Romans and other peoples. The argument here is a *reductio ad absurdum*, and again the arguments of Carneades are employed. The point of the argument is, where do we draw the line? Who is and who is not, out of all the innumerable gods and goddesses worshipped by peoples the whole world over, a god? For some reason this section is the longest (and the most tedious) in the whole of Cotta's speech. It was one, incidentally, that the early Christian apologists were to pick up and use against polytheism, though they paid singular little attention to the other arguments in Cotta's speech!

There next follows an attack on the misuses of reason among mankind—the point being to suggest what the Stoics claim to be God's greatest gift to man is to a great extent his worst enemy. If the gods gave man reason, they made him a villain, Cotta concludes. To claim that man is responsible for this misuse of reason and its attendent calamities is, argues Cotta, the same as arguing that the pilot of a ship is responsible for the storm. No, evil is endemic to the world and the conclusion must be that no god is therefore responsible for it, a conclusion which is reinforced if we take into account the evils which we read about in history or consult our own experience of the bad prospering and the good suffering, the former unpunished and the latter unaided by any god.

Here Cotta, somewhat abruptly, ends his case, but he has given us enough evidence to conclude that the religious apologists did not have it all their own way in the ancient world. Anti-religious arguments there certainly were and, as the above account shows, they were extremely powerful and subtle. They were to be used time and again throughout the course of the Western theistic tradition.

Cicero himself, who it may be recalled, is the witness of this imaginary argument, sums up very briefly – so much so that it would appear that Cicero grew tired of the work and left it unfinished. His own conclusion was that having listened to all the arguments 'around it and around' he himself was inclined, despite the formidable arguments of Cotta, to the Stoic views expressed by Balbus.

How far Cicero is being sincere here has been a matter for dispute. Lactantius, writing in the fourth century AD, certainly thought that Cicero's real opinion was that of an agnostic, if not of an outright atheist. He wrote that:

> Cicero was well aware that the objects of human worship were false for after saying a number of things tending to subvert religion, he adds that 'these matters should not be discussed in public, as such discussion might destroy the established religion. (*Institutorum* II, 3. 2)

And the argument has continued. We must, however, in the absence of evidence to the contrary, accept Cicero's own account of his opinions at their face value. As one of the foremost Ciceronian scholars of our own day has expressed it, Cicero,

> whilst not prepared to offer dogmatic assertions about the nature of the gods – strongly believed that the universe is governed by a divine plan, and this belief is reflected in the *Dream of Scipio*.... When he looked round him at the marvels of the cosmos he could only conclude, adopting the 'argument from design', that they must be of divine origin. [Grant here refers us to Cicero's *Tusculan Disputations* 1, 29, 70]. He was happy to adopt this form of religion, purified and illuminated by the knowledge of nature, [a reference here to *On Divination* 11, 72, 148 etc], because it justified his confidence in human beings, which was based... on the conviction that the mind of soul of each individual person is a reflection, indeed a part, of the divine mind. (Grant 1971a: 8)

This said, we should note also that, as Grant has mentioned earlier in the essay from which we have quoted, 'Cicero believed in human beings. He believed in their rights and their responsibilities and their freedom to make decisions without detailed interference from heaven of destiny' (*Ibid.*: 7). Grant further points out that Cicero's influence has bequeathed to us much of the vast range of ideas suggested by words like humanity and humanism. And in another essay he speaks of Cicero's accepting the Greek Stoic belief that high moral standards, the determination to live up to them, and the emotional restraint needed to do so were the most important things in the world (Grant 1971b: 12). A truly humanistic ideal – and one that is reinforced by a reading of Cicero's *Tusculan Disputations* where he asserts that all human beings, however humble, count for something and have inherent value in themselves. He also believed that affection is one of the basic impulses of mankind. It is natural to man and his nature is basically good. Man's first rule, therefore, must be regard for his fellow man and the avoidance of any personal gain through harming others. This theme runs throughout Cicero's ethical writings, and is fundamental to Western humanism.

To conclude, Cicero stands about halfway between the secular humanist, who asserts that man can be truly good without adherence to a clearly defined religion, and those religious people who would deny this. He is concerned, as Grant says, 'first and foremost with men and he throws moral responsibility on man's shoulders, and he believes that man can make decisions without detailed interference by gods or Providence' (*Ibid.*: 13). His life's work, as he himself conceived it, was to help man fulfil this truly humanistic task and his influence on the development of humanism in the West has become second to none.

But there we must leave him and turn, briefly, to his older contemporary Lucretius.

If Cicero is the protagonist of the philosophy of the Academy and to a lesser extent of Stoicism, Lucretius is equally the chief protagonist, in the same Roman world, of Epicureanism. We have already had occasion to refer to his eulogy of Epicurus in our treatment of that philosopher. But although Lucretius' entire philosophy is derived from Epicurus, he has the distinction of being the only European writer who has ever put a philosophical system – as distinct from a theological one – into great poetry. He is also, when Epicureanism is revived in Europe by Gassendi in the seventeenth century, the medium by which that philosophy was reborn into the mainsteam of European thinking.

His poem *De Rerum Natura*, which he never finished, is a didactic poem in six books setting forth, in outline, a complete science of the universe, based upon the philosophies of Democritus and Epicurus. The overriding purpose of the work, however, was to prove, by investigating the nature of the world in which man found himself, that all things – including man – operate according to their own laws and are not in any way influenced by supernatural powers. Lucretius hoped thereby – as had Epicurus – to free both himself and all men from the yoke of religion and the fear of death.

The poem is arranged as follows:

Book I: The whole of nature is made up of eternal atoms moving in infinite space.

Book II: The entire world is made up of material substances formed through the joining together of these atoms.

Book III: Mind and spirit also arise from these same atoms – though from exceedingly subtle ones. At death the individual soul is dispersed as its imperishable atoms fly apart.

Book IV: Sensation, perception and thought are all produced by images, which are emitted by external surfaces.

Book V: The world, as we know it, was created by a fortuitous concourse of atoms.

Book VI: All natural phenomena can be explained according to this atomic theory.

This bare outline does little justice, of course, to a poem in which the scientific and philosophical argumentation often rises to magnificent heights of emotional power, intensified by an eloquent simplicity of diction and by Lucretius' overriding and passionate conviction that such a view of the universe can alone set men free.

> And now pay special attention to what follows and listen more intently. I am well aware how full it is of obscurity. But high

hope of fame has struck my heart with its sharp goad and in so doing has implanted in my breast the sweet love of the Muses. That is the spur that leads my spirit strength to pioneer through pathless tracts of their pierian realm where no foot has ever trod before. What joy it is to light upon virgin springs and drink their waters. What joy to pluck new flowers and gather for my brow a glorious garland from fields whose blossoms were never yet wreathed by the Muses round my head. This is my reward for teaching on these lofty topics, for struggling to loose men's minds from the tight knots of superstition.

O Joyless hearts of men! O minds without vision! How dark and dangerous the life in which this tiny span is lived away. Do you not see that nature is clamouring for two things only, a body free from pain, a mind released from worry and fear for the enjoyment of pleasurable sensations.

Can you doubt then that this power rests with reason alone? All life is a struggle in the dark. As children in blank darkness tremble and start at everything, so we in broad daylight are oppressed at times by fears as baseless as those horrors children imagine coming upon them in the dark. This dread and darkness of mind cannot be dispelled by the sunbeans, the shining shafts of day, but only by an understanding of the outward form and inner workings of nature. (*De Rerum Natura*, I. 921-935; II. 14-19; 55-63 [Lathan 1951])

Man, Lucretius believes, will become reconciled to life by the calm contemplation of law as it operates throughout the universe and by the realisation that he need fear no supernatural power and that all life ends in death.

Poor humanity, to saddle the gods with such responsibility and throw in a vindictive temper. What griefs they hatch for themselves, what festering sores for us, what tears for our prosperity! This is not piety, this oft repeated show of bowing a veiled head before a graven image; this bustling to every altar; this kow-towing and prostration on the ground with palms outspread before the shrines and the gods; this deluging of vow on vow. True piety lies rather in the power to contemplate the universe with a quiet mind. (*De Rerum Natura*, V. 1194-1203)

Tradition has it that Lucretius committed suicide in 55 BC, but there is no substance in the legend, relayed by Tennyson in his dramatic monologue Lucretius, that it was in a fit of insanity induced by a love potion given him by his wife!

5.3 THE EARLY EMPIRE

In *The Conflict of Religions in the Early Roman Empire* (1909) T.R. Glover, after noting the attempt of Augustus to restore the fortunes of Rome upon the basis of a revival of the state religion, wrote that

> an antiquarian interest in ritual is not inconsistent with indifference to religion ... so far as the literature of the last century BC and the stories current about the leading men of Rome allow us to judge, it is hard to suppose that there has ever been an age less interested in religion. (1909: 10)

'No society', Glover claims, 'could be more indifferent to what we call the religious life. In theory and practice, in character and instinct, they were thoroughly secular' (*Ibid.*). Cicero, for instance, wrote to his wife from his journey into exile on the 30th of April 58 BC that

> If these miseries are to be permanent, I only wish, my dearest, to see you as soon as possible and to die in your arms, since neither the gods whom you have worshipped with such pure devotion, nor men whom I have always served, have made us any return. (Cicero, *ad Fam.*, XIV. 4, 1 [Glover 1909: 10])

Horace, whose *Odes* only occasionally support the official restoration of religion, is every whit as secular minded. For the most part he laughs at superstition and ridicules the idea of a divine interest in men. Glover's judgement on him is that:

> No one was ever more thoroughly Epicurean in the truest sense of the word: no one ever urged more pleasantly the Epicurean theory *Carpe Diem*; no one ever had more deeply ingrained in him the belief *Mors ultima linea rerum est.* (1909: 10)

Yet if men were conscious of decay in the sanction which religion had once given to life there was still a good deal of vague religious feeling about as indeed the sociologists of religion tell us that there is today, in our own post-Christian society. This is borne out by the rise of the mystery religions and by the numbers who flocked to imported oriental cults and, a little later during this period, to the newly established Christian religion. Philosophy and ethics, which acted as a substitute religion, were for the few.

Direct statements about the gods and man's relationship to them are, however, rare during this period, and it would seem that the whole question was so remote from the central concerns of life that writers only spoke of the gods when they consciously assumed an orthodox air for political or aesthetic reasons. One significant pronouncement, therefore, is that of Pliny the Elder, for whom God and Nature are so closely assimilated that he can be considered a practical if not a theoretical atheist. Certainly his attitude to religion is indifferent, as the following quotation shows: He writes:

> I therefore deem it a sign of human weakness to ask about the shape or form of God. Whoever God is, if any other God [than the universe] exists at all, and in whatever part of the world he is, he is all perception, all sight, all hearing, all soul, all reason, all self. (*Natural History*, II.V.; cf. Rackham 1938: 178-9)

Pliny then passes in review the popular notions of the gods, dismissing them out of hand, with the single exception, of course, of the worship of the genius of the Emperors. Providence he does not acknowledge at all and his conclusion is that

> To imperfect human nature it is a special consolation that God

> also is not omnipotent [he can neither put himself to death, even if he would, though he has given man that power and it is choicest gift in this punishment which is life: nor can he give immortality to mortals or call the dead to life; nor can he bring it to pass that those who have lived have not lived, or that he who has held honourable offices did not hold them]; and that he has no power over the past than that of oblivion; and that [in order that we may also give a jesting proof of our partnership with God] he cannot bring it about that twice ten is not twenty, and more of the same sort – by all of which the power of Nature is clearly revealed, and that it is this we call God. (*Ibid.*; cf. Rackham: 187)

This is Stoic pantheism carried to its logical conclusion, and it is the position reached by the vast majority of educated Romans under the influence of Hellenistic philosophy at the beginning of the Christian era. Everything was thrown onto the individual will. As Glover writes:

> If the gods, as Seneca claims, lend a hand ... the climber has to make his own way by temperance and fortitude. The 'holy spirit within us' is after all hardly to be distinguished from conscience, intellect and will. God, says Epictetus, ordains that if you wish for good, get it for yourself. (*Discourses*, i, 29 [Glover 1909: 65])

Seneca utters a similar sentiment. 'What do you want with prayers?', he asks, 'make yourself happy' (*Epistles*, 31. 5 [Glover 1909: 66]).

The Stoicism of this period is thoroughly pantheistic. 'God', 'the gods', 'Zeus' are used interchangeably and are, more often than not, a merely poetic or rhetorical device, interchangeable, wherever they are used, by such terms as 'fate', 'nature' or 'the universe'. Stoicism thus fell between two stools. On the one hand it could not give support to traditional popular religion and on the other it did not have the resolution to dispense with it. It vacillated. Its greatest representative, the Emperor Marcus Aurelius, who lived in the second century of the Christian Era (121-180 AD) and who became Emperor in 161, exemplifies the agnosticism and practical atheism of the age to a marked degree. F.W. Myers, in fact, called this studious and solitary

Emperor 'the saint and exemplar of Agnosticism', and T. R. Glover says that 'he is a man who neither believes nor disbelieves – 'either gods or atoms' seems to be the necessary antithesis, and there is so much to be said for and against each of these alternatives that decision is impossible' (1909: 198).

The poets of the first two centuries of the Christian Era further exemplify the general mood of agnosticism and cynicism towards religion. Oenomas in his drama *The Swindlers Unmasked* violently attacks the oracles as a priestly fraud. Lucian regards religion as a fitting subject for his light satires. Some have compared him indeed to Voltaire, but he differs from that great Frenchman in having few principles and no purpose. His drama *Lover of Lies* takes the gods at their face value and reduces situations described in traditional religious stories to absurdity. Zeus, for instance, at one point most amicably allows him to watch him at work – hearing prayers as they come up through a speaking tube, settling some auguries and arranging the weather. His *Zeus Tragoedus* has a vignette where the gods are pictured sitting lazily around listening to a debate on earth concerning their existence – a debate which they finally settle with a liberal shower of thunderbolts.

Lucian is not to be dismissed, however, as some scholars are inclined to do, as a superficial thinker whose questions are lightly asked and lightly answered (cf. Glover 1909: 215). His dialogue *Hermotimus* – an abridged version of which was translated and incorporated by Walter Pater into his novel *Marius the Epicurean* – is a superb apology for Scepticism. Certainly here, as in the dramas aforementioned, we have playful irony, but behind this lies a sense of pathos and inner tragedy which are of the essence of Scepticism. No less a scholar than Edwyn Bevan once claimed that the 'edge of that light mockery bites as shrewdly, its arrows are as penetrating today ... as eighteen centuries ago' (1913: 138). Hermotimus is a man who has been searching unsuccessfully for the truth of life for well-nigh twenty years. He retains the hope that he might still find it in the next twenty years. His is the problem of pluralism – of the disagreements between the opposing schools; a problem indeed that many people feel acutely today. Which guide should he choose? And on what grounds?

His questions are certainly neither lightly asked nor can they be lightly dismissed, for they are the questions of us all.

A less palatable exponent of Scepticism is Sextus Empiricus – the last great thinker to merit our attention in this part of our study. He is the only representative of ancient Scepticism whose works have come down to us in anything like their complete form. He flourished about 200 AD, but little is known of his life, although it would seem that he was a Greek physician who had succeeded Heroditus as head of the school of medical empiricists and sceptics (hence his designation – Empiricus). His surviving works are three: *The Outlines of Pyrrhonism*, in three books; *Against the Dogmaticists*, in five books, the first two *Against the Logians*, and three and four *Against the Physicists*, the last *Against the Ethicists*; and *Against the Schoolmasters*, in six books – a book each *Against Grammarians, Rhetors, Geometers, Arithmeticians, Astrologers and Musicians*. Of these works the first, the *Outlines*, constitutes a summary of Scepticism, Book I stating and defending the Sceptical position and the remaining two books attacking Dogmatic positions. The other two books are often put together under the title *Adversus Mathematicos*, which Bury, in his Loeb Classical Library edition, construes as 'Against the Professors of all the Arts and Sciences'. They constitute a resumé and expansion of the argument of the second and third books of the *Outlines*. From our point of view, whilst of course the Sceptical position taken as a whole is important, it is the argument of the first section of Book I of *Against the Physicists* (Book IX of *Adversus Mathematicos*) which is entitled 'Concerning Gods', that is of prime interest.

Read along with Book III of Cicero's *De Natura Deorum* this section of *Adversus Mathematicos*, which does not always agree with Cicero's account, provides us with our most comprehensive survey of the debate concerning the existence of God and the gods in the ancient world. At the outset Sextus recognises the importance of the debate. He says:

> The doctrine concerning Gods certainly seems to the Dogmatic Philosophers to be most necessary. Hence they assert that 'phi-

> losophy is the practice of wisdom, and wisdom is the knowledge of things divine and human'. Accordingly if we shall establish the doubtfulness of the enquiry concerning Gods, we shall virtually have demonstrated that neither is wisdom the knowledge of divine and human things, nor philosophy by the practice of wisdom. (*Against the Physicists*, 1. 13-14 in Bury: 1936)

He then proceeds to pass in review those philosophers of the ancient world who offered a naturalistic theory of the origin of religion – Critias, Euhemerus, Prodicus of Ceos, Democritus, Aristotle and Epicurus. Although stating that they do not require refutation, he does in fact go on to refute them as inadequate. They do not, he says, explain how those who, according to these 'Dogmatic' philosophers, first put forward notions of the gods, got the concept, having no previous tradition to go on. This criticism is then applied in detail against each of theories which he had previously stated.

Sextus then passes to the question whether in fact the gods do actually exist, pointing out that 'not everything which is conceived partakes also in existence, but [that] it is possible for a thing to be conceived and not exist' (*ibid.*, 1.49). He adopts the by now classical Sceptic position, and asserts that:

> Perchance the Sceptic, as compared with philosophers of other views, will be found in a safer position, since in conformity with his ancestral customs and the laws, he declares that the Gods exist, and performs everything which contributes to their worship and veneration, but, so far as regards philosophic investigation, declines to commit himself rashly.

In true Sceptic fashion he proceeds to set forth the positions of both those who have asserted and those who have denied the existence of the gods. On the atheistic side he mentions Euhemerus – described by a quotation from Callimachus as 'a hoary braggard, penning wicked books', Diagoras of Melos, a disciple of Democritus (ca. 420 BC), Prodicus of Ceos, Theodorus of Cyrene (ca. 310 BC) and 'a host of others'. Diagoras we have not mentioned, but Sextus tells the delightful little story that he began as 'godfearing above all others', even beginning a poem 'By Heaven's will and Fortune all things are accomplished', but 'when he had been wronged by a man who had sworn falsely and suffered no punishment for it, he changed round and asserted that God does not exist' (*Ibid.*, 1.53).

The arguments for theism (or more strictly polytheism) he reduces to four – (1) the universal agreement of mankind; (2) from the orderly arrangement of the Universe; (3) from the absurd consequences which follow from the denial of deity and (4) criticism of the arguments for atheism.[5] To say that Sextus discusses these arguments would be to give his account a structure which it does not possess. What he actually does is to expound them as representing the best case that has been made for theism, occasionally adding an odd critical remark, before passing to a similar exposition of the arguments which have been adduced – mainly by Carneades – against theism. Rarely do the two cases come to grips with each other. In this respect his presentation is far less satisfactory than that of Cicero. With regard to the first argument, he does however essay the criticism that to decide truth by plebiscite, that is by reference either to the populace at large or even to the sharpest and cleverest among mankind – namely the poets and philosophers – would involve us in believing in the most patently absurd things. It is interesting also to note that in his exposition of the second argument – from the orderly arrangement of the universe – he begins by expounding a version of the Cosmological Argument which is almost word for word that which we find St. Thomas Aquinas in the thirteenth century putting forward as the first of his 'five ways' of establishing God's existence.[6] He has some interesting things to say also on the absurd consequences which some have held to follow on the denial of the gods, such as, 'If Gods do not exist, piety is non-existent, since piety is the science of serving the gods and there cannot be any service of that which is non-existent. But piety exists, so we must declare that the Gods exist' – a form of 'argument' first traditionally expounded by Zeno. Sextus in this instance mentions some counter arguments, drawing out the absurdities of this line of argument. For example: if the Gods exist they are animals – in the sense of being living beings. But if animals then they are possessed of sensation and if of sensation then of taste and so on, which leads him into an exposition of the sorites arguments of Carneades against the existence of the gods which we have considered earlier. He concludes that the only wise course for a Sceptic is to suspend judgement.

Sextus' presentation of the case against theism is by no means as strong as it might be – indeed Cotta makes a much better job of it in Cicero's *De Natura Deorum* with which Sextus must, surely, have been acquainted. His best argument, which he expounded in his brief discussion of the gods in the *Outlines of Pyrrhonism* is not reinvoked and goes unmentioned. It is, however, an argument of some force, for it concerns our attributing to that being, whom we alone can call God, the attributes of omnipotence, omniscience and goodness. As he says:

> He who affirms that God exists either declares that he has, or that he has not, forethought for the things of the universe, and in the former case that such forethought is for all things or for some things. But if he had forethought for all, there would have been nothing bad and no badness in the world; yet all things they say are full of badness; hence it shall not be said that God forethinks all things. If, again, he forethinks some, why does he forethink these things and not those? For either he has both the will and the power to forethink all things, or else he has the will but not the power, or the power but not the will, or neither the will nor the power. But if he had had both the will and the power he would have had forethought for all things; but for the reasons stated above he does not forethink all; therefore he has not the will and the power, to forethink all. And if he has the will and not the power, he is less strong than the cause which renders him unable to forethink what he does not forethink: but it is contrary to our notion of God that he should be weaker than anything. And if, again, he has the power but not the will to have forethought for all, he will be held to

> be malignant; while if he has neither the will nor the power, he is both malignant and weak – an impious thing to say about God. Therefore God has no forethought for the things in the universe. (*Outlines of Pyrrhonism* III, 9. 11 in Bury 1933)

Sextus' influence on Western thought is, however, not so much that of the anti-religious arguments which he records, as of the general Sceptical position which permeates the wholes corpus of his writings. Robert Flint says of them, in his monumental study *Agnosticism*, that 'all Greek Scepticism, all that was important in the most thorough and consistent development of agnosticism which has appeared in the world, seems to have been preserved in them' (95). Their influence was considerable and the Scepticism which was revived in Europe from about the beginning of the sixteenth century draws its inspiration, its principles, its method and its arguments from them. Montaigne and Sir Walter Raleigh quote extensively from Sextus, as did David Hume. His influence is still with us today.[7] We have seen, however, that Scepticism does not, on the whole, make for irreligion, but that, on the contrary, it acts rather as a conservative – some might even say a reactionary – force, encouraging conformity to the status quo. Established religion has little to fear, therefore, from such a philosophy.

5.4 CONCLUSION

This brings us to the end of our survey of irreligious developments during the classical period of Western culture. Four points stand out – all of them significant for the future development of Western thought consequent on the revival of classical learning after the European Renaissance of the fifteenth and sixteenth centuries.

In the first place, the near naturalistic understanding of events in the world and of the world-process itself, begun by the Ionian physical philosophers and brought to fruition in the ancient world by the Atomists, and which forms the subject of debate in the Socratic period, when taken together with the naturalistic approach to medicine of the Hippocratean authors and of history by Thucydides, is a form of understanding which will be revived and developed in Western Europe from the sixteenth century onwards. It is also not without contemporary interest, in that the issues which it raises for religion are still very much alive today. Much contemporary religious language is still mythological – unashamedly so – in that events in the world, both past and present, are interpreted in terms of a mixed, natural/supernatural language. The question is still, therefore, today as it was in ancient Greece and Rome, a question of whether events in the world are to be understood as resulting from natural causes only, or whether we can discern in events, and in the world process, divine activity and purpose. Traditional Judaeo-Christian faith, like the Stoicism which the Sceptics attacked, has answered this question in the affirmative. There is, it claims, divine purpose and providence in the world and some events are the outcome of direct divine intervention. The whole course of the development of our understanding of both the world and of history has, however, since the sixteenth century, been away from this response to the world. The origins of the alternative, naturalistic, non-mythological approach lie, as we have seen, in the Classical period of European thought. It is this period's most significant contribution to the development of irreligion.

The second point to emphasise is the growing moral criticism of traditional religion, begun by Xenophanes and continued by the dramatists and philosophers. Whilst this, to a large extent, leads to a purification of religion, in the hands of the Sceptics and Epicureans it can also lead to irreligion. This also will be the case in European thought, particularly in the eighteenth century.

Thirdly, we should note the growth of agnosticism, which reaches its zenith in the Sceptical school of Late Antiquity – the feeling, exemplified in Protagoras, that the subject matter of religion is too complex, human life too short, and opinion too divided, to admit of any firm conclusions on this matter. This too is a mood that will occur again and again in the Western tradition.

We should note, fourthly, the tendency of many in the Classical period to offer naturalistic accounts of the origin of religion. Some of these will be revived and new ones added at subsequent periods of Western thought.

We thus see that the Classical period, the period of the civilizations of Greece and Rome, is not one in which a religious approach to the world has it all its own way. Voices, powerful and insistent voices, which were to echo down the ages, are raised against the religious way of responding to the world and in some thinkers the full flowering of agnosticism and atheism can be found. On the other hand, what the vast majority of the populace thought we do not know, for they have left no memorial. If we have concentrated on the philosophers and poets only, it is not simply because their rejection or agnosticism with regard to religion is reasoned, and, therefore, still of interest to us, but rather because they alone have left us evidence of their thinking.

The closing of the pagan philosophical schools by the Christian emperor Justinian in 529 AD can be taken as marking the end of the speculative and often free-thinking period of Western thought. For almost a thousand years Western thinking will be dominated by the Christian understanding of reality. Not until the rise of heterodox Islamic thinkers in the eleventh and twelfth centuries will anything resembling the speculative intelligence of Greece reoccur. The contribution of Greece and Rome to the revival and development of Western speculation about religion from the twelfth century onwards is, however, such as to necessitate the kind of study upon which we have been engaged.

6

Appendix

6.1 ISRAEL AND THE ANCIENT NEAR EAST

6.1.1 *Ancient Israel*

The culture of the Hebrews represents one of the major tributaries from which what was to become Western culture derives. Whilst it goes without saying that Israel's most significant contribution has been to the religious life of Europe – though here that contribution has in the past been somewhat overemphasised, and cultural historians are now increasingly emphasising the contribution of both Classical Antiquity and of indigenous European cultures – a number of theologians and historians of ideas are today pointing to what one of them has termed 'the biblical sources of secularisation' (Cox 1968: 31).

Certainly within the general history of culture ancient Israel's outlook on the world presents certain unique features which make that outlook more akin to our own than to those highly mythologically inclined cultures we have so far considered. The recovery of the Hebraic world-view at the time of the Protestant Reformation did much, in fact, as is now widely recognised, to further the growth of the naturalistic outlook in Western Europe.

Israel also stands somewhat apart from the cultures we have considered in that there is nothing comparable in Hebraic culture to those naturalistic strains which we have found in ancient India, China, Greece and Rome. Israel's interest in nature and natural processes appears to have been minimal and her rejection of the older mythological response to the world was, as we shall see, based upon very different grounds from the rejection we have so far traced.

Perhaps the best way of bringing out the difference between Hebraic culture and the cultures we have so far considered is to compare the account(s) of the creation of the world which we find in the early chapters of *Genesis* with those found among Israel's neighbours – accounts which bear a remarkable similarity to those found in early India and in early Classical Antiquity. What emerges from such a comparison is that, whilst elements suggestive of the fact that at an earlier stage of Hebraic culture that culture was not very different from the culture of surrounding peoples remain, by the beginning of the first millenium BC a very different *Weltanschauung* is in the process of coming into being. Here, too, we can detect a rejection of the older mythological response to the world, but a very different rejection from that which we have traced elsewhere. Whereas in the cultures we have so far considered the rejection of the mythological outlook, in which man saw himself, the world and the gods as part of a single cosmological system, functioning as we sought in our introductory chapter to describe, was more often than not in the name of a naturalism which dispensed with the gods altogether, Hebraic culture rejected the older mythology by radically separating nature both from the transcendent god who created it and from man, whom it regarded simply as god's steward over his creation.

It is here that many contemporary theologians see the true beginnings of that desacralising of natural processes which they, together with a number of contemporary historians of science, regard as the necessary prelude to the growth of scientific naturalism. Hebraic culture refuses to see nature and natural processes as in any sense, of themselves, divine. In *Genesis*, for example, the sun, the moon and the stars are creations of the sole God Yahweh, hung in the sky, which is also his creation, to light the world for man. They certainly have no control over his life. None of the heavenly bodies, nor indeed anything in nature, can claim any right to religious awe or worship, for this belongs to Yahweh alone.

The Hebrew view of the world as created by Yahweh, and by Yahweh alone, and of man himself as similarly created and set over against nature as its steward, whilst it takes the Hebrews out of one mythological outlook implants them firmly, however, in another – something not always realised by these theologians who point, rightly, to the near naturalistic view of nature which we find among the ancient Israelites; a naturalistic view, however, which they never sought to develop.

If ancient Indian, Chinese and Graeco-Roman mythology is spatial – centred on a cyclical view of the cosmos – Hebraic mythology is centred on that peculiar view of time which emerges out of what was early believed to be, under Yahweh, the historic destiny of the Hebrew people. Yahweh had called his people out of Egypt, made a covenant with them at Sinai, given them a land previously belonging to others, and set them upon their historic mission – a mission, however, never fully articulated.

For the Hebrews, Yahweh – a transcendent supernatural being, perhaps the only supernatural being, but a supernatural being nevertheless – had spoken decisively not through natural phenomena, though, as the 'burning bush' episode in the Mosaic saga testifies, Yahweh was not above manifesting himself in natural phenomena, but through a historical event – the deliverance from Egypt. From that moment onwards, and according to Israel's own 'historians' even before that event in calling Abraham out of Sumerian civilization, Yahweh, as the Lord of History as well as of Creation, had acted and continued to act within the historical process with a purpose directed towards the nation of Israel, his 'Chosen People'. In the prophetic interpretation of history, which begins during the Davidic kingdom (about 1000 BC), all Near Eastern history is interpreted as occurring as it does relative to the nation of Israel. Yahweh raises up and brings low the great civilizations of Egypt, Assyria, Persia, Greece and Rome in order to chastise or redeem, as the case may be, his people Israel. This interaction of the divine and human in history (but often accompanied by an interference with natural processes as well) is still, however sophisticated and refined, essentially mythological, for the world process is still regarded as being admixed with supernatural forces even if, in the last resort, these are reductible to a single divine will. This was a view of history which Israel was to bequeath to the Christian Church and which was to remain a major factor in the European understanding of history until well into the eighteenth century. It is, in fact, still with us – in the Roman Catholic conception of its divine mission 'against which the gates of hell will not prevail', in Protestant notions of divine Providence, and in the Marxist transformation of it into the dialectical progress of history towards the establishment of a truly communistic society.

But it is not only in the Hebraic conception of history that the beginnings of the breakdown of the more traditional mythico-religious view of the world, found in almost all known cultures outwith Israel, can be seen. Secularization, as stated in the Preface to this present work, is not confined to the realm of thought – to man's understanding of the world process – but impinges upon his understanding of his social, economic and political life as well, and here too the beginnings of the outlook with which we are now so familiar can be found in Israel.

The nation itself begins with an act of insurrection, of civil disobedience, against the sacral king of Egypt whose relationship to the sun-god *Re* constituted his claim to political sovereignty and as such it can be said to mark the break, within the cultural traditions of mankind, of the sacral-political view of the established social order, although, as we have seen, Confucius' position with regard to the Chinese Emperor's inheriting the 'mandate of heaven', together with certain developments within Greek political theory, also mark a break with this ancient view. That it re-establishes itself in both Eastern and Western Christendom shows its persistence, and the fact that even today there are those within our own society who regard a man's station in life as that to which it has 'pleased God to call him' shows that ancient, mythological conceptions with regard to the social order are not yet a complete anachronism.

But for many in Israel, and for many since – one thinks of the English Puritans[1] – Israel's constitution as a nation, covenanted to Yahweh as its sole ruler, was taken to mean the deliverance of man from the sacral-political order into history and social change. There were many in Israel, and there have been many within Western Europe since, who have rejected kingship, and the stratified, hierachical social order which it symbolises, on the basis of Israel's constitution as a nation. The interplay within the Christian tradition, since the time of the Emperor Theodosius in the fourth century, between the mythological outlook which sees the social structure mirroring the order of the macrocosm, however differently this has been understood, and those who did not, has only finally been resolved in the democratic constitutions of our own day.

One other aspect of contemporary secularization which has its roots deep in our Hebraic past is the relativisation of all values. As the American theologian Harvey Cox has said: 'Both tribal man and secular man see the world from a particular, socially and historically conditioned point of view. But modern secular man knows it, and tribal man does not; therein lies the crucial difference' (1968: 44). The recognition that not only our clothes, our speech, our customs, but our values themselves — indeed our whole way of perceiving reality — is conditioned to a large extent by our cultural inheritance, upon which sociologists of knowledge lay so much emphasis today, begins, for Cox, with the Hebraic prohibition against 'graven images'. The enormous relevance of this prohibition, Cox argues, is often missed today. For ancient man, gods and value systems were the same thing. In forbidding his people to 'make unto themselves any graven images' Yahweh was in effect, forbidding them to worship anything constructed by themselves. The prophets of Israel did not deny the existence of the gods and their values, they merely relativised them as human projections, the work, as the writer of the latter part of what is known as the book of *Isaiah* said, of men's hands. In this he might be said to anticipate the attitude to religion of many contemporary social scientists, except that they would include his own God within the same category! It is because the ancient Hebrews believed in an utterly transcendent God that they were led to denigrate and relativise all human values and their representations. An utterly transcendent God, however, as the development of European thought from the late middle-ages onwards through to our own day shows, has the uncanny knack of becoming so utterly transcendent as to be no God at all — a situation which leaves man free to explore and experiment with the world, including the structure of human society, without any reference at all to divine interference (cf. Thrower 1971: 63 ff.). Israel, however, never reached this stage of development. The unutterably holy God was always there in the background; a judgement upon all and every human endeavour to instantiate his will in history and society and where necessary to move all too quickly from the background to the foreground to make his judgement the more effective! But the transcendalising of such a God was a necessary stage in the secularisation process. Without it, it is doubtful if we would have either science and the naturalistic outlook or the secular, social and political institutions which, to a varying degree, many of us enjoy today. But this is to anticipate developments in European thinking which fall outwith the scope of this present work. But as a contemporary theologian has said:

> The Hebraic prohibition against idolatry represents a deflation of man's natural inclination to deify himself, or his society, or the State, or his culture ... a relentless exposing of the manifold, constant proclivity to elevate the finite to the level of the infinite, to give the transitory the status of permanent, and to attribute to man qualities that will deceive him into denying his finitude. (Vahanian 1964: 24)

It is doubtful whether the ancient Hebrew would have articulated the second commandment quite like that, but the potentiality for such an interpretation is there – as subsequent history has shown.

6.1.2 *Hebraic Pessimism and Irreligion*

Whilst the Hebrews, unlike the Greeks, were not given to systematic thought about nature and the processes of nature and so never threw up, as did Greece, a naturalism which traces natural processes back to physical laws and principles thought of as uncreated, the existence of atheism does not pass unnoticed in Hebraic culture. 'The fool hath said in his heart, "There is no God"' (Psalm 53, v. 1). To whom this statement refers is now unknown, but that there were some in ancient Israel who, perhaps out of a questioning spirit and guided by their experience of life in this world – which until quite late in Hebrew culture was the only life there was – came to doubt the existence of Yahweh and his care towards them is certain. Although overt irreligion is well-nigh non-existent in Israel's culture as that culture, redacted by the official religion, has come down to us, there are some exceptions. They are to be found in what is now known as the Wisdom Literature – in the official canon, the books of *Proverbs, Job* and *Ecclesiastes.* Here we meet with a realm of discourse altogether different from anything else in ancient Judaism and they, in fact, bear unmistakably the influence of Egypt, Babylon and Greece. *Ecclesiastes* 9, v.4-5 which reads:

> For to him that is joined to all the living there is hope; for a living dog is better than a dead lion. For the living know that they shall die; but the dead know not anything, neither have they any more reward ...

is, for instance, very reminiscent of Epicurus. However, folk wisdom, much of which is enshrined in the Wisdom Literature, has its roots deep in Hebrew culture. Wisdom was the fruit of a tradition originally rooted in the mores of the family, tribe and local community and hence, to a degree, was as old as society itself. Right was the way of wisdom, wrong, the way of folly. Apt quotations of folk sayings occur throughout Israel's literature (cf. 1 Sam. 24, v13; Jer. 31, v29; Ezek. 18, v2) and the prophets Jeremiah and Ezekiel identify the wise man alongside the priest and the prophet as one of the three sources of authoritative guidance possessed by the community.

> The priest's *torah* [instruction] must not cease, nor the wise man's counsel, nor the prophet's message (Jer. 18, v18; Ezek. 7, v26)

The spokesmen of wisdom have little or nothing to say about the institutions of religion nor of the special relationship between Yahweh and his people. Rather they address, not collective Israel, but the individual man in his individuality and social relationships, and so constitute the nearest thing that we have to humanism in Israel. Unlike the priest and prophet, the wise men do not appeal to revelation but to experience. Their counsel has to do with how men ought to act in the work-a-day world, with personal character and with a way of life that is good because coherent, meaningful and valuable. Their authority lies in their own and the past communities' experience of life, taken together with a trained intelligence. Their method is that of instruction and, at a later stage of development, of persuasion and argument.

This is particularly evident in the *Book of Ecclesiastes*, known in Hebrew as *Qoheleth*. But evidence of a debate within Israel concerning God and his ways with men can also be found in *Proverbs* and of course in the *Book of Job*.

Proverbs 30, v.1-4 records the words of one who denied the possibility of man's knowledge of God – a denial which is answered, by sheer assertion, in verses 5-6 by a believer in revelation. The denial of the possiblity of religious knowledge is put into the mouth of one Agur who was a non-Israelite and his words are, of course, cited that they might be refuted. But such views must have had some currency in Israel for such refutation to have been thought necessary. The text is somewhat corrupt and the translation in the Authorised and Revised Standard Versions of the Bible is meaningless. The most convincing reconstruction is that put forward by R.B.Y. Scott in his recent book *The Way of Wisdom* (1971), and which reads as follows:

(v. 1) The words of Agur ben Yaqeh, of Massa',
The portentious saying of the man who has no God:
'I have no God, but I can' [face this *or* survive].
(v. 2) Surely I must be more brute than man,
and devoid of human understanding!
(v. 3) I have not learned 'wisdom',
nor have I knowledge of [any] holy Being.
(v. 4) Who has ascended the sky and assumed dominion?
Who has gathered up the wind in his cupped hands?
Who has wrapped the waters in his robe?
Who has fixed the limits of the world?
What is his name, and what is his son's name?
As if you knew!

And the rejoiner:

(v. 5) All that God says has stood the test;
he is a shield to those who take refuge with him.
(v. 6) Do not add to his words, lest he correct you
and you may be exposed as a liar.
(1971: 166-170)

Thus, if we accept Scott's reconstruction of the text, we have one further reference to put alongside the reference in the *Psalms* to 'the fool' who said 'There is no God.'

The Book of *Qoheleth*, or *Ecclesiastes*, like the words of Agur, sets forth a view of life diametrically opposed to the official religion of Israel, with its belief in Yahweh having chosen Israel as his special people and having made known to them his will. Like Agur, the Book of *Qoheleth* states that man cannot attain to knowledge of God either by wisdom or revelation. A significant difference, however, is that whilst the words of Agur in *Proverbs* are countered by a positive statement of belief, no such qualification – with the exception of one or two maginal comments and a final cautionary footnote, both added to the text by later redactors – can be found in the latter book.

The author is no atheist. He explicitly affirms both the existence, and indeed the power of God as the presupposition of his agnostic, fatalistic philosophy. He even encourages participation in the religious ceremonies of the community 'in order to learn'. What God is, however, remains mysterious. What he requires of man, if anything, is not known. All that men can do is to use their powers of observation, reflect upon experience and accept what cannot be alterred. All their efforts are of little avail. The same fate ultimately overtakes man and beast, the righteous and the unrighteous. In the face of death, what human values remain?

Not surprisingly apologists have been hard put to justify and explain the inclusion of this sceptical, pessimistic and fatalistic work in the Canon of Sacred Scripture. G. A. Barton, in his commentary on *Ecclesiastes* in the International Critical Commentary Series, follows the line first taken by Gregory Thaumaturgus, the third century Christian writer, who saw *Ecclesiastes* as teaching the vanity of all earthly affairs – a necessary prelude for Gregory to the beginning of the contemplative life. Scott's comment on this line of hermeneutic is very apposit. He says that if this is so, then one can only remark that it seems a remarkable example of the indirect method! (*Ibid.*, 171).

His own explanation is more to the point. For Scott, the true explanation is historical, in that *Ecclesiastes* had approved itself, in the time which had elapsed from its compilation to the making of the canon, to such an extent in the life of the community that it could not be excluded – a fact that tells us much about Israelite attitudes to life at this time, the period of late, pre-Christian Judaism. Thus, despite considerable opposition in some official circles – the school of Shammai, for example, opposed its inclusion – it was included in the Jewish canon towards the end of the first century of the Christian era and passed eventually into the Christian canon to excise its influence on the West.

The book itself appealed, no doubt, to thoughtful Jews at a time when Judaism, following upon Alexander's conquest, was becoming acquainted with foreign and more particularly Greek ideas. The likely time of its composition was, therefore, during the latter part of the third century BC (Anderson 1959: 200).

Though with considerably more structure than, say, *Proverbs*, *Ecclesiastes*, as is to be expected from what is probably no more than a collection of teacher's sayings, possesses no overall unity other than its general mood of sceptical pessimism. Speaking very generally, the first six chapters set forth the philosophy of the 'teacher' and the last six his ethical conclusions and counsel. Encasing the whole is the famous amphorism 'Vanity of vanities, all is vanity', which opens and closes the 'teacher's' words. It is a succinct summary of his philosophical outlook and it is accompanied by arguments and illustrations followed by counsel on the attitudes and behaviour which the 'teacher' believes to be appropriate to such an outlook on life.

Six themes predominate: (1) philosophical statements which bear on the overall thesis; (2) evidence drawn from general observation; (3) evidence drawn from the 'teacher's' own experience; (4) supporting evidence from folk sayings acknowledged as authoritative; (5) direct admonitions and precepts with supporting arguments and illustrations, and (6) indirect admonitions through proverbs, illustrations and comments (Scott 1971: 174-175).

With these schemes – drawn from R. B.Y. Scott – in mind, let us now outline the progression of the book and state its main teachings.

1:2	The thesis that all that man sees, knows and does is vain, empty and ephemeral (1)
1:3-11	Effort is useless, nothing is changed, nothing is new (2)
1:12-18	The search for wisdom is frustrating (3)
2:1-11	The search for pleasure brings no lasting satisfaction (3)
2:12-17	The superiority of wisdom over folly is cancelled by death – the common fate (3)
2:18-23	Work and achievement are ultimately futile (3)
2:24-26	The only good is present enjoyment – and this comes only when and if God wills (1, 2, 3)
3: 1-8	Everything must happen at its appropriate time (1)
3: 9-15	God determines what happens and man can neither change nor understand his fate (1, 3)
3: 16-4: 3	Injustice and oppression show that men are no more than animals (1, 3)
4: 4-8	Work and ambition are fruitless (1, 2, 3)
4: 9-12	Friendship, however, mitigates, though it also emphasises, man's helplessness (6)
4: 13-16	Power and position are ephemeral (1, 3)
5: 1-7	Be circumspect in religious observation (5)
5: 8-9	Do not yield to anger at injustice, rather reflect on its outcome (5)
5:10-6: 9	The struggle for wealth is futile; such happiness as God permits is to be relished; wealth, honour, and a long life are worthless without contentment (1, 2, 3, 6)
6: 10-12	Fate governs all and is incomprehensible
7: 1-22	See life in perspective and behave with moderation (5, 6)
7: 23-8: 1	Wisdom is indefinable except in contrast with folly; all women and most men are fools (1, 3)
8: 2-9	Do not challenge irresistible powers (1, 2, 3, 5)

8:10-9:12	Men are rewarded not according to their moral behaviour but suffer a common fate; God's ways are inscrutable; happiness is incidental and to be enjoyed gratefully (1, 2, 3, 4, 5)
9:13-10:1	Wisdom is only valuable when applied and can be counteracted by folly (3, 4, 6)
10:2-11:6	Miscellaneous reflections and admonitions (2, 3, 5, 6)
11:7-10	The positive worth of youth and life (5, 6)
12:1-8	An admonition to reflect followed by a metaphorical poem on the swift approach of death (5, 6)

This bare outline of *Ecclesiastes* throws into sharp relief the pessimistic and negative philosophy for the 'teacher', which is so out of keeping with the overall Hebraic approach to life. This difference is in large part due to *Ecclesiastes* being a philosophical work, motivated by a search for an understanding of human experience through the application of reason. Revelation is excluded and reason's verdict on the human condition is that there is no meaning to human life beyond the momentary enjoyment of pleasure. Youth, therefore, is to be especially prized. Whether or not, outwith this work, the 'teacher' accepted the orthodox Hebraic understanding of life derived from Revelation we do not know – but a reading of his sayings as preserved in *Ecclesiastes* would suggest not.

Although Greek influence is strong[2] it is not predominant – the teacher's own experience of life and that of the community in which he lives is sufficient. His deepest roots, as we shall see shortly, are however in the scepticism and pessimism native to one strain in the thought of the Ancient Near East and also in the Hebraic tendency, to which we have referred, to so exhalt the transcendent God above his creation that he becomes mysterious and inscutable to a degree that leads inevitably to practical atheism.

If this pessimistic, fatalistic outlook on life were all that there was to *Ecclesiastes* it would be hard to understand how, along with the rest of the Wisdom Literature, it has been thought to express what is called the 'humanism of Israel' (Rankin, 1936). It is not unknown, of course, for modern Humanists to express sentiments similar to those of the 'teacher' in *Ecclesiastes* – H. G. Well's *Mind at the End of its Tether* and H. J. Blackham's paper, 'The Pointlessness Of It All' (in Blackham, 1963) are cases in point, but Humanists are usually more positive in their approach to life – as indeed overall were Wells and Blackham – and so is the 'teacher'. Far from suggesting the rejection of life, let alone self-destruction, he affirms life in spite of everything:

> Sweet is the light of day, and it is good to see the sunshine with one's eyes. If a man live many years, let him be happy in them all. (*Ecclesiastes*, 11: 7-8)

'Beyond Despair' might thus be an alternative title for his book, for in the latter chapters the author passes from agnosticism and pessimism to positive ethical affirmation. He tells us that he was indeed driven, for a time, to despair, the more so after the failure of his experiment with pleasure and of his attempt to justify rationally the superiority of wisdom over folly.

> So I came [he says] to hate life, because it depressed me that all man's activities under the sun are only a breath and a clutching at the wind. (*Ecclesiastes*, 2: 17)

But after all, he goes on to ask himself, why should a man think he is wise enough and good enough to be autonomous and self-sufficient? Within the limits of his knowledge, ability, circumstances and brief life-span he does have relative freedom. He can, at least, choose to be as wise as he can rather than an utter fool. He can learn to live within the limitations life imposes and, above all, he can enjoy good fortune if and when it comes. He can relish the satisfactions and joys of life even whilst he knows that he cannot count on them. The good to be had is more than enough to make life worth living. His counsel to the young is, therefore, to revel in the days of their vigour, to think for themselves, to face up to the facts of life's uncertainties and perplexities, to accept their contingency, and to abandon commonly accepted beliefs which will not stand up under examination, such as that virtue is always rewarded and vice always punished. Happiness comes unawares and we must watch and wait and then seize the moment and enjoy it. Further, the inevitable must be accepted and life lived with what cannot be changed. Man has no choice but to accept the crooked with the straight and death ends all. There are, however, compensations – life, especially when young, can be joyous and one should savour such joys while they last, for he who does not savour present joys will live to regret that it has passed unnoticed:

> Better a joy at hand than a longing for distant pleasures. (*Ecclesiastes*, 6: 9)

and again:

> So then, eat your bread with cheerfulness and drink your wine with a glad heart .... At all times let your clothing be white, and perfumed oil on your head not be lacking. Enjoy life with the woman you love all the fleeting days that God grants you under the sun, for it is your rightful portion .... Everything your hand finds to do, do with all your full strength, for there is no doing or thinking, knowledge or wisdom in Sheol whither you are bound. (*Ecclesiastes*, 9: 7-10)

– words highly reminiscent of those from the Babylonian *Epic of Gilgamesh* that we shall give in our next section. The words, also, of a true humanist, and appropriate ones with which to conclude our brief look at the minimal irreligious strain in Hebraic culture.

6.2 BABYLON

The world-weariness which we find in the Book of *Ecclesiastes* is not confined to Israel. Centuries before the Persian poet Omar Khyam gave near definitive expression to such pessimism, many in the ancient world gave eloquent utterance to the feeling that life here and now, and such enjoyment as can be snatched from it, is the most that a man may hope for. We have quoted already the unknown Indian poet who wrote:

> While life is yours, live joyously;
> None can escape Death's searching eye:
> When once this frame of ours they burn,
> How shall it e'er return?
> (Quoted by Mhadavacarya in his *Śarva-saṃgraha darśana*)

Similarly in ancient Babylon we find this moving testimony to the transience of life in the *Epic of Gilgamesh* composed as early as the beginning of the second millenium BC:

> Gilgamesh, whither are you wandering?
> Life which you look for, you will never find.
> For when the gods created man, they let
> death be his share, and life
> withheld in their own hands.
> Gilgamesh, fill your belly –
> day and night make merry,
> let days be full of joy,
> dance and make music day and night.
> And wear fresh clothes,
> and wash your head and bathe.
> Look at the child who is holding your hand,
> and let your wife delight in your embrace.
> These things alone are the concern of men.
> (Frankfort 1949: 226)

As Mesopotamean civilization drew to its close towards the middle of the first millenium BC, scepticism, doubt and indifference began to undermine the spiritual structure of that civilization – scepticism such as found expression, for instance, in the long dialogue between a master and his slave known as the *Dialogue of Pessimism.*

The structure of this dialogue is simple. The master proposes to his slave that he intends to do such and such. The slave encourages him by enumerating the pleasures which will acrue from his so doing, though by this time the master has changed his mind and states that he will no longer do as he originally intended, whereupon the slave then enumerates all the unpleasant consequences that would have resulted had the master followed out his original intention. Thus there are passed in review all the activities of a Mesopotamian nobleman and all are found wanting. There is nothing which is inherently good and worthwhile. Love, for example, is dismissed as follows:

> 'Servant, agree with me!' 'Yes, my lord, yes!'
> 'I will love a woman!' 'So love, my lord, love!
> The man who loves a woman forgets want and misery!'
> 'No, slave, I will not love a woman!'
> 'Love not, my lord, love not!
> Woman is a snare, a trap, a pitfall;
> woman is a sharpened iron sword
> which will cut a young man's neck!
> (Langdon 1923: 35-66)

The nearest thing to anti-religious sentiments that we find occur in the dismissal of piety. The dialogue runs as follows:

> 'Slave agree with me!' 'Yes, my lord, yes!'
> 'Straightway order me water for my hands,
> and bring it hither. I will make a libation to my god!'
> 'Do, my lord do! As for the man who makes a libation
> to his god, his heart is at ease;
> he makes loan upon loan!'
> 'No, slave, I will not make a libation to my god!'
> 'Make it not, my lord, make it not!
> Teach the god to run after thee like a dog
> and when he demands, be it "my service", be it "thou hast
> not asked," be it anything else from thee.'
> (Langdon 1923: 67-81)

We have also from Babylonian culture a number of compositions dealing with the ethical and theological problem of the suffering of the innocent, and indeed it may well be that Babylonian thinkers were the first to raise this question – a question which has played a very large part in the critique of theistic religion from their time to our own. Lambert quotes from a Sumero-Babylonian text which states:

> I have been treated [by life], as one who has committed a sin against a god.
> (1960: 10-11)

Lambert further notes the recurrence in this text of the name *Mina-arni*, which means 'What is my guilt?' – a question of life which Franz Kafka was to ask so articulately in his novel *The Trial*.

Two further treatments of this theme can be found in documents from the Cassite period (1500-1200 BC) of Babylonian culture. The first, known from its opening lines as *I Will Praise the Lord of Wisdom* (*Ibid.*, 21-62), tells how the sufferer feels that he has been forsaken by both the gods and men, how he has been afflicted with dreadful diseases, and how he can find no answer in prayers and sacrifices. Yet, like Job, our questioner ends his complaint by praising the inscrutable god for his mercies towards him! The second document, often called *The Babylonian Theodicy* (Lambert 1960: 63-91), also bears a remarkable resemblance to the debate about Yahweh's ways with men which we find in the book of *Job*. Like Job, the sufferer in this Babylonian work is desperate and without hope. Like Job he cries out for some answer as to the cause of his misery and yet again, like Job, he ends by pleading for divine mercy and forgiveness. Rebellion against traditional religious teaching is, however, beginning.

6.3 EGYPT

6.3.1 *Ancient Egypt*

Ancient Egypt too is certainly not without its free speculative spirits. Alongside a conservative tradition of wisdom literature, which seeks to pass on the moral norms of the ancient social tradition, we have a more intellectual and speculative tradition which questions traditional values and beliefs and which at least toys with the possibility of an alternative mode of existence.

There is little, however, with the possible exception of ancient Egyptian medical practice, to correspond in Egypt with those movements towards a systematic naturalistic interpretation of life such as we have seen developing in ancient India, China and Greece. *Ma'at*, the Egyptian conception of an order of truth, justice and goodness underlying the world-process, never becomes depersonalised, for instance, as did conceptions of *Ṛta*, *Tao* and *Moira* among the ancient Indians, Chinese and Greeks. It was, throughout Egyptian culture, continuously thought of as a divine reality creating and upholding the *cosmos* and the world of men. Such determinism as emerges in ancient Egypt is similarly linked continually, as in other religiously dominated cultures, with the will of a god or gods.

In the upset which followed upon the collapse of the monarchy and of the Old Kingdom, and which was brought about by the ever-growing decentralisation of government, in 3335 BC, documents which have survived show that many at this time found only the negative answers to life's problems of scepticism and despair. Some turned to suicide. One of the finest texts of ancient Egyptian literature comes from this period and records a debate of a would-be suicide with his *ka* or soul. The *ka*, which according to traditional teaching should have helped guide him through life, wavers and can offer no satisfactory answer to his melancholic determination to have done with this life. What the *ka* advises is that the man forget his cares and that he seek for sensual enjoyment in the immediate present. The *ka* does, however, after the man has contrasted the misery of life on earth with the possible sober pleasures of the world after death, agree to make a home with him come what may. It would appear that at this time there was no answer in Egypt to the problems of life except that this world is so bad that the next must be a release.

The verses which urge on the man the ephemeral enjoyments of this world express an age-old Hedonism and are, in fact, the earliest recorded instance of such a response to life. They read as follows:

> Generations pass away and others go on since the
> time of the ancestors .... They that built buildings,
> their places are no more. What has been done with them?
>
> I have heard the words [of past sages] Imhotep and
> Hardedef, with whose sayings men speak so much –
> but what are their places [now]? Their walls are
> crumbled, their places non-existent, as if they had
> never been.
>
> No one returns from [over] there, so that he might
> tell us how they are, that he might still our hearts
> until we [too] shall go to the place where they have gone.
>
> Since that wisdom which was so highly prized in the
> earlier age has not guaranteed for the wise a visible
> survival in well-kept tombs, and since it is
> impossible to tell how the dead fare in the other world,
> What is left for us here? Nothing, except to snatch at
> the sensual pleasures of the day.
>
> Make a holiday and weary not therein! Behold, it is
> not given to a man to take his property with him.
> Behold, no one who goes [over there] can come back again.
> (Frankfort 1949: 114-115)

This is a response to life which we have seen emerging in almost all of the cultures we have considered. It is found again in ancient Egypt in the well-known *Song of the Harper* about the beginning of the second millenium:

> Make a good day, O holy father!
> Let odours and oils stand before thy nostril!
> Wreaths of lotus are on the arms and bosom of thy sister,
> Dwelling in thy heart, sitting beside thee.
> Let song and music be before thy face,
> And leave behind these evil cares!
> Mind thee of joy till cometh the day of pilgrimage
> When we draw near the land which loveth silence.
> [Stern]

6.3.2 *Egyptian Medical Practice and the Beginnings of Naturalism*

There is one area of Egyptian thought, however, where naturalistic tendencies are particularly strong and where some have seen the beginnings of a break with the magico-religious understanding of life and the development of a scientific and empirical naturalism, and that is in Egyptian medicine. Unfortunately, our knowledge of Egyptian medical practice, though considerable for one particular period — the Renaissance following upon the explusion of the Hyksos about the sixteenth century BC — is not sufficient for us to trace, with any degree of accuracy, its chronological development, and certainly not to argue, as some have been tempted to argue, for a simple progression from a magico-religious approach to a scientific, naturalistic one.[3] In all the medical papyri — with one important exception — magic, religion and empirical, naturalistic approaches are admixed. The problem is compounded by the fact that the one exception — the *Edwin Smith Papyrus*[4] — where objective, scientific medicine predominates, comes from exactly the same period as do those other papyri where magic, religion and proto-scientific medicine are admixed. The most that this papyrus can suggest is that in the minds of some ancient Egyptian practitioners of the art of medicine, 'objective and scientific medicine, devoid of theories and of magic ...

and based upon the attentive and repeated observation of the patient, on bedside experience, and on a hitherto unsuspected knowledge of anatomy' – to quote Ghalioungui's description of this papyrus – predominated (1963: 58).[5]

This conclusion is reinforced by the fact that the *Ebers Papyrus*, which bears the date of the ninth year of the reign of Amenophis I (1550 BC) and so comes from about the same period as the *Edwin Smith Papyrus*, though it opens with an introduction aimed to reassure its users of its divine origin, and attributes many of its prescriptions to the gods, does not in the prescriptions themselves refer at all to prayers and magic-religious formulae. As Ghalioungui says:

> Whereas ... previous papyri are mainly collections of prescriptions, the 877 paragraphs of this compilation contain, besides the therapeutic recipes, diagnostic notes ... for the first time in history, theoretical considerations on the problems of life, health and disease devoid of religious or magical considerations. (1963: 51)

A similar admixture of magico-religious with objective, scientific practice can be observed in European medicine up to and including the present day. The ultimately strategic significance of medicine in the growth of irreligion in Europe I have argued elsewhere (Thrower 1976a) and certainly, as we have noted, Greek medicine, influenced as many believe by the practices of ancient Egypt, was a not inconsiderable factor in the ongoing progress of naturalism in that culture.[6] Ancient Egyptian medicine, if perhaps at second-hand, did, therefore, play its part in furthering the break, in a very important sphere of life, with the magico-religious understanding.

Postscript

We have now come to the end of our survey of the criticism of religion in the ancient world and it behoves us to cast our minds back, briefly, over the ground we have surveyed and to see what, if anything, might be concluded from our enquiry.

The earliest recorded critical response to a religious interpretation of life is the cry *carpe diem* – a cry which is, I suspect, more subversive of living religion than any and all theoretical critiques. It is one that continues throughout history.

Theoretical criticism begins, certainly in ancient India and ancient Greece, and to a more limited extent in ancient China, with a critique of traditional polytheism and of the traditional mythico-religious response to which it is allied, and which sees the world as admixed with personalised, supernatural forces. Such a critique is also, more often than not, combined with positive speculation into the origin of the world and into natural processes. It is here, I would maintain, that we see the first glimmerings of the alternative tradition – that tradition which, as more and more areas of our understanding of the world and of man come to be interpreted without reference to religion, and which I have called naturalism, finally reaches fruition in our own day.

Whilst, in the ancient world, the growth of this tradition is fitful and stunted, and the critique of established religion leads, on the whole, towards more refined and more sophisticated (if attenuated) forms of religion, there have been movements which, within the limitations of their time, have produced near-systematic naturalistic interpretations of the world. This, as we have seen, was the case in India, China and Greece.

Further, such movements have often come to the same conclusions with regard to living as those put forward by the pessimistic poets, in that they have recommended some form of hedonism – not necessarily crude – as the only sensible form of life in this, often tragic, world. Rarely, however, in the ancient world is such an outlook on life combined with a determination to alleviate the lot of one's fellow sufferers. Social concern is not something that we find to the fore in the ancient world. Only when men break with an understanding of life which sees man's destiny lying beyond history, or cease to look for divine intervention to put things to right, would it seem at all possible to contemplate changing this world. Some words of Karl Marx are apposite, I feel, at this point. They were written at the outset of his revolutionary career:

> Criticism has plucked the imaginary flowers from the chain not so that man will wear the chain without any fantasy or consolation but so that he will shake off the chain and cull the living flower. The criticism of religion disillusions man to make him think and act and shape his reality like a man who has been disillusioned and has come to reason, so that he will revolve round himself and therefore round his true sun .... The task of history, therefore, once the world *beyond the truth* has disappeared, is to establish the truth of this world. The immediate *task of philosophy*, which is at the service of history, once the *saintly form* of human self-alienation has been unmasked, is to unmask self-alienation in its unholy forms. Thus the critique of heaven turns into the critique of earth. (Marx 1975- , Vol. 3: 176)

It is in nineteenth century Europe that we find the rejection of religion issuing in passionate effort to change this world into a world where all might find – if only temporary – fulfilment. The prelude to this passionate concern with life in this world, however, is the growth of that alternative tradition whose beginnings I have sought to chart and which, from about the time of the eighteenth century European *Aufklärung*, began to oust the mythico-religious understanding of reality – however sophisticated – from the dominance it had hitherto enjoyed. That process, needless to say, is not, as yet, complete.

Bibliography

Allchin, Bridget and Allchin, Raymond (1968), *The Birth of Indian Civilization*. London, Penguin Books.

Anderson, G.W. (1959), *A Critical Introduction to the Old Testment*. London, Lutterworth Press.

Aquinas, Thomas, *Summa Theologica*.

Aristophanes, see under Rogers.

Aristotle, see under W. D. Ross, and J. A. K. Thompson.

Armstrong, A. H. (1965), *Introduction to Ancient Philosophy*. London, Methuen.

Augustine, *Confessions*.

Bacon, Francis, *Essays*.

Bailey, D. Shackleton (ed.) (1965-1970), *Cicero: Letters to Atticus* (Cambridge Classical Texts and Commentaries), 7 vols. Cambridge, Cambridge University Press.

Baillie, John (1962), *The Sense of the Presence of God*. London, Oxford University Press.

Ballantyne, J. R. (ed. and trans.) (1885), *The Sāṇkhya Aphorisms of Kapila*, 3rd. edition. London, Trübner Oriental Series.

Banergee, Sarat Chandra (1909), *The Sāṇkhya Philosophy*. Calcutta.

Basham, A. L. (1951), *History and Doctrines of the Ājīvikas*. London, Luzac & Co.

— (1954), *The Wonder that was India*. London, Sidgwick and Jackson.

Barton, G. A. (ed.) (1908), *Ecclesiastes* (International Critical Commentaries). Edinburgh, T. and T. Clark.

Bary, William Theodore de (ed.) (1960), *Sources of the Chinese Tradition*, 2 vols. London, Columbia University Press.

— (1964), *Sources of the Indian Tradition*, 2 vols. London, Columbia University Press.

Beattie, John (1964), *Other Cultures*. London, Routledge & Kegan Paul.
Belvalkar, S.K. and Renade, R.D. (1926), *History of Indian Philosophy*, Vol. 2. Poona.
Berger, Peter (1969), *The Social Reality of Religion*. London, Faber & Faber.
Bevan, E.R. (1913), *Stoics and Sceptics*. Oxford, Clarendon Press.
Blackham, H.J. (ed.) (1963), *Objections to Humanism*. London, Penguin Books.
—(1968), *Humanism*. London, Penguin Books.
Bouquet, A.C. (1956), *Comparative Religion*. London, Penguin Books.
—(1966), *Hinduism*. London, Hutchinson.
Bowra, C.M. (1959), *The Greek Experience*. New York, Mentor Books.
Braithwaite, R. (1955), *An Empiricist's View of the Nature of Religious Belief*. Cambridge, Cambridge University Press.
Brandon, S.G. (ed.) (1970), *Dictionary of Comparative Religion*. London, Weidenfield & Nicolson.
Buber, Martin (1937), *I and Thou*. Edinburgh, T. and T. Clark.
Bühler, G. (ed. and trans.) (1886), *The Laws of Manu* (Sacred Books of the East, Vol. XXV). Oxford, Clarendon Press.
Bultmann, Rudolf (1960), *Jesus Christ and Mythology*. London, SCM Press.
Burnet, John (1914), *Greek Philosophy*. London, Macmillan.
—(1930), *Early Greek Philosophy*, 4th edition. London, A. and C. Black.
Bury, R.G. (ed. and trans.) (1933-1949), *Works of Sextus Empiricus* (Vol. 1, 1933; Vol. 2, 1935; Vol. 3, 1936; Vol. 4, 1949). London, Heinemann.
Chan Wing-Tsit (ed.) (1963), *A Source Book of Chinese Philosophy*. Princeton N.J., Princeton University Press.
Chattopadhyaya, D. (1959), *Lokayata: a Study in Ancient Indian Materialism*. New Delhi, Peoples' Publishing House.
—(1969), *Indian Atheism*. Calcutta, Manisha Granthabya.
Cicero, see under Bailey, Grant, and McGregor.

Clement of Alexandria, see *Patrologia Graecia*, ed. by J.-P. Migne, Vols. 8 and 9. Paris, 1857- .

Colebrooke, H.T. (ed.) (1873), *The Sāṉkhya Karika.* Oxford, Clarendon Press.

—(1873), *Miscellaneous Essays*, Vol. 1. London, W.H. Allen & Co.

Copleston, F. (1962), *History of Philosophy*. Vol. 1, pt. 1: Greece and Rome. New York, Image Books.

Cornford, F.M. (1952), *Principium Sapientae.* Cambridge, Cambridge University Press.

—(1957), *From Religion to Philosophy*. New York, Harper.

Coulson, Charles (1958), *Science and Christian Belief*. London, Collins.

Couvreur, F.S. (1951), *Texte chinois avec traduction française*, 3 vols. Paris, Belles Lettres.

Cowell, E.B. (1862), 'The Charvaka system', *Journal of Asiatic Society of Bengal*, Vol. 31.

Cox, Harvey (1968), *The Secular City*. London, Penguin Books.

Creel, H.G. (1953), *Chinese Thought from Confucius to Mao Tsetung*. Chicago, University of Chicago Press.

Dasgupta, S.N. (1923-1940), *History of Indian Philosophy* (Vol. 1, 1923; Vol. 2, 1932; Vol. 3, 1940). Cambridge, Cambridge University Press.

Daumas, F. (1956), in *Journal des savants* (Paris), octobre-décembre, 1956.

Davids, T.W.R. Rhys (1889, 1910, 1921), *Dialogues of the Buddha* (Sacred Books of the East), Vols. I, II and III. Oxford, Clarendon Press.

Dickinson, G. Lowes (1941), *The Greek View of Life*. London, Methuen.

Diels, H. (1934-1954), *Die Fragmente der Vorsokratiker*, (Ed. by W. Kranz). Berlin.

Douglas, Mary (1966), *Purity and Danger*. London, Routledge & Kegan Paul.

Drachmann, A.B. (1922), *Atheism in Pagan Antiquity*. Copenhagen, Gyldendal.

Dubs, H.H. (1946), 'Han Yu and the Buddha's relic: an episode in

medieval Chinese religion', *Review of Religions*, Vol. 5.
Dutt, M. N. (ed. and trans.) (1906-1912), *Rigveda: Texts with Sayana's Commentary, and a Literal Prose Translation*, 4 vols. Calcutta, R. P. Mitra.
—(1953), *The Ramayana and the Mahabharata*. London. Dent (Everyman Library).
Eliade, Mircea (1960), *Myths, Dreams and Mysteries*. London, Collins.
—(1964), *Myth and Reality*. London, George Allen & Unwin.
Epicurus, see under Usener.
Evans-Pritchard, E. E. (1934), 'Levy-Bruhl's theory of primitive mentality', *Bulletin of the Faculty of Arts, Cairo*, Vol. 2, part 1.
—(1937), *Witchcraft, Oracles and Magic among the Azande*. Oxford, Clarendon Press.
—(1965), *Theories of Primitive Religion*. Oxford, Clarendon Press.
Faddigon, B. (1918), *The Vaiçesika System*. Amsterdam, K. Muller.
Farrington, Benjamin (1961), *Greek Science*. London, Penguin Books.
Forke, A. (1907-1911), *The Lu Hêng: Philosophical Essays of Wang Ch'ung*, 2 vols. London, Luzac.
—(1938), *Geschichte der mittelalterlichen chinesischen Philosophie*. Hamburg, De Gruyter.
Frankfort, Henri (ed.) (1949), *Before Philosophy: The Intellectual Adventures of Ancient Man*. London, Penguin Books.
Frazer, James (1927), *The Gorgon's Head*. London, Macmillan.
Freeman, K. (1946), *Companion to the Pre-Socratic Philosophers*. Oxford, Clarendon Press.
—(1948), *Ancilla to the Pre-Socratic Philosophers*. Oxford, Clarendon Press.
Fung, Yu-Lan (1951), 'Mao Tsê-Tung's "On Practice" and China's Philosophy', *Peoples' China*, Vol. 4, No. 10.
—(1952), *A History of Chinese Philosophy*, 2 vols. Princeton, N.J., Princeton University Press.
Geden, A. S. (1909), 'Buddha', in J. Hastings (ed.), *Encyclopaedia of Religion and Ethics*, Vol. 3, 881-885. Edinburgh, T. and T. Clark.
Ghalioungui, Paul (1960), 'Des papyrus égyptiens à la médecine grec-

que', in *XVIIe Congrès International d'histoire de la médecine, Communications.* Athens-Cos, pp. 296-307.

—(1963), *Magic and Medical Science in Ancient Egypt.* London, George Allen & Unwin.

Glover, T. R. (1909), *The Conflict of Religions in the Early Roman Empire.* London, Methuen.

Grant, Michael (trans. and ed.) (1971a), *Cicero: On the Good Life.* London, Penguin Books.

—(1971b), *Cicero: Selected Works.* London, Penguin Books.

Gray, John (1969), *Near Eastern Mythology.* London, Paul Hamlyn.

Griffith, R. T. H. (1920-26), *The Hymns of the Rigveda*, 2 vols., 3rd edition. Benares.

Guthrie, W. K. C. (1950), *The Greeks and their Gods.* London, Methuen.

Guthrie, W. K. C. *History of Greek Philosophy*, 4 vols. Cambridge, Cambridge University Press.

—(1962), Vol. 1: *The Earlier Pre-Socratics and Pythagoreans.*

—(1965), Vol. 2: *The Pre-Socratic Tradition from Parmenides to Democritus.*

—(1969), Vol. 3: *The Fifth Century Enlightenment.*

—(1974), Vol. 4: *Plato – The Man and his Dialogues, Earlier Period.*

Hallpike, C. R. (1975), 'Is there a primitive mentality?', *Times Higher Education Supplement*, 7 November 1975.

Hastings, James (ed.) (1908-1926), *Encyclopaedia of Religion and Ethics*, 13 vols. Edinburgh, T. and T. Clark.

Hicks, R. D. (1910), *Stoic and Epicurean.* London, Oxford University Press.

—(ed. and trans.) (1925), *Diogenes Laertius: Lives of the Ancient Philosophers* (Loeb Classical Library). London, Heinemann.

Hooke, S. H. (1934), *Myth and Ritual.* Oxford, Clarendon Press.

—(1935) *The Labyrinth.* Oxford, Clarendon Press.

Hooker, Richard, *Lawes of Ecclesiasticall Politie.*

Horton, Robin (1967), 'African traditional thought and western science', *Africa* (London), Vol. 37, pp. 50-71 and 155-187.

Hume, David (1911 edition), *Treatise on Human Nature* (Everyman Library). London, Dent.
—(1935 edition), *Dialogues Concerning Natural Religion*, Ed. N. Kemp Smith, Oxford, Clarendon Press.
Hume, R. E. (1921), *The Thirteen Principal Upanisads*. London, Oxford University Press.
Hummel, A.W. (ed.) (1944), *Eminent Chinese of the Chhing Period*. Washington D. C., Library of Congress.
Hunt, H. A. K. (1953), *The Humanism of Cicero*. Carlton, Vic., Melbourne University Press.
Jacobi, Hermann (1884, 1885), *Jaina Sutras* (Sacred Books of the East, Vols. XXII, XLV). Oxford, Clarendon Press.
Jaeger, Werner (1948), *The Theology of the Early Greek Philosophers*. London, Oxford University Press.
Jahoda, Gustav (1970), *The Psychology of Superstition*. London, Penguin Books.
Jaini, J. L. (1916), *Outlines of Jainism*. Cambridge, Cambridge University Press.
James, E. O. (1958), *Myth and Ritual in the Ancient Near East*. London, Thames & Hudson.
Jha, Ganganatha (1934), *The Tattva-kaumundī*. Poona. Oriental Book Agency.
Jones, W. S. (1923-1931), *Hippocrates* (Loeb Classical Library), 3 vols. London, Heinemann.
Kahn, Charles H. (1960), *Anaximander and the Origins of Greek Cosmology*. New York, Columbia University Press.
Kant, Immanuel (1934 ed.), *Critique of Pure Reason*. London, Dent (Everyman Library).
—(1838-1842), 'Beantwortung der Frage: Was ist Aufklarung?' *Werke*, vol. IV. Leipzig.
Keith, A. B. (1918), *The Sāṃkhya System*. Calcutta, Association Press.
—(1921), *Indian Logic and Atomism*. Oxford, Clarendon Press.
Kirk, G. S. and Raven, J. E. (eds.) (1957) *The Pre-Socratic Philosophers*. Cambridge, Cambridge University Press.
Kitto, H. D. F. (1951), *The Greeks*. London, Penguin Books.

Knowles, David (1962), *Evolution of Medieval Thought*. London, Longmans.

Lactantius, *Institutorum*, in W. Fletcher (1871), *Works*, (Ante-Nicene Christian Library, Vols. 21 and 22). Edinburgh, T. and T. Clark.

Laertius, Diogenes. See under Hicks.

Lambert, W. G. (ed.) (1960), *Babylonian Wisdom Literature*. Oxford, Clarendon Press.

Langdon, Stephen (1923), *Babylonian Wisdom*. London.

Latham, R. E. (ed. and trans.) (1951), *Lucretius: On the Nature of the Universe*. London, Penguin Books.

Legge, James (1861), *The Chinese Classics*. Vol. 1: *Confucian Analects* etc.; Vol. 2: *The Works of Mencius*. London, Trübner.

— (1872), *The Chinese Classics*. Vol. 5, pts. 1 and 2: *The 'Ch'un Ts'eu, with The 'Tso Chuen'*. London, Trübner.

— (1885), *The Texts of Confucinism*. Pt. III: *The Li Chi* (Sacred Books of the East, Vols. XXVII and XXVIII). Oxford, Clarendon Press.

— (1891), *The Texts of Taoism* (Sacred Books of the East, Vols. XXXIX and XL). Oxford, Clarendon Press.

Lévy-Bruhl, Lucien (1935), *La mythologie primitive*. Paris, F. Alcan.

— (1936), *How Natives Think*. London, G. Allen & Unwin.

Lindsay, A. D. (1910), *Five Dialogues of Plato*. (Everyman Library Edition). London, Dent.

Lucian, *Works*. Ed. A. M. Harmon and M. D. McLoed (1913-67) (Loeb Classical Library). London, Heinemann.

Macaulay, *Essay on Milton*.

Macdonnell, A. A. (1917), *A Vedic Reader*. Oxford, Clarendon Press.

— (1922), *Hymns from the Rigveda*. London, Oxford University Press.

— (1929), *A History of Sanskrit Literature*. London. Heinemann.

Macfarlane, Alan (1970), *Witchcraft in Tudor and Stuart England*. London, Routledge & Kegan Paul.

McGregor, H. P. (ed.) (1972), *Cicero: On the Nature of the Gods* [*De Natura Deorum*]. London, Penguin Books.

McInerny, Ralf M. (1963), *History of Western Philosophy*. Vol. 1:

From the Beginnings of Philosophy to Plotinus. London, Notre Dame Press.

McPherson, T. (1965), *Philosophy of Religion*. London, Van Nostrand.

Mahabharata. See under Dutt (1953).

Majumbar, R. C. (1951), *The Vedic Age*. London, G. Allen & Unwin.

Malcom, Norman (1958), *Ludwig Wittgenstein: A Memoir*. London, Oxford University Press.

Malinowski, Bronislaw (1954 edition), *Magic, Science and Religion*. New York, Doubleday Anchor Books.

Marshall, John (1931), *Mohenjo-daro and the Indus Civilization ...* . London, A. Probsthain.

Marx, Karl and Engels, Fredrich, (1975 -), *Collected Works*. London, Lawrence and Wishart.

Morell, Thomas (ed. and trans.) (1786), *Seneca: Epistles*, 2 vols. London.

Muir, J. (1862), 'Verses from the Sarva-darsana-sangra, the Vishnu Purana, and the Ramayana, illustrating the tenets of the Chārvakas, or Indian Materialists, with some remarks on freedom of speculation in ancient India', *Journal of the Royal Asiatic Society*, Vol. 19, pp. 299-314.

Müller, F. Max (1878), *Lectures on the Origin and Growth of Religions, as illustrated by the Religions of India* (Hibbert Lectures, London 1878). London, Longmans.

—— (ed.) (1879-1910), *Sacred Books of the East*, 50 vols. Translated by various Oriental scholars. Oxford, Clarendon Press.

—— (1879), *The Upanishads Translated*, Part I (Sacred Books of the East, Vol. I). Oxford, Clarendon Press.

—— (1884), *The Upanishads Translated*, Part II (Sacred Books of the East, Vol. XV). Oxford, Clarendon Press.

—— (1891), *Vedic Hymns*, Part I (Sacred Books of the East, Vol. XXXII). Oxford, Clarendon Press.

—— (1897), *Vedic Hymns*, Part II (Sacred Books of the East, Vol. XLVI). Oxford, Clarendon Press.

Nashe, Thomas (1976 edition), *Pierce Penniless*. London, Penguin Books.

Needham, J. (1956), *Science and Civilization in China.* Vol. 2: *The History of Scientific Thought.* Cambridge, Cambridge University Press.

Neilson, Kai (1973), *Scepticism.* London, Macmillan.

Paley, William (1802), *Natural Theology.* London.

Pater, Walter (1885), *Marius the Epicurean.* London, Macmillan.

Patai, R. (1947), *Man and Temple in Ancient Jewish Myth and Ritual.* London & New York, T. Nelson.

Perrin, B. (ed.) (1915), *Plutarch: Life of Pericles* (Loeb Classical Library, Vol. 3). London, Heinemann.

Piaget, J. (1929), *The Child's Conception of the World.* London, Kegan Paul.

Plato (1892 edition), *Works,* 5 vols., ed. B. Jowett, 3rd edition. Oxford, Clarendon Press; see also under A. E. Taylor and A. D. Lindsay.

Plutarch. See under Russel and Perrin.

Pohlenz, M. (1953), '*Nomos* und *Physis*', in *Hermes,* 418-438.

Pritchard, James B. (ed.) (1955), *Ancient Near Eastern Texts.* Princeton, N. J., Princeton University Press.

Rackham, H. (1938), *Pliny: Natural History,* Bks. I-II (Loeb Classical Library). London, Heinemann.

Radhakrishnan, S. (1933 and 1948), *Indian Philosophy,* 2 vols. London, G. Allen & Unwin.

Radhakrishnan, S. and Moore, (1973), *A Source of Indian Philosophy.* Princeton, N. J., Princeton University Press.

Raju, P. T. (1971), *The Philosophical Traditions of India.* London, G. Allen & Unwin.

Rankin, O. S. (1936), *Israel's Wisdom Literature.* Edinburgh, T. and T. Clark.

Riepe, D. (1961), *The Naturalistic Tradition in Indian Thought.* Seattle, University of Washington Press.

Rist, J. M. (1972), *Epicurus.* Cambridge, Cambridge University Press.

Robin, Léon (1928), *Greek Thought and the Origins of the Scientific Spirit.* London, Kegan Paul, Tronch, Trübner & Co.

Rogers, B. B. (1924), *Works of Aristophanes* (Loeb Classical Library, 3 vols.). London, Heinemann.

Rolfe, J. C. (1921), *Sallust* (Loeb Classical Library). London, Heinemann.

Rose, H. J. (1946), *Ancient Greek Religion.* London, Hutchinson.

Ross, J. M. (1972), 'Introduction', in McGregor (ed.), *Cicero: On the Nature of the Gods.* London, Penguin Books.

Ross, W. D. (ed.) (1908-1952), *Works of Aristotle*, 12 vols. Oxford, Clarendon Press.

Roy, M. N. (1951), *Materialism: an Outline of the History of Scientific Thought.* Calcutta.

—(1952), 'Radhakrishnan in the perspective of Indian philosophy' in P. A. Schlipp (ed.), *The Philosophy of Sarvepali Radhakrishnan.* New York, Tudor Publishing Co.

Ruben, Walter (1954), *Geschichte der Indischen Philosophie.* Berlin, Deutscher Verlag der Wissenschaften.

—(1956), *Begin der Philosophie in Indien: Aus den Vedan*, Vol. 1. Berlin, Akademie-Verlag.

Russel, D. A. (ed. and trans.) (1971), *Plutarch: Moral Essays.* London, Penguin Books.

Sallust, see under Rolfe.

Sanders, N. (1971), *Myths of Heaven and Hell from Ancient Mesopotamia.* London, Penguin Books.

Sarton, G. (1931), *Introduction to the History of Science*, Vol. 2. Baltimore, Williams and Wilkins.

Scott, R. B. Y. (1971), *The Way of Wisdom in the Old Testament.* New York, Macmillan.

Seal, Brajendranath (1915), *The Positive Sciences of the Ancient Hindus.* London, G. Allen & Unwin.

Shastri, D. R. (1930), *A Short History of Indian Materialism, Sensualism and Hedonism.* Calcutta.

—(1937), 'The Chārvāka philosophy', in *The Cultural Heritage of India.* Calcutta.

Shastri, H. P. (1925), *Lokāyāta*. Dacca.

Shastri, S. N. and Sakena (eds.) (1940), *Tattvopaplavasimha.* Baroda.

Shastri, S. S. (1935), *Sāṁkhya-Kārika of Iśvata Kṛṣna.* Madras, University of Madras Press.

Sinha, Nandalal (1915), *Sāṃkhya-pravacana-sūtra.* (Sacred Books of the Hindus). Allahabad.

Smart, Ninian (1964), *Doctrine and Argument in Indian Philosophy.* London, G. Allen & Unwin.

—(1973), *The Phenomenon of Religion.* London, Macmillan.

Strenlow, Carl F. T. (1907-1920), *Die Aranda-und Loritja-Stämme in Zentral Australien*, 5 vols. Frankfurt-am-Main, J. Baer & Co.

Taylor, A. E. (1926), *Plato: The Man and his Work.* London, Methuen.

—(1960 ed.), *Plato: Laws* (Everyman Library). London, Dent.

Taylor, J. (ed.) (1811), *Kṛṣṇa Misra: Prabodha-candrodaya.* Bombay.

Thibaut, George (1890, 1896), *The Vedānta Sūtras with the Commentary by Sankarācārya* (Sacred Books of the East, Vols. XXXIV and XXXVIII). Oxford, Clarendon Press.

Thomas, Edward J. (1923), *Vedic Hymns.* London, K. Paul, Trench, Trübner & Co.

Thomas, F. J. (ed. and trans.) (1921), *Brihaspati Sutra.* Lahore.

Thomas, Keith (1970), 'The relationship of social anthropology to the historical study of English witchcraft', in Mary Douglas (ed.), *Witchcraft Confessions and Accusations.* London, Tavistock.

Thomas, J. A. K. (ed. and trans.) (1953), *Aristotle: Nichomachean Ethics.* London, Penguin Books.

Thrower, James (1971), *A Short History of Western Atheism.* London, Pemberton.

—(1973), 'Peter Abelard and the growth of European rationalism', in Hector Hawton (ed.) *Question 6.* London, Pemberton, 58-68.

—(1976a), 'Medical science and the growth of irreligion', in Hector Hawton (ed.), *Question 9.* London, Pemberton, 13-23.

—(1976b), 'Irreligia i ateizm', *Euhemer* (Warsaw), No. 102, Vol. 4, 19-28.

Tucci, G. (1925), 'F. W. Thomas: the Brihaspati Sutra', in *Proceedings of the Indian Philosophical Congress, 1925.*

—(1926), 'Linee di una storia del materialismo indiano', *Atti della Reale Accademia Nazionale dei Lincei*, Serie 6, Vol. II. Rome.

Tylor, Edward (1871), *Primitive Culture*, 2 vols. London, John Murray.

Umasvamin (n.d.) *Tartvārthādhigama-sūtra*, Eng. trans. Arrah, Bihar, Central Gira Publishing House.

Unamuno, Miguel de (1962), *The Tragic Sense of Life in Men and Nations*. London, Collins.

Usener, Hermannus (1887), *Epicurea*. Leipzig.

Vahanian, Gabriel (1964), *Wait without Idols*. New York, George Brazillet.

Waley, Arthur (1934), *The Way and its Power*. London, G. Allen & Unwin.

—— (1938), *Analects of Confucius*. London, G. Allen & Unwin.

Warren, H. C. (1915), *Buddhism in Translations* (Harvard Oriental Series, Vol. 3). Cambridge, Mass., Harvard University Press.

Weber, Max (1930), *The Protestant Ethic and the Spirit of Capitalism*, trans. Talcott Parsons. New York, Scribners.

—— (1951), *The Religion of China: Sociology of Confucianism and Taoism*, trans. Hans Gerth. Glencoe, Ill., Free Press.

—— (1958), *The Religion of India: Sociology of Hinduism and Buddhism*, trans. Hans Gerth and Don Martindale. Glencoe, Ill., Free Press.

Wells, H. G. (1945), *Mind at the End of its Tether*. London, Heinemann.

Wender, Dorothea (ed. and trans.) (1973), *Hesiod: Theogony; Works and Days; Theogonis: Elergies*. London, Penguin Books.

Wheeler, Mortimer (1953), *The Civilization of the Indus Valley and Beyond*. Cambridge, Cambridge University Press.

Wilson, Bryan R. (ed.) (1974), *Rationality*. Oxford, Blackwell.

Witt, N. W. de (1954), *Epicurus and his Philosophy*. Minneapolis, University of Minnesota Press.

Wright, A. F. (1951), 'Fu Li and the rejection of Buddhism', *Journal of Historical Studies*, Vol. 12, No. 33.

Zaehner, R. C. (1966), *Hindu Scriptures* (Everyman Library). London, Dent.

Zimmer, H. (1951), *Philosophies of India*, ed. Joseph Campbell. London, Routledge & Kegan Paul.

Notes

NOTES TO CHAPTER 1: 'INTRODUCTION'

1. As a Christian apologist, however, Rudolf Bultmann, in his now famous demythologising programme, was not content simply to *describe* the traditional Christian approach but, through the medium of Heidegger's existential analysis of the human condition, to *re-interpret* its meaning for today.
2. The designation 'modern man' in the writings of Bultmann, and in the present work, is of course, simply an abstraction to indicate the predominant outlook on the world in contemporary (Western) society. It is not intended – by me at least – to be taken in any normative sense. Bultmann, however, does give the impression of so using it.
3. I am thinking here particularly of the work of Bronislaw Malinowski and of the late Sir Edward Evans-Pritchard and the Oxford School of Anthropology which he created.
4. The debt to current anthropological work on witchcraft is explicitly acknowledged, for example, in Alan Macfarlane's fine study, *Witchcraft in Tudor and Stuart England* (1970), and by Keith Thomas in a paper entitled 'The relevance of social anthropology to the historical study of English witchcraft', in M. Douglas (ed.), *Witchcraft Confessions and Accusations* (1970).
5. For the terminology used here the reader is referred to Martin Buber's seminal work, *I and Thou* (original German edition, 1923).
6. The 'animistic' theory of the origin of religion was first put forward by Sir Edward Tylor in the second volume of his *Primitive Culture* (1871).
7. It would have been more correct, as is now widely recognised by social anthropologists and historians of religion, if Malinowski had used the composite term 'magico-religious' rather than

'magical'; the distinction between 'magic' and 'religion' being a feature of our own, rather than of 'primitive' cultures.

8. This fact was first brought to the attention of students of ancient society by the Oxford 'Myth and Ritual' School. Cf. S. Hooke (ed.), *Myth and Ritual* (1934), and *The Labyrinth* (1935), although it had been known to anthropologists for some time. Cf. E. O. James, *Myth and Ritual in the Ancient Near East* (1958).
9. For a detailed description of the Akitu Festival cf. John Gray, *Near Eastern Mythology* (1969), pp. 26f.; E. O. James (1958), pp. 55f.; N. Sanders, *Myths of Heaven and Hell from Ancient Mesopotamia* (1971).
10. This point has been forcibly made by Gustav Jahoda in his book, *The Psychology of Supersition* (1970), pp. 109f. Cf. also Robin Horton, 'African traditional thought and western science', *Africa*, Vol. 37 (1967), pp. 50-71 and 155-187.
11. In this connection cf. C. R. Hallpike, 'Is there a primitive mentality?' in *The Times Higher Education Supplement* for 7.11.75, pp. 9f.
12. The reader is referred to Mary Douglas, *Purity and Danger* (1966), for a detailed study of this aspect of 'primitive' thinking.
13. Cf. the closing sections of *The Protestant Ethic and the Spirit of Capitalism.* Weber's phrase is *Entzauberung der Welt.*
14. For a fuller treatment of the 'legitimating' function of religious mythology, cf. Peter Berger, *The Social Reality of Religion* (1969).
15. This has been largely the case in Chinese and Indian cultures as well. The continued persistence of the hierarchical caste system in Indian society is due in no small measure to the fact that it is held to have been divinely instituted. Cf. *Bhagavad-Gīta*, IV: 13.

NOTES TO CHAPTER 2: 'INDIA'

1. Those who accept the authority of the Vedas are known as *āstikas*, those who reject it as *nāstikas*.
2. For accounts of the religion of the Indus Valley civilization, cf. R.

C. Majumbar, *The Vedic Age* (1951), pp. 185-189; A. H. Basham, *The Wonder that was India* (1954), pp. 22-24; Bridget Allchin and Raymond Allchin, *The Birth of Indian Civilization* (1968), ch. 12; Sir John Marshall, *Mohenjodaro and the Indus Valley Civilization* (1931), 2 vols.; and Sir Mortimer Wheeler, *The Indus Valley Civilization and Beyond* (1953).

3. The hymns which form the *Ṛg Veda Samhitā* were not, of course, all composed at the same time but represent a religious development stretching over a long period – from before the Aryan conquest of India until well into the period of conquest itself. In the main, however, they represent that period when the Aryans found their way into India from their original home, i.e. from about the beginning of the second millenium BC.
4. The surname in brackets after *Ṛg Vedic* and *Upaniṣadic* references is that of the translator. For more complete reference see Bibliography.
5. Literature which was eventually to become part of the sacred scriptures.
6. W. Ruben, *Geschichte der Indischen Philosophie* and *Beginn der Philosophie in Indien: Aus den Vedan*, Vol. 1. Ruben also holds Uddālaka to be an historical person and dates him about the 7th century BC.
7. If a very late date – say 400 BC – is accepted for this *Upaniṣad* then it may be that the systems of Cārvāka and Sāṃkya are being referred to.
8. In 1921 F. W. Thomas recovered and published a certain *Bṛihaspati Sūtra*, but whilst this may contain quotations from the lost work of that title, as it stands it is almost certainly the work of a later hand. Cf. C. Tucci, in *Proceedings of the Indian Philosophical Congress* (1925).
9. Erroneously attributed to Śankara. Śankara did, however, as we will see, comment on Lokāyāta in his *Commentary on the Bṛhama Sūtra*.
10. Cf. S. Radhakrishnan, *Indian Philosophy*, Vol. 1; S. N. Dasgupta, *A History of Indian Philosophy*, Vol. 3, pp. 512 ff.; J. Muir, 'Verses from the Śarua-darśana-sangraha ... with some remarks on free-

dom of speculation in Ancient India', *J. R. A. S.*, Vol. 19 (1862); T.W. R. Rhys Davids, *Dialogues of the Buddha*, Vol. 1, p. 166; R. Shastri, *A Short History of Indian Materialism, Sensationism and Hedonism* (1930); H. P. Shastri, *Lokāyāta* (1925); G.Tucci, *Proceedings of the Indian Philosophical Congress* (1925).

11. Note also that Cārvāka – the (later) alternative name for Lokāyāta – appears in the *Mahābhārata* as a name of a demon (*asura*) in disguise – at XII, 1f.
12. Chattopadhyaya's argument can be found on pp. 49 ff of his book *Lokāyāta*, and his description of Tantrism on pp. 269-358.
13. Chattopadhyaya underestimates the extent to which Lokāyāta became an articulate anti-Vedic philosophy. He is also far too sceptical of the value to be ascribed to the later and polemical accounts of philosophical Lokāyāta. All that is necessary to reconcile his account of early Lokāyāta with the accounts given by later writers (due weight certainly being given to the fact that they were writing from a biased and prejudiced point of view) is to postulate that Lokāyāta, like Sāṃkhya, which he derives from the same source, became more and more philosophical and perhaps dropped in so becoming (at least among its more philosophical exponents) its earlier ritual practices. These, of course, may have survived among certain sections of its adherents. Chattopadhyaya also underestimates the amount of philosophical (and speculative) material which the ancient sources attribute to the Asuras.
14. Silanka in his commentary on the *Sutra-Kṛtanga-Sutra* identifies them with the Lokāyātikas.
15. It is, perhaps, in their accounts of the ethical system of Cārvāka/Lokāyāta that most allowance for the idealistic bias of the later commentators needs to be made.
16. Written by Kṛṣṇa Miśra of Mirhila to expose, ridicule and criticise the ideas of Buddhists, Jains, Cārvākas, Kapalikas and other sects which had taken hold of the people of his day. It is, of course, a caricature, and should not be taken too seriously.
17. Chattopadhyaya argues that the Sāṃkhya system originated as did the Cārvāka in Tantrism, cf. 1959, pp. 359 ff, where he pro-

duces some interesting evidence for this. His argument that Sāṃkhya was originally atheistic can be found on pp. 363f.

18. The old Indian philosophical tradition certainly viewed it as atheistic for it was persistently called *nirisvara pradhāna karana vada* – the godless doctrine of primordial matter. It is also interesting to note that the *Brahma Sūtra* (ca. 200 BC) understood Sāṃkhya to be a materialistic system and sought to refute it as the most important challenge hitherto to the Idealist position.
19. Zimmer, in his *Philosophies of India* (1951), argues that Sāṃkhya, Jainism and Buddhism originated with the early pre-Aryan Indus Valley Civilization which, he holds, was also atheistic, but few scholars follow him in this.
20. So Śankara in his *Commentary on the Brahma-Sūtra*, C 11.2.7 Max Müller (1889-1926), Vol. 34, p. 374. Cf. also *Sāṃkhya Karīka* of Īśvara Kṛṣna, p. 20.
21. Cf. W. Paley, *Natural Theology* (1802), pp. 5-6. That this is a mistaken interpretation of Paley is argued (I think convincingly) by T. MacPherson in his *Philosophy of Religion* (1965), pp. 77 ff.
22. Cf., for example, *Marābhārata*, xii.318, also xii.203, 204, where *paruṣa* is said, according to Sāṃkhya, to issue forth from *prakṛiti*.
23. Śankara concludes the above quotation, 'for the purpose of affecting the highest end of mankind'. However, this theological view of nature would appear to be a later (and unnecessary) importation into early Sāṃkhya.
24. This is a commentary of a much later date than Kapila (probably ca. AD 1400; cf. McDonnell, *A History of Sanskrit Literature*, 1929, p. 393), and it is very doubtful whether even the aphorisms go back to Kapila himself.
25. It has, however, been argued by Professor Smart (*Doctrine and Argument in Indian Philosophy*, 1964, p. 81) that this does not mean that nature is devoid of purpose, since for Sāṃkhya, nature contains an inherent teleology – not only in the way in which outer and inner worlds are mutually adaptive, but also because the whole process of nature is thought of as subserving the ultimate interests of individual souls, which are gradually taught by nature that empirical existence is sorrowful and so acquire that

distaste for life which is the first step towards their eventual liberation. He goes on to point out that it was a common criticism of Sāṃkhya that it posited an inherent teleology in nature whilst holding that nature was unconscious. Far better surely, said its opponents (in the Vaisnavite school) to externalize this teleology and posit a personal God who directs the whole process. However, it is not so certain that Sāṃkhya does posit an inherent teleology. For this school, as we have seen, souls and nature just are eternally. That nature causes the soul suffering need not imply conscious intention on nature's part. The soul can learn from nature without nature, as it were, consciously teaching the soul that this is so, and so begin to achieve liberation. This is the way that things are and Sāṃkhya could reply that 'there's an end of it'.

26. It was in fact, as Chattopadhyaya notes, the Sāṃkhya system which provided Indian culture with the ideas of positive science, the most important of which were a theory of nature, a theory of causality, a theory of knowledge, and and theory of evolutionary process (1959, p. 363). B. N. Seal noticed this too. He wrote, 'The Sāṃkhya system possesses a unique interest in the history of thought as embodying the earliest clear and comprehensive account of the process of cosmic evolution, viewed not as a mere metaphysical speculation but as a positive principle based upon conservation, the transformation and the dissipation of energy' (*Positive Sciences of the Ancient Hindus*, 1915, p. 2).
27. In the early eighteenth century a break-way sect led by one Vīrajī rejected both temple-worship and religious iconography.
28. A very common line of argument among the Jains. One type of substance, they held, cannot produce another with completely different characteristics.
29. The Greek Fathers of the Christian Church were to face a similar question.
30. The three aims of man according to traditional Hindu classification are righteousness (*dharma*), profit (*artha*) and pleasure (*kāma*).
31. An attack upon the Vedantic doctrine of creation, as arising out of *lila* (sport).

32. This, of course, was the traditional Christian answer to the question.
33. So Majjkima-nikaya 7.483.8. This passage, which deals with the Buddha's teaching concerning 'questions which tend not to edification', can be found in M. C.Warren, *Buddhism in Translation* (1915), pp. 123f.

NOTES TO CHAPTER 3: 'CHINA'

1. Tso Ch'iu's enlargement of the *Spring and Autumn Annals* – a work which records the events in the state of Lu during the 'Spring and Autumn' period and attributed to Confucius, who was a native of the state of Lu. Compiled between 430-250 BC.
2. Cf. the passages quoted by Fung Yu-Lan (1952), Vol. 1, pp. 33-42.
3. *Analects* or *Lun Yu*. This work, compiled shortly after the death of Confucius by his disciples, preserved a record of his teachings.
4. Cf. V.12 where it is stated that he would not discuss 'The Way of Heaven'.
5. Cf. for example: *Analects* XIV, 37; LI,4; LX, 5; etc., in Legge (1861).
6. So Mencius, *Works of Mencius* (trans. Legge, 1861), Vol. 2; (1) 4.6.
7. The phrase is Needham's – 1956, p. 38.
8. For the contribution of religious mysticism to the rise of empirical science both in ancient China and in 16th and 17th century Europe the reader is referred to Needham (1956), pp. 89ff.
9. For a fuller account of Wang Ch'ung's world-view cf. A. Forke in the introduction to his translation of the *Lu Hêng, Philosophical Essays of Wang Ch'ung*, pt. 1.
10. Needham (1956), pp. 374-375. Wang Ch'ung's arguments can be found in ch. 43 and ch. 71 of the *Lun Hêng* (cf. Forke, 1907).
11. Cf. Cornford (1957), p. 5 and 55, for examples from early Greek culture; and for Jewish examples, R. Patai (1969).
12. Cf. especially ch. 44 and 64. Tung Chung-Shu's dates are 179 BC-104 BC.

13. For a European parallel one might cite the *Constitution* of the Emperor Theodosius in the fourth century, where there is a passage forbidding anyone to practice augury on penalty of high treason. Cf. *Cod. Theod.*, XVI, x, 12.
14. It should be stated, however, that Wang Ch'ung did give limited credence to astrology – that is, to the influence of the stars upon one's destiny, though he tried to explain this naturalistically. Cf. Needham (1956), p. 383.
15. Cf. A. F. Wright, 'Fu Li and the rejection of Buddhism', *Journal of Historical Studies*, Vol. 12, No. 33 (1951).
16. Cf. H. H. Dubs, 'Han Yu and the Buddha's relic: an episode in medieval Chinese religion', *Review of Religions*, Vol. 5 (1946).
17. Needham compares him with Herbert Spencer and Whitehead; see Needham (1956), pp. 455-485.
18. There is some evidence to suggest that he met the Western traveller, Matthew Ricci – although his thought shows little or no signs of Western influence.
19. Cf. Fung Yu-Lan, 'Mao Tse-Tung's "On Practice" and China's philosophy', *People's China*, Vol. 4, No. 10 (1951).

NOTES TO CHAPTER 4: 'GREECE'

1. For a more detailed account of the religion of the Greeks, cf. H. J. Rose, *Ancient Greek Religion* (1946), and W. K. C. Guthrie, *The Greeks and their Gods* (1950).
2. Cf. A. H. Armstrong, *Ancient Philosophy* (1965), pp. 1-2, and Benjamin Farrington, *Greek Science* (1961), Vol. 1, p. 29.
3. For a discussion of the sources of our knowledge of Thales and the pre-Socratics, cf. Kirk and Raven, *The Pre-Socratic Philosophers* (1957), pp. 1-7.
4. Cf. J. Burnet, *Greek Philosophy* (1914), pt. 1, pp. 5 f.; Léon Robin, *Greek Thought and the Origin of the Scientific Spirit* (1928), pp. 30 ff.
5. Cf. Cumont, in *Neue Jahrbücher*, Vol. 24 (1911), p. 4.
6. All quotations from Aristotle, unless otherwise indicated, are

from W. D. Ross, *The Works of Aristotle* (1908-1952).

7. The reference to Pohlenz is to his paper, '*Nemos* und *Physis*' (1953), in which he argues that the conception of *φύσις*, meaning 'nature' both as it is, as it has evolved, and as it originally was, is the creation of Ionian science. Pohlenz distinguishes the concept of *φύσις* from that of matter.
8. Both Burnet and A. E. Taylor dispute this dating, and on evidence derived from Plato's dialogue *Protagoras*, where Protagoras is depicted as an old man, they put the date of his birth at about 500 BC. Cf. A. E. Taylor, *Plato* (1926), p. 236, note.
9. Cf. Cornford's remarks on the Hippocratic school in *Principium Sapientae* (1952), pp. 31 ff.
10. For a review of the evidence, cf. de Witt, *Epicurus and his Philosophy* (1954), pp. 340-344.
11. Cf. Cicero, *De Natura Deorum*, III; Sextus Empiricus, *Ad. Math.* IX.
12. For a recent appeal to this argument, cf. John Baillie, *The Sense of the Presence of God* (1962).
13. Cicero, *De Natura Deorum*, III, 43; Sextus Empiricus, *Ad. Math.* IX.
14. Thomas Nashe in *Pierce Penniless* (1592) and Thomas Hooker in *Laws of Ecclesiastical Politie* (1593) both claim that religious disputation makes for religious unbelief, and Francis Bacon in his famous essay, *On Atheism* (1625), notes such controversy as the first cause of atheism.
15. It is interesting to note that the contemporary Marxist journal of *Religionswissenschaft* published in Poland is called *Euhemer*.

NOTES TO CHAPTER 5: 'ROME'

1. Cf. J. M. Ross in his introduction to the Penguin Classics edition of Cicero's *The Nature of the Gods* (ed. H. C. P. McGregor), pp. 8-9.
2. The British humanist H. J. Blackham claims that 'Cicero himself is the most representative and influential single figure in the

broad humanist tradition' (*Humanism*, 1968, p. 110).

3. Trans. H. C. P. McGregor, Penguin Classics; all quotations from *De Natura Deorum* are taken from this translation.
4. Cf. Kant, *Critique of Pure Reason*, Transcendental Dialectic I, III, VI.
5. Sextus' discussion of these arguments can be found as follows: (1) 1.61-74; (2) 1.75-122; (3) 1.123-190; (4) not discussed.
6. Cf. Sextus, *Ibid.*, 1.75, 76, with St. Thomas Aquinas, *Summa Theologica* 1.2.3.
7. A recent book, Kai Neilson, *Scepticism* (1973), contains extensive references to him.

NOTES TO CHAPTER 6: 'ISRAEL AND THE ANCIENT NEAR EAST'

1. The reader is referred to Macaulay's fine desciption of the Puritan approach to politics in his *Essay on Milton.*
2. The Epicurean flavour of 9 vv. 4-5 has already been mentioned. Scholars have also detected a reference to Heraclitus's view that all things are in perpetual flux in *Ecclesiastes*' opening reflections on the restless cyclical motions of the natural world and the passing of human generations (1 vv. 4-11). The verse, 'Whatever has been is what will be, and whatever has been done is what will be done' (1 v. 9), recalls, some have thought, the Stoic theory of world cycles, and the verse, 'Everything has its season ... and proper time' (3 v. 1), the Stoic doctrine of living according to nature. The Hedonistic doctrines of popular Epicureanism are seen as influencing the saying of the 'teacher' that 'There is nothing better for a man to do than to eat and drink and enjoy himself in return for all his labours' (2 v. 24).
3. For the most thorough discussion of ancient Egyptian medicine available, cf. Paul Ghalioungui's *Magic and Medical Science in Ancient Egypt* (1963).
4. Translated by J. H. Breasted, 1932.
5. This description, however, refers to only one of the papyrus's three parts, 'The book of wounds'.

6. Cf. Ghalioungui (1963), pp. 61 and 164ff.; *XVII*[e] *Cong. Int. d'Hist. de la Med.*, Athens, 1960, p. 296; F. Daumas in *Journal des Savants* (Paris), octobre-décembre 1956, p. 165.

Index